Responsible Assertive Behavior

Cognitive/Behavioral Procedures for Trainers

Arthur J. Lange Patricia Jakubowski

with a chapter by Thomas V. McGovern

Research Press
2612 North Mattis
Champaign, Illinois 61820

4

To Janet Clark Loxley,
Arthur and Helen Lange, and Sterling Dean Whitley

To Frances, John, Jerome,
Christine, and Barbara Jakubowski

Contents

Illustrations

Foreword
by Albert Ellis

I rarely feel as enthusiastic about a book as I feel about Dr. Arthur J. Lange and Dr. Patricia Jakubowski's *Responsible Assertive Behavior.* It describes a highly important area of human relations and it does so in an unusually competent and comprehensive manner. I can imagine few readers, from professional trainers who want to learn how to run assertion training groups to lay readers who want to increase their own assertion skills and get over some of their personal hangups in this area, who will not appreciably benefit from reading this book.

First of all, Drs. Jakubowski and Lange really tell you almost everything you would possibly want to know about assertion training. They include a wide variety of techniques, and very precisely outline these methods and give detailed examples (including suggested dialogs) and exercises. They show why these methods work—and why other methods do not. They cover special methods, such as theme-oriented groups, which virtually no other books in the field even mention. They end each chapter with pertinent and valuable questions for trainers. They have a detailed discussion of the ethical considerations in assertion training and in the training of trainers. They talk about assessment procedures and relate them to research studies. They discuss many different kinds of applications of assertion training.

Secondly, *Responsible Assertive Behavior* clearly defines assertion training terms and relates assertion to humanistic goals and values. Following the pioneering work of Alberti and Emmons and of rational-emotive therapy, Lange and Jakubowski show no interest in espousing forms of assertiveness that do not include great respect for the rights of others, that do not aid communication and mutuality between people with opposing desires, and that do not consider the advisability of rational forms of compromise. Throughout the book, they consistently demonstrate that assertion does not mean aggression; and they define it as "a *direct, honest,* and *appropriate* expression of opinions, beliefs, needs, or feelings." Naturally, I greatly like this kind of definition, since it endorses my own contention that we have two fairly distinct forms of emotion—appropriate and inappropriate; and that anger, hostility, resentment, and rage almost invariably comprise inappropriate feelings, while assertion, determination, annoyance, displeasure, and irritation may well comprise appropriate feelings.

The authors, in other words, see assertion as a mode of helping people to survive in a difficult world and to do so in a healthier, happier, and usually more relaxed manner. They show that you do not *have* to express your feelings, act assertively, or get what you want in life, however *desirable* you may find such goals. They do not view assertiveness, as do many other "leaders" in the field, as a thing in itself, but solidly place it as part of human personality, aliveness, and goal-seeking. Quite a different outlook from that presented in various other articles and books!

Finally, I find even more to my liking Jakubowski and Lange's unique emphasis on the cognitive and rational-emotive aspects of assertion training. Whereas most works in this area give lip service to this exceptionally important side of assertion training, they cover it unusually well. They include the philosophy and homework assignments that I and my associates have used in rational-emotive therapy for a good many years now to get at and change the basic irrational cognitions that people use to keep themselves unassertive; and they also employ some of the cognitive methods outlined by Rimm and Masters, Donald Meichenbaum, and other advocates of cognitive-behavior therapy. Along with Drs. Janet L. Wolfe and Iris G. Fodor of the Institute for Advanced Study in Rational Psychotherapy in New York City, Drs. Lange and Jakubowski unquestionably lead the field, in my estimation, in applying cognitive-behavioral techniques to assertion training. Although most assertion training workshops do not, as the authors point out, amount to formal psychotherapy, an assertion training workshop led by or conducted along the lines of the Jakubowski-Lange procedures can well turn into a highly therapeutic experience for the participants.

Can I cavil at all with *Responsible Assertive Behavior?* Not easily. I will say, however, that the book really includes two separate texts: a manual for assertion trainers and self-help book for readers who want to apply much of the material presented to their own lives. In both respects, it provides more than enough effective and responsibly presented information. I do think, however, that the authors could well get around, eventually, to a specific manual that would serve the purposes of the general reader a little better. Even in its present form, *Responsible Assertive Behavior* has fine self-help possibilities. But I do hope that Drs. Lange and Jakubowski will refine these possibilities in another volume designed specifically for public consumption.

Albert Ellis
Institute for Advanced Study in
Rational Psychotherapy
New York City

Foreword
by Arnold A. Lazarus

Assertion training has become a booming, blustering business. There has been a rash of books (popular and professional), journal articles, seminars, symposia, and widespread coverage in several popular magazines, prominent newspapers and prime television shows. There is even a quasi-professional newsletter devoted solely to "assertiveness." Furthermore, assertion training groups abound, replete with a new brand of paraprofessional—"assertion workshop leaders." The result? Benefits have accrued to some timid, reticent and inhibited people who have learned that they have certain rights, and that interpersonal gratification calls for the expression of these rights. But we have seen several psychiatric casualties, and encountered a host of obnoxious trainers and trainees who fail to separate "assertion" from "aggression." Many have become bewildered and disappointed to discover that assertiveness is not a panacea, and that assertive people do not always get what they desire.

Under the auspices of a competent professional, assertion training is an important treatment process. It rarely comprises the sole treatment program but is generally part of a wider strategy designed to overcome anxiety, depression, hostility, and other problems of communication. Major setbacks can occur when people prematurely try out their new-found assertiveness only to receive swift retaliatory reactions.

There are many circumstances when wisdom decrees that *unassertive* behaviors are more adaptive than assertive responses. Yet when perusing the literature, one comes across many inflammatory and ill-advised examples under the guise of "assertiveness." For instance, a handbook produced by the Seattle-King County National Organization for Women, cites the case of a policeman who had stopped a woman for a traffic violation. Upon inspecting her driver's license, he referred to her as "Mary," while she obviously would have preferred being addressed by her surname. When the policeman said, "Well, Mary, do you know what you did?" the book advised the following response: "Officer, I would appreciate being referred to as Ms._____." This response would seem to guarantee the officer's antagonism and the most stringent traffic summons permissible by law!

In some circles, so-called assertion has become a fetish. People will argue at length over petty principles, harass exhausted salespeople, and upbraid defenseless subordinates. I have heard people actually boast about pushing little old ladies to the back of lines! Some of these compulsively "assertive" individuals go through life busily chalking up interpersonal "victories" while remaining puzzled by their consequent lack of emotional intimacy. Assertion not only calls for considerable skill in knowing how to express one's needs, but also implies full knowledge of when and when not to exercise one's rights.

And in assertiveness, *style* is all-important. Some people learn the essentials of assertive behavior—"I messages," "feeling talk," "self-disclosure," "honest feedback," etc.—and yet manage to elicit nothing but stark antagonism from others. When properly taught and intelligently practiced, assertiveness results in mutual trust, emotional togetherness, and personal caring.

Given the foregoing caveats, it is heartening to read a book on *responsible* assertive behavior. The very title implies that not *all* assertive behavior is responsible or desirable. Drs. Jakubowski and Lange are professionals who see assertiveness in its proper interpersonal context.

There are several factors that make this book unique. Among them is the fact that despite the plethora of literature on the subject, there is no other book that can actually equip therapists to practice assertion training. *Responsible Assertive Behavior* goes far beyond the usual descriptive components of assertiveness. It includes piecemeal and systematic strategies, and a variety of "how to" exercises and examples. Drs. Lange and Jakubowski offer more than general guidelines. They provide preplanned responses across a variety of conditions, coupled with transcripts and dialogs that permit the reader to understand the concept of assertion and its situational implementation. Furthermore, the authors have integrated the cognitive and behavioral components of assertive reactions and interactions, thereby producing a synthesis that adds impetus to their detailed examples. The net result is bound to be a more enlightened and elegant approach to this significant area of human conduct.

Arnold A. Lazarus, Ph.D.
Professor
Graduate School of Applied
and Professional Psychology
Rutgers University

Preface

We approach assertiveness and assertion training from a personal as well as a professional perspective. Over the years, we have successfully worked on all kinds of changes for ourselves from assertively initiating conversations with men and women, disagreeing with respected colleagues about professional issues, negotiating salary increases, responding to persons who would like us to feel guilty, inferior, or helpless to dealing with a close friend's continual pressure to eat various forms of eggplant. In addition to our own efforts to behave more assertively, we have conducted over a hundred assertion groups and workshops. As a result of these experiences and our professional investigations, we have developed a variety of principles and procedures for conducting assertion training groups.

As is often the case with significant social interventions, the concept of assertiveness has attained greater popular support than have the specific methods for developing assertiveness. This book is our effort to provide a rationale and specific procedures for conducting assertion training, particularly in groups.

Through assertion training, people in all sorts of contexts are learning cognitive, affective, and behavioral procedures for increasing their interpersonal effectiveness. Group members have learned to discriminate between assertive, nonassertive, and aggressive behavior; developed belief systems which support their own personal rights and the rights of others; recognized and changed their irrational thinking and self-statements; modified the resultant excessive anger, guilt, or anxiety; and increased their repertoire of assertive behaviors.

This book is primarily intended for those persons who wish to learn how to conduct assertion training groups in a wide variety of contexts. We also believe that people who are generally interested in becoming more assertive can profit from reading this book.

We believe that thinking, feeling, and behaving are all components of assertiveness. Our approach to training is an integrative model utilizing cognitive restructuring procedures and behavior rehearsal techniques. We believe that people are more likely to change when they learn to control what they say to themselves as well as how they overtly feel and behave. This book presents a variety of procedures and techniques to help people develop an awareness of and control over what they say to themselves, how they feel, and how they behave. The old dichotomy between cognitive and behavioral approaches to change is now being reconceptualized, thus facilitating the development of models for personal growth. Assertion training is a most likely context for this marriage of therapeutic orientations.

The first three chapters present a rationale for assertion, discuss the causes of aggression and nonassertion, and describe an assertive belief system which maintains a high regard for personal rights as well as the rights of others. The next chapters present a series of structured exercises for assertion training groups, and detailed models for conducting cognitive restructuring and behavior rehearsal procedures. Specific types of assertion training groups are also dealt with: the theme-oriented group and consciousness-raising in conjunction with assertion training. The stages of planning and conducting a group, as well as assessment procedures, are also presented. Thomas McGovern of Southern Illinois University, Career Planning and Placement Center, has written a detailed account of the application of assertion training procedures to training job interviewers and interviewees; he also describes the use of assertion procedures for both management and staff personnel in business. Finally, we are especially concerned with a number of ethical issues which have emerged for trainers as assertion training has grown in popularity. Thus, the chapter on ethical concerns raises these issues and offers some resolutions. The extensive Reference section cites the research and descriptive literature on assertion training, approximately 85 percent of which has appeared in the last six years.

In regard to writing style, the terms "participant" and "group member" are used interchangeably. Secondly, we have balanced the use of feminine and masculine pronouns throughout the book. The term nonassertion is defined in Chapter 2 and is distinguished from assertion and aggression. In this book, the term "unassertion" refers both to nonassertion and aggression and is distinguished from assertion. Thus, unassertion might refer to either nonassertive or aggressive behavior.

Any situations cited in this book which were taken from the authors' clinical experiences and any other actual experiences have been disguised by using fictitious names and changing various circumstances.

This book has been written in a manner which emphasizes that readers should try *doing* the procedures presented throughout. Each chapter is highly descriptive, including demonstrative case transcripts employing specific cognitive and behavioral procedures. In addition, the chapters include "homework" activities, both for trainers and participants as well as a series of review questions to help the reader recap the important procedures and techniques. We believe that assertion trainers must not only know the theoretical and procedural bases of training, but they must also practice the *art* of doing assertion training.

We have attempted to make this book as complete and detailed as possible in order to meet the needs of less knowledgeable readers. In some cases, the text elaborates considerable detail which might be most appreciated by the less experienced trainer. We decided that a truly comprehensive and detailed presentation of assertion procedures would be of greatest value to all.

This book has been a joint effort on the part of both authors. We have both contributed substantial thought and energy to its development and completion. A flip of the coin determined senior authorship.

We wish to recognize Janet Clark Loxley, Rita Whiteley, Thomas McGovern, Albert Ellis, David Rimm, and Donald Meichenbaum whose stimulating discussions with us led to greater clarity and insight. We especially wish to thank Ann Wendel at Research Press for her important support and technical assistance in the completion of this book. We would also like to express our thanks to Karen Anderson, Robin Cecile Alward, Sally Nusbaum, and Margie Kemp for their assistance in the typing of the manuscript.

We firmly believe that greater understanding and new insights result from dialog and experience as well as serious reading. We invite you, the reader, to communicate with us in the hope that through such dialog we will all achieve greater clarity and understanding. Moreover, we encourage assertion trainers to attend experiential workshops. Workshops afford the opportunity to see experienced trainers in action and, in some cases, to actually conduct assertion procedures under supervision. In addition, ongoing supervision and training from competent trainers is recommended.

It is our hope that this book will help trainers to conduct effective assertion training groups, and that the participants in those groups will assertively act on their own personal rights with high regard for the rights of others.

Patricia Jakubowski*
University of Missouri-St. Louis

Arthur J. Lange
University of California-Irvine

* Formerly published under the name of Patricia Jakubowski-Spector

1
An Overview

Assertion training has a long history. As early as 1949 Andrew Salter in *Conditioned Reflex Therapy* described an early form of assertion training. However, the major credit for the current development of assertion training is generally given to Joseph Wolpe (1958) and Arnold Lazarus (Wolpe & Lazarus, 1966), who more clearly differentiated assertion from aggression and used various role play procedures as part of their assertion training.

Nonetheless, only since 1970 have many professionals become greatly interested in assertion training and started to refine and expand its procedures. The growing interest in assertion training on the part of both professionals and the lay public is not a fad. Instead this interest is a natural outgrowth of cultural changes which occurred in the Sixties.

Two important cultural changes seem to have taken place in the Sixties. First, personal relationships began to be highly valued. Perhaps because it became more difficult to achieve self-worth through traditional sources—job security, job advancement, marriage—people began looking for alternative ways of improving the quality of their personal lives. Personal relationships began to be valued as a major source of self-worth and satisfaction in life. But many people found themselves lacking the skills to improve their personal relationships. Second, the range of socially acceptable behavior was considerably widened; for example, alternative life styles became more acceptable. But many people found themselves lacking the skills to make choices about how to behave. They also lacked the cognitive and behavioral skills to act on their choices and to defend these choices when they were criticized or blocked by other people.

1

Now in the Seventies, more and more people are seeking increased personal effectiveness, which involves active, practical ways of standing up for themselves and using their abilities for personal growth and the enhancement of personal relationships. It is within this cultural context that the interest in assertion training has grown—not as a passing fad, but rather as a set of effective procedures whose time has come. Assertion training meets a strong and pervasive cultural need.

WHAT IS ASSERTION TRAINING?

At this point there is no agreement as to the set of procedures which constitute assertion training. This is not surprising in view of the fact that how assertion training is conducted varies as the needs of individuals vary. Assertion training with psychiatric patients is likely to deal with different situations, behaviors, beliefs, and needs than assertion training carried out with homemakers, business people, or college students. Furthermore, different groups of people may require additional special techniques, e.g., homemakers who have become overly invested in their families may require special techniques to help them get in touch with themselves and identify their own needs, while psychiatric patients may require special procedures to help reduce their excessive anxiety and to better test reality. Lastly, many new role playing procedures and modeling techniques are now being developed. Since research is inconclusive about which combination of techniques is most effective, different trainers use a wide variety of procedures in their assertion training.

Despite the lack of general agreement on the procedures which constitute assertion training, there is a great need to define what assertion training is. Many therapeutic procedures—from bio-energetics training to transactional analysis—could be purported as assertion training simply because they may result in greater assertiveness on the part of individuals. However, assertion training, in our view, generally incorporates four basic procedures: (1) teaching people the differences between assertion and aggression and between nonassertion and politeness; (2) helping people identify and accept both their own personal rights and the rights of others; (3) reducing existing cognitive and affective obstacles to acting assertively, e.g., irrational thinking, excessive anxiety, guilt, and anger; and (4) developing assertive skills through active practice methods (Jakubowski-Spector, 1973a; Jakubowski, in press, b).

Stated most simply, assertion training is a semi-structured training approach which is characterized by its emphasis on acquiring assertive

2

skills through practice. The practice may be direct by actually role playing alternative assertive responses, or it may be indirect by vicariously acquiring assertive skills through observing models who demonstrate these behaviors. Although insight and exhortation to be more assertive may be present in a particular assertion training program, they are not the main ways through which individuals are helped to become more assertive. When a person becomes more assertive simply through insight or exhortation, that person has received "assertive awareness exposure" rather than assertion training.

GROUP ASSERTION TRAINING

Assertion training may be done individually or in groups. While research has yet to compare the relative effectiveness of group assertion training with individual training, we believe that group training is generally more effective:

1. Assertion trainees often can more easily accept assertion rights when other group members provide their own personal rationales for accepting these rights and give examples of how they have assertively acted on such rights.
2. In the group setting, participants may engage in nonassertive and aggressive behaviors which would not occur in individual training. For example, individuals who monopolize, intellectualize, or offer controversial opinions may trigger various nonassertive or aggressive reactions on the part of the other group members. These real-life behaviors can then be immediately worked on in the group.
3. An individual can practice assertive responses with a variety of people in the group. This may facilitate the generalization of practiced assertive behaviors to others outside of the group.
4. The group can often devise creative assertive responses which had not even occurred to the trainer. In addition, members' assertive skills may be strengthened through their modeling assertive responses for another group member.
5. More people are available to encourage and reinforce a member's assertion attempts. Getting reinforcement from several peers at one time usually makes a greater impact on an individual. In addition, some members accept reinforcement from other group members more easily than they accept similar remarks from a trainer.

Although group assertion training has these general advantages, it should be noted that some people may derive more benefit from individual assertion training. Individual training has the advantage of providing a safe environment for those people who are very anxious in groups. It also enables a trainer to work more intensively. Thus it is more appropriate for those people who are in a crisis situation which requires immediate assertion skills, or for those people who have complicated psychological problems in addition to assertion problems.

TYPES OF ASSERTION TRAINING GROUPS

There are four basic types of assertion training groups: (1) exercise-oriented groups in which all the group members initially participate in a pre-set series of role play exercises and in later sessions the members generate their own behavioral rehearsal situations; (2) theme-oriented groups in which each session is devoted to a particular theme (e.g., giving constructive criticism) and behavior rehearsal is used, though the role plays may not be highly structured exercises; (3) semi-structured groups which use some role play exercises in combination with other therapeutic procedures, such as consciousness-raising discussion, values clarification, parent effectiveness training, empathy training, fair fight training, negotiation skills training, conflict resolution training, transactional script analysis; and (4) unstructured groups in which the role play experiences are based entirely on whatever needs the members present at each session. This latter group will not be specifically elaborated upon in this book because any of the cognitive-behavioral techniques described in this book may be used in the unstructured groups.

Whether training is done individually or in groups, we believe that the following process goals are critical considerations for successful assertion training: (1) identify specific situations and behaviors which will be the focus of training; (2) teach the participants how to ascertain if they have acted assertively rather than aggressively or nonassertively; (3) help individuals to accept their personal rights and the rights of others; (4) identify and modify the participants' irrational assumptions which produce excessive anxiety and anger and result in nonassertion and aggression; (5) provide opportunities for the participants to practice alternative assertive responses; (6) give specific feedback on how the members could improve their assertive behavior; (7) encourage the members to evaluate their own behavior; (8) positively reinforce successive improvements in assertive behavior; (9) model alternative assertive responses as needed; (10) structure the group procedures so that the members' involvement is widespread and supportive; (11) give considerable permission and encouragement for the participants to behave assertively within and outside of the group; and (12) display leadership behavior which is characterized by assertion rather than aggression or nonassertion.

Assuming that the participants have experienced the process we have described, how will they change after assertion training? We believe that the participants would ideally develop a wider repertoire of assertive responses to specific situations; recognize their own aggressive and nonassertive behavior; maintain a belief system which highly values their own personal rights and those of others; recognize and change whatever irrational thinking they do in specific situations; feel less anxious and more self-confident in those situations as well as in others which require assertive behavior; and lastly, that in their personal lives the participants would encourage others to be equally assertive.

SUMMARY

Although assertion training has a long history, only recently have professionals and the lay public become interested in it. This interest is the natural outgrowth of certain cultural changes which occurred in the Sixties.

Assertion training incorporates four basic procedures: (1) teaching people the differences between assertion and aggression, nonassertion and politeness; (2) helping people identify and accept their own personal rights as well as the rights of others; (3) reducing existing cognitive and affective obstacles to acting assertively; and (4) developing assertive skills through active practice methods.

Assertion training can be done on an individual or group basis, although group training is considered generally more effective. There are four types of assertion training groups: exercise-oriented, theme-oriented, semi-structured, and unstructured.

REVIEW QUESTIONS

1. Is assertion training a brand new technique?

2. Is assertion training simply another passing fad? Why or why not?

3. Why is there no general agreement on the set of specific techniques that comprise assertion training?

4. What is assertion training?

5. If you simply encourage a person to act more assertively and as a result the person becomes more assertive, have you done assertion training with that person?

6. Describe some advantages of group assertion training. What are the four basic types of assertion training groups?

7. Ideally, how will participants change after assertion training?

2
Assertive, Nonassertive, and Aggressive Behavior

Trainers who want to help group members learn to distinguish between assertion and aggression, nonassertion and politeness must themselves thoroughly understand these differences. This chapter examines these differences in some detail and includes a Discrimination Test for the trainer (see Table 1, p. 41). A later chapter (Chapter 4) describes an exercise which can be used to help group members learn these distinctions.

OVERVIEW OF ASSERTION, NONASSERTION, AND AGGRESSION

Assertion involves standing up for personal rights and expressing thoughts, feelings, and beliefs in *direct, honest,* and *appropriate* ways which do not violate another person's rights (Jakubowski, in press, a). The basic message in assertion is: This is what I think. This is what I feel. This is how I see the situation. This message expresses "who the person is" and is said without dominating, humiliating, or degrading the other person.

Assertion involves respect—not deference. Deference is acting in a subservient manner as though the other person is right, or better simply because the other person is older, more powerful, experienced, or knowledgeable or is of a different sex or race. Deference is present when people express themselves in ways that are self-effacing, appeasing, or overly apologetic.

Two types of respect are involved in assertion: respect for oneself, that is, expressing one's needs and defending one's rights, as well as respect for the other person's needs and rights. An example will help clarify the kind of respect involved in assertive behavior.

7

A woman was desperately trying to get a flight to Kansas City to see her mother who was sick in the hospital. Weather conditions were bad and the lines were long. Having been rejected from three standby flights, she again found herself in the middle of a long line for the fourth and last flight to Kansas City. This time she approached a man who was standing near the beginning of the line and said, pointing to her place, "Would you mind exchanging places with me? I ordinarily wouldn't ask, but it's extremely important that I get to Kansas City tonight." The man nodded yes, and as it turned out, both of them were able to get on the flight.

When asked what her reaction would have been if the man had refused, she replied, "It would have been OK. I hoped he would say yes, but after all he was there first" (Jakubowski, in press, a).

In this example the woman showed self-respect for her own needs by asking whether the man would be willing to help her. Also, she respected the man's right to refuse her request and not fulfill her need.

How is respect shown when refusing another's request? It depends on how that request is refused. A request may be refused aggressively: "What do you mean you want to borrow my car! I don't know where you get your nerve!" Such aggressive refusals involve only one-way respect; that is, respect for one's right to refuse but not for the other person's right to ask. A request may also be refused nonassert-ively: "What can I say. . .I feel just awful saying this, really bad. . .I can't loan you my car. Oh gee, what a terrible thing to say!" Here the person refused the request, but did it in a way that showed lack of self-respect: It suggested that the refuser was a bad person who should not have denied the request. In addition, the nonassertive refusal did not respect the other person's right to be treated as a capable person who can handle a disappointment. In contrast, an assertive refusal would be: "I'd like to help you out, but I feel uncomfortable loaning my car." The assertive refusal shows the two-fold respect: self-respect in the self-confident way the request is refused and respect for the other person's right to ask.

In our view, the goal of assertion is communication and "mutual-ity"; that is, to get and give respect, to ask for fair play, and to leave room for compromise when the needs and rights of two people conflict. In such compromises neither person sacrifices basic integrity and both get some of their needs satisfied. The compromise may be one in which one person gets her needs taken care of immediately while the other party gets taken care of a little later. For example, one weekend the friends see a movie and the next weekend they bowl. Or the compromise may involve both parties giving up a little. They attend *part* of an outdoor concert and then take a *short* walk and talk. When personal integrity is at stake, a compromise is inappropriate and nonassertive.

We are opposed to viewing assertion as simply a way "to get what one wants" for three reasons. First, this view emphasizes success in attaining goals. Thus it can cause people to become passive when they believe that acting assertively will not get them what they want. Second, this view concentrates only on the asserter's rights and not on the personal rights of both parties. Such an attitude increases the chances of people using aggressive or manipulative methods to get what they want. Third, it may lead to irresponsible behavior in which assertion is used to take advantage of other people. We have frequently heard people say that they can assertively ask for favors and it's just too bad that the other person is not strong enough to refuse their requests. In contrast, we advocate *responsible* assertion which involves mutuality, asking for fair play, and using one's greater assertive power to help others become more able to stand up for themselves. Interestingly, a by-product of responsible assertion is that people often do get what they want. Why? Because most people become cooperative when they are approached in a way which is both respectful of self and respectful of others.

Nonassertion involves violating one's own rights by failing to express honest feelings, thoughts, and beliefs and consequently permitting others to violate oneself, or expressing one's thoughts and feelings in such an apologetic, diffident, self-effacing manner that others can easily disregard them (Jakubowski, in press, a). In the latter type of nonassertion, the total message which is communicated is: I don't count—you can take advantage of me. My feelings don't matter—only yours do. My thoughts aren't important—yours are the only ones worth listening to. I'm nothing—you are superior.

Nonassertion shows a lack of respect for one's own needs. It also sometimes shows a subtle lack of respect for the other person's ability to take disappointments, to shoulder some responsibility, to handle his own problems, etc. The goal of nonassertion is to appease others and to avoid conflict at any cost.

Aggression involves directly standing up for personal rights and expressing thoughts, feelings, and beliefs in a way which is often dishonest, usually inappropriate, and always violates the rights of the other person. An example of "emotionally dishonest" aggression is a situation where individuals who feel saddened by another person's mourning for the death of a loved one sarcastically degrade the mourner ("That's just what I like to see—a grown person sniveling like a two-year-old brat"), instead of revealing their own sad and helpless feelings.

The usual goal of aggression is domination and winning, forcing the other person to lose. Winning is insured by humiliating, degrading, belittling, or overpowering other people so that they become weaker and less able to express and defend their needs and rights. The basic message is: This is what I think—you're stupid for believing differently. This is what I want—what you want isn't important. This is what I feel—your feelings don't count.

Nonverbal Components of Assertive, Nonassertive, and Aggressive Behavior

So far we've discussed the verbal components of assertive, nonassertive, and aggressive behavior. The nonverbal components of these behaviors are equally important, if not more so. Research (e.g., Mehrabian, 1972) has shown that the vast majority of our communication is carried out nonverbally. Take a moment to consider how the statement "I like you" can be said as a sincere statement, a question, or a sarcastic remark, by simply changing voice inflection, facial expression, and hand gestures. Likewise, an otherwise verbal assertive statement can become nonassertive or aggressive depending on the nonverbal behaviors which accompany the verbal statement.

Eisler, Miller & Hersen (1973) have pinpointed some of the nonverbal behaviors which may be important in assertion: duration of looking at the other person, duration of speech, loudness of speech, and affect in speech. Research has generally supported the importance of these nonverbal behaviors (e.g., Hersen, Eisler & Miller, 1973), with the exception of length of time it takes the person to respond to the other individual (Galassi, Galassi & Litz, 1974). Other nonverbal behaviors which may be important in assertion, nonassertion, and aggression are described below.

In assertive behavior, the nonverbals are congruent with the verbal messages and add support, strength, and emphasis to what is being said verbally. The voice is appropriately loud to the situation; eye contact is firm but not a stare-down; body gestures which denote strength are used; and the speech pattern is fluent—without awkward hesitancies—expressive, clear, and emphasizes key words.

In nonassertive behavior, the nonverbal behaviors include evasive eye contact, body gestures such as hand wringing, clutching the other person, stepping back from the other person as the assertive remark is made, hunching the shoulders, covering the mouth with a hand, nervous gestures which distract the listener from what the speaker is saying, and wooden body posture. The voice tone may be singsong or overly soft. The speech pattern is hesitant and filled with pauses and the throat may be cleared frequently. Facial gestures may include raising of the eye brows, laughs, and winks when expressing anger.

In general, the nonassertive gestures are ones which convey weakness, anxiety, pleading, or self-effacement. They reduce the impact of what is being said verbally, which is precisely why people who are scared of acting assertively use them. Their goal is to "soften" what they're saying so that the other person will not be offended.

In aggressive behavior, the nonverbal behaviors are ones which dominate or demean the other person. These include eye contact that tries to stare down and dominate the other person, a strident voice that does not fit the situation, sarcastic or condescending tone of voice, and parental body gestures such as excessive finger pointing.

Individuals may display idiosyncratic nonverbal behaviors which are important besides those described above. It is important that trainers attend to, and teach group members to attend to, their own individual nonverbal behaviors. Both trainers and group members need to continually assess the impact of the members' nonverbal behaviors. Chapter 4 describes two exercises for helping the group members to become aware of their nonverbal behaviors.

Table 2 (p. 53) summarizes the basic differences between assertive, nonassertive, and aggressive behavior.

Examples of Assertive, Nonassertive, and Aggressive Behavior

In each example, the first response is aggressive, the second, nonassertive, and the third is assertive.

Confronting a professor who gives inappropriate and excessive amounts of work—

11

1. Dr. Jones, you have some nerve giving me this kind of work. I know you have control over me, but I don't have to take this stuff. You professors think you can use grad students for anything you please—Well not this time!
2. OK, Dr. Jones, I'll do it. I guess you must have a reason for asking me to do this stuff. . .even if it isn't related to my assistantship. I don't suppose you'd consider letting me off the hook this time? Huh?
3. Dr. Jones, when you give me work that's not related to your class, I'd have to put in extra hours beyond what's appropriate for my assistantship. For those reasons I need to say no on this extra work.

Talking with someone who has just made a sexist remark—
1. Who the hell do you think you are! God's gift to women?
2. Oh come on (ha ha). You know how much that irritates me when you say things like that (ha ha).
3. Frankly, I think that remark demeans both of us.

Refusing an extra helping of food at a dinner party—
1. You'd just love me to put on a few pounds of fat!
2. Gee . . . ah . . . Well, since you insist . . . I'll change my mind. Yeah, give me another piece.
3. That food does look good but I don't want any more.

Trying to get a group on the subject after they've wandered into tangential areas—
1. Can't you people get back to work and stop this goofing off?
2. I guess it's just my hang-up. Do you think it'd be OK if we got back to the original subject? I've forgotten it myself (ha ha).
3. What we're talking about is interesting; however, I'm feeling the need to get back to the original subject.

ASSERTIVE BEHAVIOR

Reasons for Acting Assertively

Assertion rather than nonassertion / Losing other people's approval is usually a major issue for people who are often nonassertive. In a way it's like believing "I will only survive if I have other people's approval." However, nonassertion does not guarantee approval. People may pity rather than approve of nonassertion; often this pity eventually turns into irritation and finally disgust (Jakubowski-Spector, 1973b).

A major reason for acting assertively is that it increase *one's own self-respect.* Indeed, an unpublished study by Judy Demplewolff (1974) showed that group members' self-concepts significantly changed after assertion training. A second reason is that assertion eventually results in greater self-confidence which can then reduce the need for others' approval. Third, while it is true that people will sometimes disapprove of assertion, usually other people respect and admire those who are responsibly assertive, show respect for self and others, have the courage to take stands, and deal with conflict openly and fairly. Lastly, assertion—more frequently than nonassertion—results in individuals getting their needs satisfied and preferences respected.

Assertion rather than aggression | A major fear of people who are frequently aggressive is that they will become more vulnerable and lose control over other people. It's like believing "I can only survive if I'm invulnerable and able to control people." That aggression does not guarantee successful control over other people is usually overlooked. When people apparently acquiesce under aggression, often they simply have gone "underground" and subtly sabotage the aggressor's control. (This sabotage process is described more fully later in this chapter.)

A major reason for acting assertively is that it increases *one's control over oneself,* which feels good. Second, assertion eventually results in greater feelings of self-confidence which reduces insecurity and vulnerability. Third and very importantly, assertion rather than aggression results in closer, more emotionally satisfying relationships with others. Fourth, while it is true that assertion will mean that sometimes individuals will not achieve their objectives and "win," assertion maximizes the likelihood that both parties can at least partially achieve their goals and get their needs met.

There are many different ways of acting assertively. It is important that the trainer know the various types of assertion so that group members can be helped to find better alternatives when one type of assertion is inappropriate or does not meet a member's needs. The different types of assertion are more accurately thought of as principles to help guide the person's assertion instead of as techniques to use *on* other people.

Types of Assertion:

Basic Assertion

Basic assertion refers to a simple expression of standing up for personal rights, beliefs, feelings, or opinions. It does not involve other social skills, such as empathy, confrontation, persuasion, etc. Examples of basic assertions are:

When being interrupted—
Excuse me, I'd like to finish what I'm saying.

When being asked an important question for which you are unprepared—
I'd like to have a few minutes to think that over.

When returning an item to a store—
I'd like my money back on this saw.

When refusing a request—
No, this afternoon is not a good time for me to visit with you.

When telling a parent you don't want advice—
I don't want any more advice.

Basic assertion also involves expressing affection and appreciation toward other people:

I like you.
I care for you a lot.
Having a friend like you makes me feel happy.
You're someone special to me.

The following is a particularly touching example of assertively expressing affection:

A father overheard his five-year-old child saying to a playmate: "Are you having a good time?" When the playmate replied "Yes," the child continued, "I am too. I'm so glad that I invited you to come over and play!"

Empathic Assertion

Often people want to do more than simply express their feelings or needs. They may also want to convey some sensitivity to the other person. When this is the goal, the empathic assertion can be used. This type of assertion involves making a statement that conveys recognition of the other person's situation or feelings and is followed by another statement which stands up for the speaker's rights (Jakubowski, in press, a). Examples of empathic assertions are:

> *When two people are chatting loudly while a meeting is going on—*
> You may not realize it, but your talking is starting to make it hard for me to hear what's going on in the meeting. Would you keep it down.

> *When having some furniture delivered—*
> I know it's hard to say exactly when the truck will come, but I'd like a ball park estimate of the arrival time.

> *When telling a parent that you don't want advice—*
> I know that you give me advice because you don't want me to get hurt by mistakes I might make. At this point in my life, I need to learn how to make my own decisions and rely on myself, even if I do make some mistakes. I appreciate the help you've given me in the past and you can help me now by not giving me advice (Jakubowski, in press, a).

There is considerable personal power in the empathic assertion because other people more easily respond to assertion when they have been recognized first. This power, however, should not be used as a manipulation to merely gain one's own ends, without genuine respect for the other person. Repeatedly saying, "I understand how you feel but. . ." can be just "mouthing" understanding and conning other people into believing that their feelings are being taken into account when in fact their feelings are really being discounted. Such behavior does not involve empathic assertion.

Another important benefit of the empathic assertion is that it causes the speaker to take a moment to try to understand the other person's feelings before the speaker reacts. This can help the speaker keep perspective on the situation and thus reduces the likelihood of the speaker's aggressively overreacting when irritated.

Escalating Assertion
According to Rimm & Masters (1974), escalating assertion involves starting with a "minimal" assertive response that can usually accomplish the speaker's goal with a minimum of effort and negative emotion

and a small possibility of negative consequences. When the other person fails to respond to the minimal assertion and continues to violate one's rights, the speaker gradually escalates the assertion and becomes increasingly firm. We have observed that often it is not necessary to go beyond the initial minimal assertion; but if it is necessary, the person can become increasingly firm without becoming aggressive. The escalating assertion can occur from a request to a demand, from a preference to an outright refusal, or, as the following example illustrates, from an empathic assertion to a firm basic assertion.

> *The speaker is in a bar with a woman friend, and a man repeatedly offers to buy them drinks—*
> That's very nice of you to offer, but we came here to catch up on some news. Thanks, anyway!
>
> No, thank you. We really would rather talk just to each other.
>
> This is the third and last time I am going to tell you that we don't want your company. Please leave! (Jakubowski, in press, b).

In this example, the final blunt refusal was appropriate because the earlier escalating assertions were ignored. If the woman had started with the highly escalated assertion the first time the man had approached, her response would have been inappropriate. Since assertion involves direct, honest, and *appropriate* expressions of thoughts and feelings, her reaction would be aggressive, rather than assertive. Likewise when a person has not objected to taking the minutes of a meeting, but one day suddenly says, "I'm getting sick and tired of being the secretary just because I'm the only woman in the group," her response would be aggressive, rather than assertive. Only if her comment had been preceded by successively escalated assertions which had been ignored would her comment be appropriate and assertive.

A final point about the escalating assertion is that just before making the final escalated assertion, we suggest that one consider offering a "contract option," in which the other person is informed what the final assertion will be and is given a chance to change behavior before it occurs. For example, when a repair shop repeatedly refuses to settle an unreasonable bill, one may say, "I'm being left with no other alternative other than to complain to the Better Business Bureau and your distributor. I'd prefer not to do that but I will if this is the only alternative I'm left with." Often people only recognize that one means business at the contract option point.

Whether the contract option is simply a threat depends on how it is said. If it is said in a menacing tone of voice which relies on emotionality to carry the argument, it is a threat. When the contract option is carried out assertively, it is said in a matter-of-fact tone of voice which simply gives information about the consequences which will occur if the situation is not equitably resolved.

Confrontive Assertion

Confrontive assertion is used when the other person's words contradict his deeds. This type of assertion involves objectively describing what the other person said would be done, what the other actually did do, after which the speaker expresses what he wants (Jakubowski, in press, a). The entire assertion is said in a matter-of-fact, nonevaluative way, as the examples below show:

> I was supposed to be consulted before the final proposal was typed. But I see the secretary is typing it right now. Before he finishes it, I want to review the proposal and make whatever corrections I think are needed. In the future, I want to get a chance to review any proposals before they're sent to the secretary.

> I thought we'd agreed that you were going to be more considerate towards students. Yet I noticed today that when two students asked for some information you said that you had better things to do than babysit for kids. As we discussed earlier, I see showing more consideration as an important part of your job. I'd like to figure out what seems to be the problem.

> I said it was OK to borrow my records as long as you checked with me first. Now you're playing my classical records without asking. I'd like to know why you did that.

The above are examples of initial confrontive assertive statements. In most cases the ensuing conversation would be an extended interaction between the two people. This is particularly true in the last two examples in which the speaker wanted additional information and the resulting discussions would be problem-solving ones.

17

In contrast to assertive confrontation, aggressive confrontation involves judging other people—rather than describing their behavior—and trying to make others feel guilty. For example:

> Hey, those are my records! Evidently your word means absolutely nothing to you! Just for that I want my records right now and in the future you're going to find them locked up. Then you'll *have* to ask me first.

I-Language Assertion

I-language is particularly useful as a guide for helping people to assertively express difficult negative feelings. In addition, the principles in I-language can help individuals learn how to determine when their feelings stem from some violation of their rights and feelings, or whether their negative feelings are due to their trying to impose their own values and expectations on other people.

I-language assertion is based on the work of Thomas Gordon (1970) and involves a four-part statement:

> *When* . . . (speaker objectively describes the other person's behavior).
> *The effects are* . . . (speaker describes how the other person's behavior concretely effects his life or feelings).
> *I feel* . . . (speaker describes feelings).
> *I'd prefer* . . . (speaker describes what he wants).

Three points merit further comment. First, we believe that the "I feel . . ." part of the statement is optional. Saying, "I feel . . ." does clarify for oneself and for others just precisely what one's feelings are and thus it may reduce misunderstandings about the nature of one's feelings. However, describing one's feelings may be inappropriate in some situations, e.g., business. Second, we believe that the "I prefer . . ." part of the statement is also optional. As Gordon cogently notes, excluding it gives the other person maximum opportunity to offer his own ideas for dealing with the situation. However, including it gives the other person some information as to what the speaker, at least, would like to see happen. Third, I-language assertion is initially presented as a formula. After individuals feel comfortable using the formula, they may wish to intermix the four components so that it matches their own natural style of speaking.

18

The following example illustrates I-language assertion in which one expresses irritation and describes the concrete effect of the other person's behavior. A desk is shared by two people, one of whom is disorganized and the other is neat.

Today I saw Ms. Van Buren to give her my report and I didn't have all of it because my papers got mixed up with yours. The disorganization on this desk has gotten to be a real problem for me and I'm getting upset. I'd like to hear your suggestions so that this problem doesn't come up again.

Depending on the speaker's wants, alternative ending assertions could be:

I'd like to talk to Ms. Van Buren about our getting separate desks, or Would you be willing to keep your side of the desk more organized?

The example below illustrates how the I-language assertion could be done when the effect of the other person's behavior is less concrete:

When your half of the desk is so disorganized, I find it hard to think and concentrate on my work because I'm worried that my papers may be mixed with yours. This is really bothering me. Do you think we could work something out to help me?

Does the following statement identify a concrete effect?

When your half of the desk is so messy, I start feeling angry and that upsets me. I'd like you to be more neat and organized.

No. The speaker has not specified a concrete effect but rather has attempted to impose the speaker's own idiosyncratic values on the other person—all under the guise of being assertive.

In contrast to assertively expressing irritation in terms of I-language, aggressively expressing irritation tries to make the other person responsible for having caused the bad feelings and uses You-language instead of I-language. In the following example, the first statement is aggressive, and the second statement is assertive.

You make me mad when you always butt in! What's wrong with you anyway!

When I'm constantly interrupted, I lose my train of thought and begin to feel that my ideas aren't important to you. I start feeling hurt and angry. I'd like you to make a point of waiting until I'm finished speaking.

Assertion and Persuasion

Often individuals lack information about how to be influential in groups and maximize their impact—without being aggressive. While much has been written about persuasion, little has been said about ways of being assertive and persuasive. At the present time, we've identified two principles which may maximize a person's impact when giving opinions in task-oriented groups, such as small faculty meetings, PTA committee meetings, etc. The two principles concern how to use *timing* and *tact* in expressing honest opinions.

Timing / Before deciding when is the best time to assert their opinions, individuals need to decide which of all the many issues that are raised in a meeting have top priority for them and warrant taking an assertive stance. People who fail to decide their top priority issues may end up being "assertive for the sake of being assertive" and talking far too long about virtually every issue that is raised. The consequence of such behavior is that the rest of the committee members view the individual as being on an ego trip. Once individuals have become so labeled, their opinions are not listened to seriously. When they do raise cogent points on an important issue, their opinions are likely to be ignored by the group.

After people identify their own priority issues, timing of the opinion becomes important. Observation leads us to believe that it is generally more effective to express an opinion after a third to a half of the committee members have already expressed their positions. At that point in the meeting, individuals have a better sense of the group's position and they can more easily address themselves to the points which thus far have been raised. Furthermore this timing reduces the risk of the group members' making up their minds before one lets one's position be known.

When individuals express their opinions, in order to achieve maximum impact, these opinions should be stated clearly, cogently, and with few self-depreciatory remarks. For example, saying, "I sure don't understand what's wrong with this proposal. Maybe it's just me, but I kind of feel something's wrong with the whole thing," implies that the speaker is inadequate. It is generally more effective to present oneself as a capable person. For example, "The way I see it there's a flaw in this

20

proposal that's hard to pin down. Does anyone else sense that too?" Needless to say the nonverbal behaviors which accompany opinions are extremely important. Losing eye contact, speaking softly, in a whining or belligerent tone of voice, covering one's mouth with a hand, etc., all reduce the potential impact of a statement.

Tact / Tact becomes very important when taking a position which is contrary to either the rest of the group or to a powerful group member. In assertive persuasion, tact involves a specific type of empathic assertion of "stroking" which is said *before* stating an opinion. Stroking does not mean using flattery or making ingratiating comments, but rather finding something that is genuinely good about the other person's point. In the following examples the stroking statements are italicized.

> *Your point about the lack of interest in student government is well taken. The students have been apathetic.* But if we bow to apathy we'll never get anywhere. I say let's try to get a student questionnaire developed anyway and find out just how much support we've got.

> *I agree that the time-flex planning has not been widely used and the bugs haven't been completely worked out of the system.* However, the experimental results have been encouraging to the point where I think the system's worth trying.

NONASSERTIVE BEHAVIOR

Reasons Why People Act Nonassertively
There are at least five major reasons for nonassertive behavior. The first of these concerns the failure to distinguish assertion from aggression and nonassertion from politeness.

Mistaking firm assertion for aggression / To many individuals, firm assertive behavior sounds like aggression. Their own unique learning backgrounds have caused them to equate any show of assertive firmness or anger with aggression. Furthermore, the culture at large has not sufficiently distinguished between assertion and aggression—indeed, neither have some prominent behaviorists (e.g., Salter, 1949)! Thus, individuals mislabel their own natural assertive impulses as dangerous urges which are to be severely controlled. Women in particular may be told that their natural assertive behavior is aggressive and masculine.

21

Mistaking nonassertion for politeness | Many people act non-assertively under the mistaken notion that such behavior is really just being polite and considerate. They may have been taught that it is not polite to end a telephone call when the other person called first, to use the word "I" to interrupt someone even if the other person talks ad nauseam, to disagree with someone who's older, disabled, or has higher status, to refuse food at someone's home, to ask guests to leave when the evening has worn thin, to agree with a compliment, or to compliment oneself, etc.

There are several ways leaders can help group members to differentiate between so-called "politeness"—which is really disguised non-assertion—and genuine consideration for others. One way is to help members pay attention to their own body signals. When people are nonassertive, their bodies often signal tension. These signals may be a churning stomach, a headache, facial muscles freezing, breathing faster, and the like. Sometimes the body reacts more quickly to nonassertion than the intellect!

A second way to help people become aware of nonassertion which masquerades as politeness is to ask whether they are likely to remind other persons of their previous behaviors which were politely disregarded when they occurred. One example would be when a friend has borrowed some records and returned them warped. The owner says nothing at the time but knows that in the midst of some future disagreement, the issue may be brought up:

> Do you remember the time you borrowed my records and got them warped and I said nothing! That's the kind of friend I am. And you mean to tell me that you don't want to double date with me!

If people are likely to throw up such incidents later to the person, their original failure to complain about someone else's misdeed was not polite, it was nonassertive.

A third way is to ask the members to reflect on how their relationship with the other person is likely to change if they fail to honestly express their feelings and instead "politely" keep silent.

> A friend had frequently borrowed small amounts of money from his roommate and had failed to pay it back. The roommate decided to be "polite" and did not ask for repayment. After a while, the roommate found himself making jokes that had an

unexpected barb, avoiding his friend at times he thought his friend would be short of cash, and lying about having no money. The roommate's so-called politeness was starting to wreck a good relationship.

This is an example of the nonassertive circle in which one acts nonassertively so as not to hurt the relationship; the nonassertion, in fact, ends up hurting the relationship.

Another classic situation occurred with a woman who was dating an older man who rapidly fell in love with her. After a few days, he started asking her questions like, "Do you miss me as much as I miss you?" "Do you love me as much as I love you?" "Did you think about me this afternoon?" Not wanting to hurt the man, she distantly replied yes to all his questions hoping he would realize she did not feel all that her words suggested. However, the man felt encouraged by her responses and continued to press for a more involved relationship. Within a week, the woman was disgusted with herself for lying, and blamed the man for causing her to be deceitful and feeling pushed into a corner. She started to avoid him, did not answer the phone, and eventually stood him up. The result was that the relationship ended. The man was deeply hurt and felt misled and foolish. The woman felt guilty, nasty, and fearful of other relationships.

Another way in which a leader can help members decide whether they are being nonassertive or simply considerate and generous is to describe the "hidden bargain" (Jakubowski-Spector, 1973b). A hidden bargain occurs when a person sacrifices some important rights or preferences, expecting that the other person will do something explicit in return, but without telling the other person what is expected in exchange. A classic example are employees who want a larger raise, a job promotion, or special privileges, such as coming late to work. Instead of directly asking for what they want, they overwork, expecting that the employer then *cannot* possibly refuse them a raise, promotion, or whatever. When the employees do not get the raise, they feel abused by the organization and reason that it's not worth doing anything for anybody since one just gets used in the process.

The hidden bargain also occurs in personal relationships. For example, "I won't complain to my husband about the small separation settlement and then he'll change his mind and return to me," or "I'll say nothing to my roommate when he doesn't wash the dishes and drinks my liquor and then he won't be able to object to my girlfriend staying overnight."

People can find out whether they are being polite or striking a hidden bargain by asking themselves this question: "Will I feel used if the other person doesn't do what I expect him to do?" (doesn't give me a raise, divorces me, objects to my overnight guests). If the answer is yes, a hidden bargain is in operation.

Failure to accept personal rights | A second major reason why people act nonassertively is that they do not fully accept their personal rights; in other words, they do not believe they have the right to express their reactions, to stand up for themselves, to take care of their own emotional needs. Often they do not believe that they are entitled to express certain kinds of feelings, e.g., hurt, anger, disappointment, affection. Frequently they not only believe that they should not express these feelings but that *they should not have these feelings in the first place!* Chapters 3, 4, and 10 describe some methods for helping people accept their right to have and express feelings and to take care of their own needs.

Anxiety about negative consequences | A third major reason why people act nonassertively concerns their anxiety about what would happen as a result of any assertive behavior. Common fears are that they will lose other people's affection or approval, that other people will think they are foolish, stupid, or selfish, that they will hurt other people's feelings or badly damage other's lives, and that other people will become angry or rejecting. Methods for helping people to deal with their anxieties are described in Chapter 5.

Mistaking nonassertion for being helpful | A fourth cause of non-assertion is the belief that one's nonassertion actually helps the other person. In reality such behavior involves "rescuing" the other person. Rescuing is giving help the other person actually does not need and sacrificing one's own needs. Unhealthy rescuing can be distinguished from genuine helping. In genuine helping, the receiver's behavior changes in positive ways, and at some point, the receiver no longer needs the help. In rescuing, one person eventually ends up in the victim role and then in the persecutor position (James & Jongeward, 1971, p. 87). The other person continues the same unhealthy behavior.

We've observed one such rescue in which a brother, over a period of years, kept borrowing money from his sister to the tune of $8,000.

24

Each time his plea was dramatic: Because of his gambling debts, he was in danger of being beaten up unless she would loan him the money. On the surface it might appear that the woman was a Good Samaritan. In reality she was being taken advantage of. Her brother had an excellent job, took expensive vacations, and in general just frittered away his money. In a sense the brother was living off his own income plus half of his sister's. Classically, the sister then became the "victim" and felt abused, powerless, developed marital problems, and had no money to take care of her own needs for relaxation, clothes, savings, etc. Occasionally she became the "persecutor" and aggressively attacked her brother for his failure to repay the loans. Yet every time he came begging for help, she again rescued him, and the cycle started again. As long as she was hooked into rescuing, she could not assertively refuse her brother's requests and demands for money.

The next example illustrates a less dramatic case of how non-assertion can be related to rescuing:

Though the high school teacher had laid out explicit guidelines for the term paper, the student nonassertively presented himself as a helpless victim: "I don't know where to start. How should I start off the paper? I just don't understand at all about linking the paragraphs together. What would be a good topic for the paper? Would you give me some ideas on how to end it?" The student did not even try to help himself. The teacher rescued the student, denied her own needs, and ended up essentially writing the paper for the student. The teacher then became the victim, and felt trapped, manipulated, and angry. The next time the teacher saw the student, she aggressively criticized him in class. Predictably, the student then became the aggressive persecutor, accusing the teacher of being unclear, never giving help, favoring other students, expecting too much from the student, etc.

In this case, if either the teacher or student had acted assertively, the entire scene could have been prevented. If the student had *assertively* asked for help, the teacher would not have felt manipulated and then become abusively aggressive, for example:

Student: I've started my rough draft of the paper and it's going fairly well. I've gotten stuck in one spot though and would appreciate it if you could help me learn some more interesting ways of starting off the lead sentence. I'm also having trouble linking the paragraphs together. Here's what I've done so far. How does it look to you?

If the teacher had *assertively* set limits when the student played the nonassertive victim, the rescuer-victim-persecutor triangle would have been avoided:

Teacher: I'm willing to give you help on your paper. However, I am uncomfortable giving you all the help you want when at this point you haven't done any work at all on the paper. If you would start a rough draft, I'd be willing to help you learn how you could improve it.

Deficient skills / A last major reason for nonassertion is that people may simply not know how to act otherwise. They may not have learned assertive skills because they lacked opportunities to vicariously acquire such skills by watching how other people have handled similar situations. For example, adults who as children rarely went to restaurants may simply not have learned how to request service or return badly cooked food.

Consequences of Acting Nonassertively

The usual goal of nonassertion is to appease others and to avoid conflict at any cost. Even when the nonassertion *costs people their own integrity,* the immediate consequence of allowing individuals to avoid or escape from anxiety-producing conflicts is very reinforcing. For example, even when a man's nonassertion is viewed as feminine, such punishment is usually not strong enough to counter the more immediate tension reduction which occurs when he successfully avoids a potential conflict by acting nonassertively.

In addition, people may be encouraged to be nonassertive by others who praise them for their selflessness, feminity, for being a good friend, child or student, and for being quiet, subservient, and generally agreeable and not causing problems for other people.

In the long run, however, a person who is frequently nonassertive feels a growing loss of self-esteem and an increasing sense of hurt and anger. Even more internal tension may then result. When this tension is constantly suppressed, somatic problems may develop, such as headaches, stomach aches, backaches (Jakubowski-Spector, 1973b) and sometimes even general depression (Jakubowski, in press, a). Other people who are interested in close relationships which are characterized

26

by the honest expression of thoughts and feelings may withdraw or not even start a relationship with a nonassertive person. People who feel guilty about inadvertently taking advantage of another person's non-assertiveness may withdraw from that person. Finally, although other people may initially feel sorry for the nonassertive person, their pity often turns into irritation, and finally disgust and lack of respect (Jakubowski-Spector, 1973b).

Maintaining Assertion
in the Face of Someone Else's Nonassertion

While most of the types of assertion which have been previously discussed can be helpful in dealing with someone else's nonassertion, I-language assertion is particularly effective. The following example illustrates using I-language assertion with someone who is demeaning himself.

> A man frequently cut himself down whenever his woman friend talked about anything positive in her career. Disagreeing with his self-cutting was ineffective.
>
> When the woman discovered that his behavior had become irritating and was interfering with the development of their relationship, she said, "I get uncomfortable when you negatively compare yourself to me. You don't really deserve to cut yourself down. Also, I am starting to feel like not telling you some of the good things that happen to me because it results in your negatively comparing yourself to me and cutting yourself down. When that happens, I feel like we're in some sort of competition with each other as to which of us is the more competent and successful. I'd like to be able to share my happiness with you without your cutting yourself down. I'd also like to see you feel good about yourself. You deserve to feel good about yourself. And if I can help with that, I'd like to."

In this example, the assertive woman was also helping the man to become more assertive and feel better about himself. This is a responsible use of assertive behavior in which the individual's power is used to help other people and not to take advantage of them. Other ways of encouraging a nonassertive person to become more assertive are: (1) to explain the difference between acting assertively and aggressively and being nonassertive or polite; (2) to note any assertive behavior on the part of the other and to encourage that behavior; (3) to

27

encourage other people to discuss when they are unsure whether they have the right to be assertive; and (4) to give other people the opportunity to act assertively.

AGGRESSIVE BEHAVIOR

Reasons Why People Act Aggressively

There are many kinds of cognitive, affective, and behavioral patterns which lead to aggressive behavior. Five patterns which are primarily behavioral will be described here. Chapter 5 deals with some cognitive and affective patterns associated with aggression.

Powerlessness and threat | A general cause of aggression is the feeling of being vulnerable to an anticipated or actual attack by another person. The resulting aggressive overreaction is instigated by threat and a sense of powerlessness.

Prior nonassertion | It may seem surprising that a second chief cause of much aggression is due to the person's prior nonassertion. The subtle ways in which aggression can result from nonassertion deserve some consideration.

Aggression can occur when a person has been nonassertive for a period of time, allowing rights and feelings to be violated, with the result that hurt and anger build to the point that the person finally feels justified in expressing these feelings and aggressively standing up for rights. In other cases, individuals may nonassertively allow their rights to be abused and misunderstandings grow as part of a game. After their aggressive outburst of feelings, they expect the other person to feel guilty and become more affectionate. Thus, their aggression is a kind of game to manipulate emotional closeness, rather than to directly ask for affection or act in ways that openly show their vulnerability, thus increasing closer personal relationships.

At other times people act aggressively as a way to prevent themselves from becoming nonassertive. For example, when individuals have been assertive in repeatedly refusing someone's request, they may be afraid that they will back down and accede to the request if asked once more. As a way of preventing themselves from becoming nonassertive, they may start to make themselves feel self-righteous anger and blame the other person: "Who does he think he is anyway? I've already said no three times!" These feelings then erupt into aggressive behavior.

28

Aggression and nonassertion are related in another subtle way in which individuals are nonassertive towards people who have greater power and they inhibit their hurt and angry feelings. Then they aggressively express these feelings with those people over whom they have power. The classic example of this type of aggressive-nonassertive pattern are employees who acquiesce to an employer's unreasonable requests, and then finding themselves overburdened with work, personally blame subordinates for their failure to work even harder.

Finally, aggression is related to nonassertion in that *both* involve denying certain personal rights. For example, in order to justify asking for help when individuals do not feel they have the right to be weak and need help, they may start seeing the other person as bad and selfish for not volunteering to help ("All you ever do is think of yourself! Can't you see that I need help getting the house ready for company!").

In other cases when individuals mistakenly believe that the other person had "no right" to act in a certain way, there is a strong tendency for individuals to exaggerate the supposed misdeed and to overreact in a punitive manner. For example, a person who believes that a friend does not have the right to request to borrow the car typically becomes aggressive when such a request is made. The aggressor reasons that the absurdity of such a request is so obvious that the other person should not even have had to ask! Interestingly, these aggressors almost invariably also believe that they do not have the right to make a comparable request and would never do so, regardless of how great their need was. Often persons who deny themselves the right to ask for personal favors from others deny others the same right.

Overreaction due to past emotional experiences / Thirdly, aggression may be due to a person's overreacting to a current situation because of some past unresolved emotional experience. The person reacts to the present with the emotions that are actually linked to some past experience or significant person, as the following case example illustrates:

> Sitting with her husband and woman friend, a wife was trying to explain the need for the Equal Rights Amendment. Her husband casually asked why it was needed since the issues were already covered by the other amendments in the Constitution. The wife overreacted and started to berate the husband for his ridiculous position. After the tirade, her woman friend calmly asked the

29

husband whether the wife always reacted so strongly. He responded, "Yeah, when we start talking about issues like this, Kathy gets pretty uptight." The calm way in which both her friend and husband reacted caused Kathy to realize that she had acted as though she had been personally attacked; in reality her husband had only asked for additional information. In thinking about her own overreaction, she realized that the feelings of powerlessness and personal attack she experienced were the same that she had felt as an adolescent, arguing to no avail with her unyielding father about religion and other issues. Discussing an emotionally charged issue produced feelings of powerlessness and thus triggered aggression, even though her husband did not respond like her father. In subsequent disputes she deliberately reminded herself that the other person was not her father, that she was no longer a child, etc. This self-talk helped her to maintain her perspective, composure, and assertion when presenting her opinions to potentially rejecting individuals.

Beliefs about aggression / Fourthly, aggression may result from the belief that aggression is the only way to get through to the other person. In the Sixties, for example, when college students challenged the administration and met with an unyielding stance and a complete discount of their complaints, many students became extremely aggressive upon hitting that "brick wall." A related cause of aggression is the belief that the world is hostile and one must be aggressive in order to survive.

Reinforcement and skill deficits / The fifth cause of aggression is that individuals may simply have received positive reinforcement for this behavior in their home or subculture. Also, individuals may react aggressively because they have not acquired the needed assertive skills which would be appropriate for a particular situation.

Consequences of Aggression

Since behavior is more easily influenced by immediate consequences, it is unfortunate that the most immediate consequences of aggression are usually positive, while the long-run consequences are negative. Immediate positive results include emotional release, a sense of power, and getting goals and needs met without experiencing direct negative reactions from others.

The long-term negative consequences include losing or failing to establish close relationships and feeling one has to be constantly vigilant against attack from others. Highly aggressive behavior may eventually cause individuals to lose jobs and promotions, get high blood pressure, become alienated from their children and mates, get into fights, or have trouble with the law. Because of these negative consequences, persons who are frequently aggressive eventually may feel deeply misunderstood, unloved, and unlovable.

In addition, when one is aggressive, other people may retaliate in direct or indirect ways by causing work slowdowns, property damage, by making deliberate mistakes, backbiting, through doing things that are subtly irritating, or by becoming self-destructive in an attempt to make the aggressor feel guilty.

People who are frequently nonassertive and who become aggressive only sporadically may feel immediate guilt, shame, and embarrassment after their aggression. Usually these bad feelings just make the individuals resolve to say nothing in the future because they feel they easily "get out of control" when they finally do express themselves. Unfortunately, this resolution does not solve the problem and merely sets in motion the vicious cycle of long periods of nonassertion which eventually explode in aggressive behavior.

People who are the target of aggression may experience various negative effects such as lowered morale in the family or a loss of initiative and creativity at work. The children of aggressive parents may suffer in many different ways. A son of an aggressive father who sees the most important male model in his life hurt other people, may feel ambivalent about his own masculinity, believing that "being a man" means hurting other people. An aggressive mother may cause a son to be suspicious, fearful, or hostile towards women. Similarly, the daughter of an aggressive mother may become alienated from herself as she tries to deny those parts of herself which are like her mother. When the father is aggressive, the daughter may avoid or fear men, may develop a subservient, masochistic relationship with other men, or may become hostile and rebellious towards men. Trainers can encourage group members to dwell on those negative consequences of aggression that have personal meaning to them. Chapter 5 also describes some ways of helping group members modify their aggressive behaviors.

31

Maintaining Assertion
in the Face of Someone Else's Aggression

Although the usual tendency is to flee (react nonassertively) or fight (react aggressively) when faced with aggression, it is generally important that individuals try to maintain an assertive position. This means that individuals stand their ground and defend themselves without belittling the aggressor. Such behavior frequently results in the aggressor eventually calming down and becoming more able to focus on the central issues which are at conflict.

In contrast, nonassertion merely reinforces the other person's aggression. Likewise, reacting aggressively to another's attack and using the rationale that since the other person did not respect one's rights, one does not have to respect the aggressor's personal rights frequently results in both parties losing in the process. When one reacts aggressively to another person's attack, the other person usually counter-aggresses, which leads to more aggression and so on until the two people end up tearing each other down, while the issues being argued become more and more remote from the original issues. The resulting hurt is often difficult to heal.

The following section describes ways of maintaining assertion in the face of another's aggression.

Reflection / It is often effective to simply reflect back what the aggressor is saying or feeling. This helps aggressive individuals realize that their message has been received. (Such reflection must be delicately done so that one does not give the impression of agreeing with the unwarranted aggressive criticisms.) Usually the aggressor then starts calming down, after which each person can react to what has been heard and can then state a personal position.

In the following example, the speaker makes an assertive statement which is in response to an aggressive attack. The first sentence in the statement includes a reflection, while the remaining statements include elements of self-disclosure, additional information, and limit-setting. The reflective statement is italicized.

I know that from your point of view it's completely unfair that you've received a small raise this year. Ideally, I would have liked to give you a larger raise, but right now the company has severely limited raises. We're in financial trouble, and the only way I could give a larger raise to you—and to the other people who'd like larger raises—would be to let some employees go. That's unacceptable to the company and to me, too.

Repeated assertion | Another potentially effective type of assertion is repeated assertion. This is appropriate when the other person overreacts and ignores or discounts the assertor's thoughts, feelings, or wants. Rather than countering each discount by justifying personal feelings, opinions, or wants, it is usually more effective to firmly repeat the original point *while still responding to legitimate points made by the other person.* The following example illustrates repeated assertion.

A student social worker disagreed with the staff physician about the disposition of a client's case and wanted to have a second evaluation given before a final decision was made about the kind of therapy the client would receive. The physician was sarcastic and refused to respond to the student's initial suggestion. The social worker again said, "I'd like a second opinion on this case," and finally the third time responded, "I realize that your decision is the final one, and I'm willing to abide by that, but I'd still like to have a second evaluation made of this client." The physician finally decided to act on the suggestion.

The important point here is that the assertor stuck to his position and did not directly threaten or try to intimidate the physician. He did make it clear that he was willing to accept realistic limits and that he intended to maintain his position. The repeated assertion was *not* a simple rote repetition. Instead it involved repeating the basic message while taking into consideration any legitimate points which were made by the other person. The assertor ignored all nonrelevant issues and red flag words, for example, "You social workers don't know what you're talking about." If these red flag statements are disagreed with in the middle of the argument, such disagreements usually abstract from the main issue; the two people then end up in a sand trap arguing about something far afield of the original subject.

In another example of repeated assertion, a man was asked to go to a movie. He responded by saying, "I need to study tonight but I'd also like to see you. I'd like to work out some sort of arrangement so I could do both things." When the other person said, "You don't really need to study," he firmly restated, "I do need to study tonight." If the other person continued to discount his need to study, the man could use I-language assertion rather than repeating, to an absurd point, his need to study:

> Hey, I'm getting irritated. When I tell you I need to study and you keep insisting I don't, I begin to feel like you're not interested in what my needs are. I'm willing to compromise with you, but I'm not willing to do it all your way.

A special note about broken record / Under certain circumstances, the repeated assertion may take the form of a "broken record" where the person keeps repeating the same message ad nauseam in a calm monotonous tone of voice, responding in a superficial manner, rotely repeating, "I understand how you feel . . ." (Smith, 1975). Broken record may be appropriate when the other person is extremely aggressive, destructive, manipulative, or discounting. In one such rare case, a father aggressively attacked his son whenever he saw him, finding fault in everything the son thought, felt, or did. The torrent of criticism quickly reduced the son to silence. The son consequently became depressed and anxious. Other types of assertion in response to the criticism were totally ineffective since the father completely ignored everything the son said. Finally, the son simply kept repeating in a voice loud enough to overshadow his father's, "I don't want to hear any more criticism! It hurts me!" This had to be repeated about ten times before the father stopped, and it took repeated encounters before the father would stop long enough for the son to really talk to him.

Improperly carried out, broken record can easily become an aggressive manipulation in which the person using it fails to respond to the other person's legitimate points and steamrollers the other person. In contrast to the other types of assertion described earlier, broken record is not a method which can be used at the same time by both parties of an interaction.

Broken record is similar to repeated assertion in that both require persistence on the part of the assertor. The two are different in that broken record involves a mere rote repetition which in practice essentially ignores the points made by the other person. In contrast, repetitive assertion is not carried out ad nauseam, does respond to the legitimate points raised by the other person, and may include the assertor providing some brief explanation of her own position.

Pointing out the implicit assumptions of the aggressor's position can help to diffuse the aggression. This involves listening very closely to what the aggressor is saying, hearing the implicit assumptions of the extreme position being taken, pointing out these assumptions, waiting for the aggressor's response, and then expressing one's own view of the situation. Pointing out the implicit assumptions of the aggressor's position sometimes helps the aggressor to become more objective which makes it possible for real communication to take place. In the following example, the implicit assumptions are italicized.

A man was aggressively attacked by his wife for disagreeing with her on a minor issue. The husband responded, "The message I'm getting is that *under no circumstances—regardless of what I think or feel—should I disagree with you. It's like I have no rights except to agree with you.*" The wife essentially agreed with this absurdity and continued her attack. After a short time, the man interrupted: "The way I see it, as long as I don't put you down, I have a right to express my opinion. *Just because I have a different opinion than you doesn't mean that I think you're stupid.* My opinions are my own, just as yours are. We can't always think the same way. I don't expect you to always agree with me or have the same opinion I do. And I don't think it's fair for you to lay your opinions on me either."

In another example, a counselor was trying to refer a current client to someone else because the counselor felt he lacked the skills to help the client. The client kept insisting that the counselor continue to see her, repeatedly saying that he did not really care about her. Finally the counselor commented: "What I hear you saying is that *the only way I can prove that I really do care for you is to see you in therapy.* The fact is that I've shown caring for you in the past and want to do the best for you by referring you to someone else who's more qualified. My position is being discounted as not showing caring. *The only way I can show that I care for you is to do what you want.*" From this point the counselor and client were able to get to the real issues that were bothering the client. A successful referral was eventually made.

I-language assertion is often an effective way of responding to someone's aggression.

An 18-year-old son was being severely castigated for failing to keep his room clean. The son responded, "When I'm personally cut down and accused of being totally irresponsible and selfish, I feel like I'm worthless, and there's no use in even trying. When you get mad about the way my room is, please just say, 'Jack, your room is getting pretty sloppy, and I'd appreciate your picking up your clothes off the floor.' I'd feel like cooperating with you if you talked to me like that. Would you do that—for both our sakes?"

Questions can sometimes be an effective means of helping the other person become aware of an unwarranted reaction, especially when the other person has been nonverbally aggressive. For example, when asked to wrap a package, the clerk said nothing but looked extremely irritated and muttered almost inaudibly as he wrapped the purchase. The customer responded in a puzzled, nonsarcastic tone of voice, "You got mad because I asked you to wrap the package?"

A security officer became visibly angry when a college professor, who had forgotten her office key, asked him to unlock her office door. Seeing his anger, the professor became angry, feeling that she had not asked him to do something that was unwarranted and that she didn't deserve his anger. After a few minutes, she asked in an even tone: "Tell me. *Are you angry because I asked you to come down and open my door?*" To which the officer responded with a polite but cold, "No, Madam." He paused and then continued, "Well, there are other things I could be doing besides coming here and opening up doors for teachers who don't remember their keys." The professor paused and then assertively said, "I can see where that does get irritating. I want to tell you that I don't make a habit of forgetting my key. These papers are extremely important, and I needed them today." In this situation, each party achieved more understanding of the other's behavior and established satisfactory limits.

It should be noted that in this example the professor provided information about her behavior rather than excuses for herself. Part of the distinction between an explanation and an excuse rests on how long one continues explaining one's behavior. The professor would have been making excuses if she had continued ad nauseam with explanations: "You see I left some materials for a student in my office and gave the student the key. Well, today I suddenly realized I needed these papers and being rushed I forgot I didn't have my key on my regular chain. The student left it in an envelope at home, etc."

Paradoxical statements is a rather subtle procedure which requires considerable skill for it to be assertive rather than aggressive. It involves diffusing the other person's aggression by making a statement which causes the aggressor to realize that the aggression could boomerang.

A man wearing prescription sunglasses was waiting in a restaurant lobby to be served. Suddenly an older man walked up to him and in a sarcastic tone of voice said, "What's the matter with you? Got some kind of eye disease?" The assertor responded in an even tone of voice, "Now wouldn't you feel bad if I told you I did?" The aggressor looked quite startled and simply walked away.

Arnold Lazarus (1975) has talked about the use of paradoxical statements in assertion. It should be noted, however, that not all paradoxical statements will be assertive, although they may be successful in stopping someone else's aggression.

A special caution about "fogging" / Smith (1975) has advocated "fogging" as a so-called assertive method for dealing with manipulative criticism. This procedure requires continually acknowledging the probability that there is some truth in the criticism, as the following example illustrates:

Passenger: You drive too fast.

Driver: That's probably true. I could drive slower.

Passenger: You're going to get a ticket.

Driver: Yes, I could get a ticket. That could happen.

Passenger: You're going to get us into an accident.

Driver: It's possible. Accidents do happen.

What is disturbing about this technique is that individuals do not really express their honest feelings. It is not straight communication. Carried to an extreme, it is countermanipulative and discounts possibly valid criticism of the person's behavior. Countermanipulative techniques which are manipulative themselves would seem warranted only when all other assertions have failed and the person's integrity and selfhood are at stake. Fogging was originally developed with an in-patient psychiatric population, who may be likely to live in environments where criticism, manipulation, and discounting are excessive. In such cases, fogging may be effective and even necessary to preserve integrity. Our position is that fogging as used by Smith (1975) is not an assertive method, but rather is a discounting technique which should not be confused with responsible assertive behavior.

In contrast to fogging, the following example illustrates an assertive way of responding to another's criticism which is direct and yet establishes limits:

Passenger: You're driving too fast.

Driver: I'm going at the speed limit. I don't think that's too fast. If it bothers you a lot, just tell me directly, and I'll slow down a couple of miles.

Passenger: You're going to get us into an accident.

Driver: Now wait a minute. When I start getting these criticisms of my driving, I'm getting mad and not wanting to listen to you at all. I want to have a nice time with you tonight and not have both of us mad at each other. How about it?

Passenger: That's a red light there. Slow down.

Driver: (Pulling over to the side of the road) Is it my driving that's really bothering you, or is it something else? What's going on?

SUMMARY*

Assertion involves standing up for personal rights and expressing thoughts, feelings, and beliefs in direct, honest, and appropriate ways which respect the rights of other people. In contrast, aggression involves self-expression which is characterized by violating others' rights and

* In this chapter we refer to "expressing one's needs" as part of assertion. We use the term "needs" as synonymous with "wants" or strong preferences and desires. By the term "needs," we do not intend to imply that one has a *need* to have one's needs met or that one *must* have one's needs met. We recognize that people have strong wants, which they frequently label as needs. As long as participants' use of the term "I need" does not involve catastrophizing, we are comfortable with using "need" and "want" synonymously.

demeaning others in an attempt to achieve one's own objectives. Nonassertion involves behavior which violates one's own self by failing to express honest feelings or thoughts. It may also involve diffident, overly apologetic, or effacing expression of personal rights and preferences.

It is important that assertive skills be used responsibly, that is, used in ways which treat others fairly and help facilitate others becoming more assertive.

Losing others' approval is a major fear which prompts many individuals to act nonassertively. For those who are frequently aggressive, a typical fear concerns their losing control and power over other people. A major reason for acting assertively rather than unassertively is that assertion increases one's own sense of self-respect and personal control.

There are various types of assertion: basic, empathic, escalating, I-language, and repeated. These are construed as principles which guide individuals in forming assertive responses, rather than as techniques to use on other people. Pointing out the implicit implications of an aggressor's position, appropriate use of questions, and some types of paradoxical intention may help individuals maintain a protective assertive stance while diffusing an aggressive attack.

REVIEW QUESTIONS

1. Assertion involves self-respect as well as respect for the other person. What does this mean?

2. Assertion is a method to "get what you want." Is this statement true? Why or why not?

3. In a few sentences distinguish between assertion and aggression, nonassertion and politeness.

4. Name four important nonverbal components of assertive behavior and show how these nonverbal behaviors would differ in nonassertive and aggressive behavior.

5. Why is body language important?

6. Assume that a person wants to refuse a request to babysit, borrow class notes, or play poker. Choose one of these situations and write an assertive response that would be an example of a basic assertion, empathic assertion, escalating assertion, confrontive assertion, I-language assertion, and repeated assertion.

7. How can one be assertive and persuasive?

8. Name some ways a leader can help people learn how to distinguish nonassertion from politeness.

9. Create your own example of the hidden bargain.

10. Create your own example of the nonassertive circle.

11. How can rescuing be distinguished from genuine helping?

12. How is rescuing related to nonassertion and aggression?

13. How is aggression related to nonassertion?

14. What are some reasons why people act aggressively? Nonassertively?

15. What are the immediate consequences of aggression and nonassertion? What are the long-term consequences of aggression and nonassertion?

16. Under what special conditions would "broken record" be appropriate?

17. Create your own example of "pointing out the implicit assumptions" of the other person's aggressive behavior.

18. What are some reasons for maintaining assertion in the face of someone else's aggression?

19. What is fogging? Is fogging an assertive behavior?

20. What is meant by the term "responsible assertive behavior"?

Table 1
Discrimination Test on Assertive, Aggressive, and Nonassertive Behavior

The following self-check Discrimination Test (Jakubowski, 1975) consists of 60 interpersonal situations. The responses to these situations are aggressive, assertive, or nonassertive. Twenty judges rated each of these responses, reaching 90 percent to 100 percent agreement on classifying each situation. Trainers should carefully read each situation and classify each response, as either assertive (+), aggressive (−), or nonassertive (N). The correct answers appear on page 52. A sum of 90 percent correct would indicate a satisfactory understanding of these concepts. We highly recommend that those trainers who obtain less than 90 percent re-read this chapter and analyze each of their errors to ascertain where their misunderstanding occurred, for example, mis-construing escalated assertions as aggressions, etc.

Chapter 4 describes how trainers can use this Discrimination Test to help group members refine their understanding of these basic concepts. Chapter 13 briefly describes how this test could be used to evaluate the effectiveness of assertion training.

Situation	Response	+, −, or N
1. Husband gets silent, instead of saying what's on his mind. You say,	I guess you are uncomfortable talking about what's bothering you. I think we can work it out if you tell me what's irritating you.	_____
2. A friend has asked you for the second time in a week to babysit for her child while she runs errands. You have no children of your own and respond,	You're taking advantage of me and I won't stand for it! It's your responsibility to look after your own child.	_____

Situation

3. An attendant at a gas station you frequently stop at for gas neglected to replace your gas cap. You notice this and return to inquire about it and you say,

4. You'd like a raise and say,

5. Someone asks for a ride home and it is inconvenient because you're late, have a few errands, and the drive will take you out of your way. You say,

6. Student enjoyed the teacher's class and says,

7. Your husband promised you that he would talk to your daughter about her behavior at school. The promise has not been carried out. You say,

Response

One of you guys here forgot to put my gas cap back on! I want it found *now* or you'll buy me a new one.

Do you think that, ah, you could see your way clear to giving me a raise?

I am pressed for time today and can take you to a convenient bus stop, but I won't be able to take you home.

You make the material interesting. I like the way you teach the class.

I thought we agreed last Tuesday that you would have a talk with Barb about her behavior at school. So far there's been no action on your part. I still think you should talk to her soon. I'd prefer sometime tonight.

+, −,
or N

_____

_____

_____

_____

_____

8. A committee meeting is being established. The time is convenient for other people but not for you. The times are set when it will be next to impossible for you to attend regularly. When asked about the time, you say,

Well I guess it's OK. I'm not going to be able to attend very much but it fits everyone else's schedule.

———

9. In a conversation, a man suddenly says, "What do you women libbers want anyway?" The woman responds,

Fairness and equality.

———

10. You've been talking for a while with a friend on the telephone. You would like to end the conversation and you say,

I'm terribly sorry but my supper's burning, and I have to get off the phone. I hope you don't mind.

———

11. A married man persists in asking you out for a date, saying, "Come on honey, what harm can it do to go to lunch with me just this once?" You respond,

I like our relationship the way it is. I wouldn't feel comfortable with any kind of dating relationship—and that includes lunch.

———

12. At a meeting one person often interrupts you when you're speaking. You say,

Excuse me. I would like to finish my statement.

———

13. You are in a hard-sell camera store, and you have been pressured to purchase an item. You say,

Well, OK, I guess that's pretty much what I was looking for. Yes, I suppose I'll get it.

———

43

		+, −, or N

Situation

14. A blind person approaches and asks you to purchase some materials. You respond,

15. Teenager is asked to do laundry. As the child puts laundry in the washer, parent says,

16. You have been pestered several times this week by a caller who has repeatedly tried to sell you magazines. The caller contacts you again with the same magazine proposition. You say,

17. Kids upstairs are making a lot of noise. You bang on the ceiling and yell,

18. An acquaintance has asked to borrow your car for the evening. You say,

19. Wife tells husband she'd like to return to school. He doesn't want her to do this and says,

Response

You people think that just because you're blind, people have to buy stuff from you. Well, I'm certainly not going to.

Don't forget to balance the load. Make sure you push the right buttons. You just never do things right!

This is the third time I've been disturbed and each time I've told you that I'm not interested in subscribing to any magazine. If you call again, I'll simply have to report this to the Better Business Bureau.

Hey you! Knock off the noise!

I don't know . . . Well, it's not worth getting into a fuss about it. You can borrow it, but I should warn you that I've been having trouble with the brakes.

Why would you want to do that? You *know* you're not capable enough to handle the extra work load.

20. An employee makes a lot of mistakes in his work. You say,

You're a lazy and sloppy worker.

21. Husband expects dinner on table when he arrives home from work and gets angry when it is not there immediately. You say,

I know you are tired and hungry and would like to have dinner immediately, but I have been doing some sculpting which is important to me. I will have dinner ready soon.

22. You've taken a suit to the cleaners that you plan to wear for a coming special occasion. When you go to pick it up, you find that there's a hole in it. You say,

I planned to wear that tonight. Aren't you people responsible enough to do something about it.

23. You are having trouble writing a paper and don't know exactly what further information you need. You say,

I really must be dumb but I don't know where to begin on this paper.

24. Roommate about to leave for work tells you that a friend of his needs a ride that afternoon and he has volunteered your services. You say,

You've got your nerve committing me without asking first! There's no way I'm going to the airport today. Let him take a cab like everybody else does.

25. A friend promised to come to a special party and then failed to show up. You call and after a few minutes of social conversation, you say,

I understood that you were coming to my party but you didn't come. I feel bad about not having you there. . . . What happened to you?

46

Response

Oh gee, Fran, I just know that Jerry will be mad at me if I say "yes." He says I'm always getting involved in too many things. You know how Jerry is about things like this.

No, I'm sick and tired of being the secretary just because I'm the only woman in the group.

We're supposed to be team teaching and yet I see that I am doing all the work. I'd like to talk about changing this.

What is the matter with you kids? I'm supposed to get off at the next corner!

When you're not here at the beginning of my lecture, I have to repeat parts of my lecture and that takes extra class time. I'm getting bothered by your tardiness.

Situation

26. A good friend calls and tells you she desperately needs you to canvass the street for a charity. You don't want to do it and say,

27. You are at a meeting of seven men and one woman. At the beginning of the meeting, the chairman asks you to be the secretary. You respond,

28. You are team teaching but you're doing all the planning, teaching, interacting and evaluating students. You say,

29. The bus is crowded with high school students who are talking to their friends. You want to get off but no one pays attention when you say "Out please." Finally, you say,

30. Student comes late to class for the third time. Teacher responds,

31. Man asks you for a date. You've dated him once before and you're not interested in dating him again. You respond,

Oh, I'm really so busy this week that I don't think I will have time to see you this Saturday night.

_____

32. The local library calls and asks you to return a book which you never checked out. You respond,

What are you talking about? You people better get your records straight—I never had that book and don't you try to make me pay for it.

_____

33. You are in a line at the store. Someone behind you has one item, and asks to get in front of you. You say,

I realize that you don't want to wait in line, but I was here first and I really would like to get out of here.

_____

34. Parent is talking with a married child on the telephone and would like the child to come for a visit. When the child politely refuses, the parent says,

You're never available when I need you. All you ever think about is yourself.

_____

35. Employer sends a memorandum stating that there should be no more toll business calls made without first getting prior permission. One employee responds,

You're taking away my professional judgment. It's insulting to me.

_____

36. Your husband expects dinner on the table when he arrives home from work and gets angry when it is not there immediately. You respond,

I feel awful about dinner. I know you're tired and hungry. . . it's all my fault. I'm just a terrible wife.

_____

Situation	Response	+, −, or N
37. Plans to vacation together are abruptly changed by friend and reported to you on the phone. You respond,	Wow, this has really taken my by surprise. I'd like to call you back after I've had some time to digest what's happened.	___
38. Parent is reprimanding the children when they haven't cleaned up their room and says,	You've got to be the worst kids in the whole city! If I had known parenthood was going to be like this, I would never have had any kids at all!	___
39. Your roommate habitually leaves the room a mess. You say,	You're a mess and our room is a mess.	___
40. Your husband wants to watch a football game on TV. There is something else that you'd like to watch. You say,	Well, ah, honey, go ahead and watch the game. I guess I could do some ironing.	___
41. Parent is annoyed that school counselor has not done anything about son's conflict with a teacher. Parent says,	I have asked the school to investigate the situation in my son's classroom and it concerns me that nothing has been done. I must insist that this situation be looked into.	___
42. Supervisor has just berated you for your work. You respond,	I think some of your criticisms are true, but I would have liked your being less personal about telling me about my shortcomings.	___

43. Your ten-year-old child has interrupted you three times with something that is not urgent. You've assertively asked her not to interrupt you. The child has now again interrupted you. You say,

I can't listen to you and talk on the phone at the same time. I'll be on the phone a few more minutes and then we'll talk.

_____

44. It is your turn to clean the apartment, which you have neglected to do several times in the last month. In a very calm tone of voice your roommate asks you to clean up the apartment. You say,

Would you get off my back!

_____

45. You're the only woman in a group of men and you're asked to be the secretary of the meetings. You respond,

I'm willing to do my share and take the notes this time. In future meetings, I'd like us to share the load.

_____

46. A fellow teacher always tries to get out of doing his turn of team teaching and asks you again to take his turn. You say,

Well . . . I guess that'd be OK even if I do have a splitting headache.

_____

47. An acquaintance has asked to borrow your car for the evening. You say,

Are you crazy! I don't lend my car to anyone.

_____

48. Loud stereo upstairs is disturbing you. You telephone and say,

Hello, I live downstairs. Your stereo is loud and is bothering me. Would you please turn it down.

_____

Situation

49. You have set aside 4:00 to 5:00 for things you want or need to do. Someone asks to see you at that time. You say,

50. Wife gets silent instead of saying what's on her mind. You say,

51. Husband has criticized your appearance in front of your friends. You say,

52. A friend often borrows small amounts of money and does not return it unless asked. She again asks for a small loan which you'd rather not give her. You say,

53. A neighbor has been constantly borrowing your vacuum sweeper. The last time, she broke it. When she asked for it again, you reply,

Response

Well, uh, I can see you at that time. It's 4:00 Monday then. Are you sure that's a good time for you?

Here it comes. The big silent treatment. Would it kill you to spit it out just once?

I really feel hurt when you criticize my appearance in front of other people. If you have something to say, please bring it up at home before we leave.

I only have enough money to pay for my own lunch today.

I'm sorry, but I don't want to loan my sweeper anymore. The last time I loaned it to you it was returned broken.

+, −, or N

54. A woman is being interviewed for a job, in the process of which the interviewer looks at her leeringly and says, "You certainly look like you have all the qualifications for the job." She responds,

I'm sure I am quite capable of doing the work here.

_____

55. Your mate wants to go out for a late night snack. You're too tired to go out and say,

I really don't feel like going out tonight. I'm too tired. But I'll go with you and watch you eat.

_____

56. You're walking to the copy machine when a fellow employee, who always asks you to do his copying, asks you where you're going. You respond,

I'm going to the Celtics ball game... Where does it look like I'm going?

_____

57. Parent is talking with a married child on the telephone and would like child to come for a visit. The parent says,

I had a funny dream last night. I dreamt that the grandchildren came to visit me.

_____

58. Your best friend has recently divorced. She confides that she is currently sleeping with several men and is not happy with this situation. She says that she's not sure how to handle it. You respond,

Well, I guess it's true about what they say about divorcees being an easy mark.

_____

51

59. Each night your roommate consistently slams the bathroom and bedroom doors, either keeping you awake or even if you're not sleeping, annoying you. You say,

"Please don't slam the doors—it's annoying to hear that late in the night. It wakes me up and I can't get back to sleep. _____"

60. You are asked to serve on a committee. You respond,

"I'm sorry. I'm not available to serve on that committee. _____"

Key for Discrimination Test

1. +	16. +	31. N	46. N
2. −	17. −	32. −	47. −
3. −	18. N	33. +	48. +
4. N	19. −	34. −	49. N
5. +	20. −	35. −	50. −
6. +	21. +	36. N	51. +
7. +	22. −	37. +	52. N
8. N	23. N	38. −	53. +
9. +	24. −	39. −	54. +
10. N	25. +	40. N	55. N
11. +	26. N	41. +	56. −
12. +	27. −	42. +	57. N
13. N	28. +	43. +	58. −
14. −	29. −	44. −	59. +
15. −	30. +	45. +	60. +

Table 2
Comparison of Nonassertive, Assertive, and Aggressive Behavior

	Nonassertive Behavior	Assertive Behavior	Aggressive Behavior
Characteristics of the behavior:	Emotionally dishonest, indirect, self-denying, inhibited	(Appropriately) emotionally honest, direct, self-enhancing, expressive	(Inappropriately) emotionally honest, direct, self-enhancing at expense of another, expressive
Your feelings when you engage in this behavior:	Hurt, anxious at the time and possibly angry later	Confident, self-respecting at the time and later	Righteous, superior, depreciatory at the time and possibly guilty later
The other person's feelings about herself when you engage in this behavior:	Guilty or superior	Valued, respected	Hurt, humiliated
The other person's feelings about you when you engage in this behavior:	Pity, irritation, disgust	Generally respect	Angry, vengeful

Reprinted by permission from *The Counseling Psychologist*. P. A. Jakubowski-Spector. Facilitating the growth of women through assertive training. *The Counseling Psychologist*, 1973, 4 (1), 77. Modified from R. E. Alberti & M. L. Emmons. *Your perfect right: A guide to assertive behavior*. San Luis Obispo, CA: Impact Publishers, Inc., 1970, 1974.

3
Developing an Assertive Belief System

When group members develop their own system of positive beliefs about assertion, they are more likely to engage in assertive behavior and to continue acting assertively in the face of unwarranted criticism. Furthermore, they are less likely to feel guilty after they have been appropriately assertive (Jakubowski-Spector, 1973b). Thus, in addition to helping group members acquire specific assertion skills, it is important that trainers help members develop a basic belief that *assertion—rather than manipulation, submission, or hostility—enriches life and ultimately leads to more satisfying personal relationships with people.* More specifically this means that the participants would hold beliefs* such as:

1. By standing up for ourselves and letting ourselves be known to others, we gain self-respect and respect from other people.
2. By trying to live our lives in such a way that we *never* hurt *anyone* under *any* circumstances, we end up hurting ourselves—and other people (e.g., the nonassertive circle in Chapter 2).
3. When we stand up for ourselves and express our honest feelings and thoughts in direct and appropriate ways, everyone usually benefits in the long run. Likewise, when we demean other people, we also demean ourselves and everyone involved usually loses in the process.
4. By sacrificing our integrity and denying our personal feelings, relationships are usually damaged or prevented from developing.

---

* These beliefs have been referred to elsewhere as the Tenets of an Assertive Philosophy (Jakubowski, in press, b).

Likewise, personal relationships are hurt when we try to control others through hostility, intimidation, or guilt.

5. Personal relationships become more authentic and satisfying when we share our honest reactions with other people and do not block others' sharing their reactions with us.

6. Not letting others know what we think and feel is just as selfish as not attending to other people's thoughts and feelings.

7. When we frequently sacrifice our rights, we teach other people to take advantage of us.

8. By being assertive and telling other people how their behavior affects us, we are giving them an opportunity to change their behavior, and we are showing respect for their right to know where they stand with us.

A second basic belief in an assertive philosophy is that *everyone is entitled to act assertively and to express honest thoughts, feelings, and beliefs.* More specifically this involves beliefs such as:

1. We all have the right to respect from other people.

2. We all have the right to have needs and to have these needs be as important as other people's needs. Moreover, we have the right to ask (not demand) that other people respond to our needs and to decide whether we will take care of other people's needs.

3. We all have the right to have feelings—and to express these feelings in ways which do not violate the dignity of other people (e.g., the right to feel tired, happy, depressed, sexy, angry, lonesome, silly).

4. We all have the **right** to decide whether we will meet other people's expectations or whether we will act in ways which fit us, as long as we act in ways which do not violate other people's rights.

5. We all have the right to form our own opinions and to express these opinions.

These basic rights were derived from a larger list of more than one hundred assertive rights generated in various assertion workshops. Although these five rights are seen as the basic ones, discussions about these assertive rights frequently have more meaning to people when the rights are more specific, for example, right to get what you paid for, right to make mistakes, right to dislike your relatives, right to decide how often you will visit parents, right to not laugh at jokes, right to ask for help, right to refuse loaning your car. Thus, it is often more effective for participants to create their own list of rights (see Exercise 9 in Chapter 4) than to be simply handed a list of their five basic rights.

Assertive rights are often described as "human" rights which suggests that all human beings inherently possess these rights, without any limitations imposed by one's culture. However, our view of legitimate assertive rights does at least partially reflect an American system of values. Since people often deny certain assertive rights to themselves or others because of sex, role, age, race, or status considerations, it is often more effective to describe assertive rights as "human rights." For example, a wife may deny herself the right to have her needs be as important as those of her children merely because she has the role of a mother. When a mother takes this position, she may think thoughts such as, "Kids don't ask to be brought into the world. When you're a mother, you've got to make some sacrifices; you've got other lives to consider besides your own. So take care of theirs first, and yourself last." At the same time the woman may simply accept the right of her husband to take care of his needs for rest and freedom from family distractions. Thus talking about "human rights" which she, her husband, and her children share often helps individuals feel more comfortable about accepting assertive rights.

The concept of rights also helps individuals feel that they can justify their assertive actions. For example, believing that one has "a perfect right to say that I don't like a movie" facilitates expressing such opinions instead of remaining silent. Furthermore, helping group members identify and accept their personal rights often helps reduce those internal injunctions which prohibit individuals from acting assertively. These injunctions include such thoughts as: Don't ever inconvenience other people; Don't ever refuse to help a friend; Don't ever feel mad; Don't be weak and ask for help; Don't ever make someone else feel bad. For example, participants can learn to counter the internal injunction, "Don't ever contradict a teacher," with thoughts about their personal rights: "I have a right to have my opinion given the same consideration and respect which a teacher's opinion is given." Thus the net effect of personal rights is to give individuals permission to be "themselves," in other words, to act in ways that are different from other people and to express their real thoughts, feelings, and needs.

Permission, however, is not the same as license to act any way one wishes with total disregard for other people. Depending on the trainer, the concept of personal rights could be presented in such a way that it gives license or gives permission. In our view, personal rights should be presented in a way which promotes responsible assertive behavior, where group members respect other people's rights, as well as their own. Trainers can help promote this view of assertive rights by discussing some of the responsibilities which are attached to rights (Jakubowski-Spector, 1973a). For example, the responsibilities which accompany the right to make a mistake are acknowledging the fact that a mistake was made, not making the same mistake again and again, and accepting other people's rights to make some mistakes also. When individuals accept the right to feel and express angry feelings, the attendant responsibilities are to resist dumping their anger on other people, to resist hitting other people below their "emotional belt line" (Bach & Wyden, 1968), and to assess whether their anger stems from their own imposed and critical "shoulds and oughts," or whether another person's behavior has concrete and specific effects which result in a more legitimate irritation.

CONFLICT OF RIGHTS

How conflicts between the rights of two people are handled is also an important part of a philosophy of responsible assertion. In this philosophy, an individual takes a flexible stance, not a rigid one when in conflict with another person. Furthermore, the individuals assess which situations involve personal integrity and are not appropriate for compromise, and which situations are ones in which some compromise could be equitably worked out. Finally, responsible assertion means not deliberately using personal power to manipulatively overpower weaker people in conflict situations.

A DANGER WITH RIGHTS

So far we have described all the positive effects of personal rights in terms of developing an assertive belief system. There are, however, some potential negative features as well. When rights are overly stressed in assertion training, some participants become "rights conscious" and start overreacting to every violation of their rights, often becoming aggressive in defending their own rights. It is as though they have come to believe that other people *must* treat them fairly and that it is a personal affront and an *unforgivable outrage* when other people are unfair (see Chapter 5 for a discussion of this irrational idea). Instead of focusing on their own goals, taking into consideration some aspects of the other person's situation, and determining how they could possibly assert themselves in the unfair situation, these individuals solely focus on the misdeed of the other person and the injustice of it all. What causes some individuals to develop such an attitude? In some cases, trainers themselves may be partially responsible. This is especially true when trainers overly dramatize the rights that are involved during conflicts with other people; for example, a trainer saying to a member who has been nonassertive with his employer, "You should never have let him impose on you that way. You let him *trample* on your rights! You should have stopped him immediately, the first time he mentioned the possibility of overtime without compensation. Don't you realize how you got screwed in this deal!" In other cases, certain types of individuals (perhaps those who are inclined to be very impatient and idealistic) may have certain thought patterns which make them more likely to become overly rights conscious. Trainers need to be sensitive to the danger of their group members becoming aggressive as a result of being overly rights conscious.

HELPING MEMBERS TO DEVELOP AN ASSERTIVE BELIEF SYSTEM

Developing an assertive belief system is rarely, if ever, accomplished in a single session. Instead, an assertive philosophy gradually develops throughout the course of assertion training as participants feel better about themselves as a result of their various assertive encounters with others. Although all the group sessions deal with rights to some extent, usually one of the early group sessions focuses explicitly on these issues.

Reading Material
In an early session, reading material can be used to introduce the participants to the concept of personal rights, for example, Alberti & Emmons' (1974) *Your Perfect Right*, which discusses personal rights in a way that promotes responsible assertive behavior. Besides reading material, various group exercises can be used to help members begin identifying and emotionally accepting their personal rights (see Chapter 4).

Support and Information from the Group
During the course of the various training sessions, the group itself can provide individual members with information about their rights in

particular situations. In a given session there is usually at least one member who feels comfortable about accepting a particular right which another group member has difficulty accepting. Thus one member can provide a persuasive rationale for accepting an assertive right, as the following example illustrates:

Chris had agreed to spend a Boston vacation with Therese. Now—six weeks before their scheduled departure—Chris was having second thoughts about the vacation. The last school year had been a mess and she was feeling hassled and longed for a quiet summer vacation at the sea. But her girlfriend hated the water and wanted to spend their vacation visiting museums and attending concerts. When Chris presented her problem to the group, she expressed doubt about her right to change vacation plans and thought that she'd just have to grit her teeth and bear the Boston vacation because she had made a prior commitment to her friend.

At this point another group member, Lidia, interceded with, "You know I had a similar problem last summer, only it was just the reverse situation! I gritted my teeth at the beach and hated every sunny moment of it—hated myself and *my friend too,* I might add! What a bust—I had a miserable time and made Jerry very angry too because I just couldn't get into the spirit of things. Now I think that even though I had made a prior commitment to Jerry, just like you made to Therese, we do have a right to change our minds in this situation. For us it's not like a flippant change of mind but the *circumstances are different now,* in June, than they were in February when your decision was originally made.

"I do think though that just cancelling out on Therese wouldn't be fair to her either. What do you think of just laying your cards on the table and telling her what's been going on in your life, what you need in terms of a vacation, and get her reaction? Maybe the two of you could work out a compromise and spend some time at the sea and also at Boston. Or maybe she could find somebody else to go with her—she'd still have enough time to do that.

"You know what I think? If you don't say anything at all, you'd be violating your own rights. What's more, even if you tried to cover up your feelings, your feelings would still show. Besides, Therese has a right to make this decision *together with you.* When you think of just gritting your teeth and going on with the Boston vacation, you in effect would be making this important decision *for her*—and that's not right."

In this example, Lidia did not simply say that Chris had some rights in the situation. She also provided a rationale for accepting that right, which made sense to Chris. Furthermore, the rights of *both* Chris and her friend were considered. It is through group interaction such as this that group members gradually start identifying and accepting assertive rights, and developing a belief system about responsible assertive behavior.

Trainer Modeling and Reinforcement

Another way in which trainers can help the participants develop a philosophy of responsible assertive behavior is for the trainers themselves to model such behaviors in the group and to engage in behavior which supports the principle that everybody counts, that everyone has the right to have their rights and feelings considered and respected. This can be done in such diverse ways as:

1. Encouraging the group to fairly handle conflicts that occur within the group: setting smoking limits, changing the time schedule, altering the group's activities, negotiating for extra group sessions, making time for individual members to work on idiosyncratic problems that other group members do not share.
2. Helping two group members who hold conflicting viewpoints to communicate with each other.
3. Making sure that everyone gets a chance to speak during the group.
4. Respecting a member's decision not to be assertive in a given situation.
5. Assertively disagreeing with group members' opinions and offering your own views in a straightforward and nondefensive fashion.
6. Being responsive to group or individual criticisms about your own leadership or the value of particular assertion exercises.
7. Helping members to analyze their assertive conflicts with other people and to give due recognition to the rights of both parties involved in the interaction.

8. Supportively confronting another member's repeated aggressions within the group and helping that person to change aggressive statements to more assertive statements in the group.

Challenging Socialization Messages

Finally, trainers can help the group members accept assertive rights and develop an assertive philosophy by helping the members learn how to challenge various internalized messages which have in effect denied them their rights. Some of these socialization messages are presented in Table 3 (p. 66) along with their effects on personal rights and consequent ability to act assertively. In addition, the more healthy messages which trainers can give to counteract these internalized messages are also described.

In questioning these internalized socialization messages and helping the participants to deal with their rights, trainers can use some of the following probes: "What in your background causes you to believe that you don't have these rights?" "Tell me how it is that you permit others to have these rights but you deny them for yourself?" "Can you give yourself permission to accept these rights?" "How do you go about making yourself believe you don't have these rights?" (Jakubowski, in press, b).

When group participants intellectually realize that they are entitled to a certain human right but find that they cannot emotionally accept this right, a trainer may need to use therapeutic procedures—such as Gestalt techniques—which are more emotionally involving. The following two case examples (Jakubowski, in press, b) illustrate how these procedures may be used:

> A 25-year-old woman felt that she had no right to refuse to help other people once she discerned that they were in need of some help. Her acceptance of herself was highly contingent on others: "I am only acceptable to live if I try to fulfill other people's needs." Despite these deep feelings, she stated that she would like to feel comfortable enough to accept the right to have her needs be as important as other people's.
>
> Using the empty chair technique (Perls, 1969), the client played the part of her that wanted to accept the right in one chair and the part of her that rejected the right in another chair. She started the internal dialog from the side that needed the greatest strengthening. From the sidelines she was given her

occasional prompts, e.g., "Tell her that you have a right to live too."

It should be recognized that this procedure did not result in the woman's immediate emotional acceptance of the right to refuse requests and to have her own needs satisfied. It did, however, result in the woman becoming significantly more comfortable with such ideas.

> In another case, a female graduate student did not believe that she had "the right to have rights." According to her, if she and another person had the same right and a conflict of rights resulted, this would mean that she was not entitled to the right for "it was not right to have conflict." Upon being asked where this message came from, the client immediately described how her parents bitterly quarelled. When it was pointed out that she was equating conflict with destruction and that as a child her parents' conflict had been overwhelming, but that as an adult she could act in ways that could produce nondestructive conflict, she cried.

> While the woman could not yet give herself permission to produce conflict, she was able to accept the existential proposition that she had the right to make choices even if these choices differed from those of other people.

It is obvious that trainers who work with such individuals will need to have considerable skill and knowledge in sensitively using procedures to help them develop an assertive belief system.

COMMON ISSUES RAISED BY GROUP MEMBERS

Some participants become worried about assertion leading to dead-end conflicts where both parties adamantly stick to their positions, each defending their own rights. The public too has this concern as a recent cartoon illustrates: Two women each left their separate assertion training groups, and while driving down the road toward each other, came to an impasse. A ridiculous argument ensued as to which person had the right of way. Crowds of people quickly converged and they also argued about their own rights. In our view, people get into such dead-end conflicts when both parties take the position that "I am 100 percent right and you're 100 percent wrong" and neither party will budge an inch. They get locked into a power conflict instead of generating other possible ways of resolving the conflict. Furthermore, such power conflicts are more likely to occur when people are being assertive "simply for the sake of being assertive."

A second common issue concerns the question whether one must always assert one's rights. Individuals are always free to choose not to assert themselves, assuming that they are willing to take the responsibility of whatever consequences may then occur.

Sometimes group members even ask for the right to be nonassertive. What they frequently mean is that they'd like to have the permission to decide for themselves when and how to be assertive, rather than feel that they are now stuck with a new set of rules to live by and that they should feel badly about failing these rules: "Thou Shalt Be Perfectively Assertive All the Time or Else You Have Failed and Should Feel Guilty." Trainers need to be very careful that they do not inadvertently promote such perfectionism and guilt on the part of their group members.

A final common issue concerns *when* assertive behavior should be used. Here it is helpful to have the participants use some self-assessment questions: (1) How important is this situation to me? (2) How am I likely to feel afterwards if I don't assert myself in the situation? (3) How much will it cost me to assert myself in this situation? The decision to assert oneself also involves a sense of what is appropriate in a given situation. For example, when an aged grandfather comes for his once-a-year, two-day visit, and asks how you like his garish tie that he so proudly picked all by himself, is telling him that you think it's ugly a remark that is necessary or appropriate?

SUMMARY*

Teaching a system of positive beliefs about assertion involves helping the participants to develop two basic beliefs: First, assertion—rather than manipulation, submission, or hostility—enriches life and ultimately leads to more satisfying personal relationships with people. Second,

---

* Several issues regarding the basis and nature of personal rights merit consideration. At this point, we believe that people have the right to "want" and assume that others will respect their personal rights. Moreover, people can ask and even insist that others respect their rights. However, if the other person continues not to respect one's personal rights, condemnation of the other person is not warranted since we surely have *no inalienable right to have others act correctly.*

The question of the origin or specific nature of personal rights remains unresolved. Are any of these rights inalienable? Are they inherent simply because we are human? What is the functional-pragmatic basis of personal rights? At this stage, these fundamental issues are still unresolved for us. The nature of personal rights leads one to consider the very nature of one's values and beliefs about mankind, thus requiring a broad axiological analysis which is beyond the scope of this book.

everyone is entitled to act assertively and to express honest thoughts, feelings, and beliefs.

The concept of human rights or personal rights helps individuals to feel better about their assertive actions and to counteract various internal messages which prohibit specific assertive acts. Thus assertive rights help give individuals "permission" to act assertively. Such permission, however, should not be construed as license to act any way one wishes with total disregard for other people's rights in the situation.

Various methods for helping group members develop an assertive belief system were presented. Some methods simply involve giving information, while other methods include exercises which are more emotionally involving.

REVIEW QUESTIONS AND EXERCISES

1. What is meant by the term "responsible assertive behavior"?

2. What are the advantages of the term "human rights"?

3. How can assertive rights be used to counteract internal injunctions?

4. What is the difference between permission and license?

5. What are some dangers of the concept of assertive rights?

6. What are some common issues raised by participants about the whole concept of assertive rights?

7. For each of the eight basic tenets of an assertive philosophy, develop a practical example which demonstrates the validity of these tenets.

8. Read Alberti & Emmons' book, *Your Perfect Right.*

9. Develop your own list of assertive rights and identify the responsibilities which may accompany these rights.

10. Prepare a short lecture on what responsible assertive behavior involves.

Table 3
How Socialization Messages May Negatively Effect Assertion

Socialization Message	Effect on Rights	Effect on Assertive Behavior	Healthy Message
Think of others first; give to others even if you're hurting. Don't be selfish.	I have no right to place my needs above those of other people's.	When I have a conflict with someone else, I will give in and satisfy the other person's needs and forget about my own.	To be selfish means that a person places his desires before practically everyone else's desires. This is undesirable human behavior. However, all healthy people have needs and strive to fulfill these as much as possible. Your needs are as important as other people's. When there is a conflict over need satisfaction, compromise is often a useful way to handle the conflict.
Be modest and humble. Don't act superior to other people.	I have no right to do anything which would imply that I am better than other people.	I will discontinue my accomplishments and any compliments I receive. When I'm in a meeting, I will encourage other people's contributions and keep silent about my own. When I have an opinion which is different from someone else's, I won't express it; who am I to say	It is undesirable to build yourself up at the expense of another person. However, you have as much right as other people to show your abilities and take pride in yourself. It is healthy to enjoy one's accomplishments.

		that my opinion is better than theirs?	
Be understanding and overlook trivial irritations. Don't be a bitch and complain.	I have no right to feel angry or to express my anger.	When I'm in a line and someone cuts in front of me, I will say nothing. I will not tell my girlfriend that I don't like her constantly interrupting me when I speak.	It is undesirable to deliberately nit-pick. However, life is made up of trivial incidents and it is normal to be occasionally irritated by seemingly small events. You have a right to your angry feelings, and if you express them at the time they occur, your feelings won't build up and explode. It is important, however, to express your feelings assertively rather than aggressively.
Help other people. Don't be demanding.	I have no right to make requests of other people.	I will not ask my girlfriend to reciprocate babysitting favors. I will not ask for a pay increase from my employer.	It is undesirable to incessantly make demands on others. You have a right to ask other people to change their behavior if their behavior affects your life in a concrete way. A request is not the same as a demand. However, if your rights are being violated and your requests for a change are being ignored, you have a right to make demands.

Socialization Message	Effect on Rights	Effect on Assertive Behavior	Healthy Message
Be sensitive to other people's feelings. Don't hurt other people.	I have no right to do anything which might hurt someone else's feelings or deflate someone else's ego.	I will not say what I really think or feel because that might hurt someone else. I will inhibit my spontaneity so that I don't impulsively say something that would accidentally hurt someone else.	It is undesirable to deliberately try to hurt others. However, it is impossible as well as undesirable to try to govern your life so as to *never hurt anyone.* You have a right to express your thoughts and feelings even if someone else's feelings get occasionally hurt. To do otherwise would result in your being phoney and in denying other people an opportunity to learn how to handle their own feelings. Remember that some people get hurt because they're unreasonably sensitive and others use their hurt to manipulate you. If you accidentally hurt someone else, you can generally repair the damage.

Reprinted with permission from Charles C. Thomas, Publisher. P. A. Jakubowski. Assertive behavior and the clinical problems of women. In D. Carter & E. Rawlings (Eds.), *Psychotherapy with women.* Springfield, IL: Charles C. Thomas, in press.

4
Structured Exercises

The assertion training format described in Chapters 4, 5, 6 and 7 is somewhat structured in that there is a clear focus on (1) specific assertion problems, (2) a set of procedures for working on those concerns, and (3) a number of initial skill-building exercises. At the same time, however, there is a great deal of flexibility in these exercises.

In conducting assertion training groups, we have found that most people are unprepared to begin immediately with behavior rehearsals. At first group members also tend to be hesitant, anxious, have a low energy level, and are minimally involved. Since training itself should be a successful experience, it is often premature to attempt the complex cognitive restructuring and behavior rehearsal procedures described in the next chapters. Moreover, at the start of the first session, participants are likely to be silently sitting around the edges of the meeting room, avoiding contact with each other in every way. Until a trainer leads a group, it may be hard to appreciate the communication difficulties which persons lacking in assertive skills experience. For example, many new group participants seem to pay little attention to the impact they have on others and are not clearly aware of what they react to in others. Some participants may have the necessary skills, but they are too anxious to effectively use them. The exercises in this chapter are designed to: (1) maximize participant learning and use of skills, (2) help the members become more comfortable and involved in the group, (3) focus on specific aspects of assertive behavior, and (4) prepare participants for the cognitive and behavioral procedures which come later in the group sessions. Each of the exercises described in this chapter includes the procedure, specific outcome goals, the issues to be raised while conducting the exercise, and some nuances of conducting the exercise.

We do *not* support the use of structured exercises as the sole format for an assertion training group. Assertion training should ultimately focus on those needs and situations which are identified by the participants, and use the appropriate cognitive and behavioral interventions described in later chapters.

EXERCISE 1
Introductions

We strongly believe in identifying and expressing the strengths of group members particularly in the first session. If the focus is on pointing out group members' deficiencies, trainers will be doing just what the group members fear. The result will then likely be their avoiding the exercises and increasing self-depreciation. Ineffective behaviors are not avoided or denied by the trainer. At first, however, we set a supportive atmosphere which is conducive to risk-taking.

Since a group has to begin in some way, introducing ourselves to one another is a logical starting point. This process can be ineffectual if individuals simply state their names in order around the group, while they focus on the rug, ceiling, or the leader. Instead, we ask someone to begin by making eye contact and introducing himself to someone across the group and have that person respond (simply exchanging names, e.g., "Hi, I'm Art;" "Hi, Art, my name is Pat"). The person who receives the introduction then introduces herself to someone else in the group, who has not yet been introduced. This exchange continues until each member has responded to an introduction *and* then introduced himself to *another participant*. (Be sure people respond by stating their names in each introduction so that two people are actually interacting before the respondent moves on to the next introduction.) As the introductions progress, some participants may forget who has not yet been introduced. The trainer can simply ask those persons to raise their hands. When trainers are "matter of fact" about such concerns, they can reduce the participants' discomfort, while modeling assertive behavior within the group.

Then ask each person, beginning with the first *respondent,* to tell the *introducer* something specific she *liked* about the *way* the person introduced himself (e.g., "Art, I really liked how you smiled and your voice was easy and smooth"). The focus is on the nonverbal qualities since very little is actually being said. Even within such a brief interaction there is always something good each person can say. It is extremely important that this feedback be positive and as behaviorally specific as possible (saying "I liked your vibes" is complimentary but not as clear as "I liked your smile and how you looked straight at me"). Before initiating the feedback, the trainers might give a few examples of the types of behaviors that participants might focus on: eye contact, facial expression, body and hand positions, voice qualities.

We often ask if anyone can remember all the names of the group members (usually someone is willing to try but most participants find they cannot). After someone tries, we explain that a lot of people immediately forget newly introduced names. They may "catastrophize" that somehow this implies the introducee is terribly unimpressive or that the introducer is awfully stupid. Consequently, on future occasions people may make believe they remember the person's name or they may avoid talking with the other person. Finally, we note that it is really OK to have forgotten another's name. We then take a few seconds for everyone simultaneously to ask the names of those persons they did not remember. This breaks some of the "structured" ice and people seem to enjoy it. At the beginning of the next group session, the trainer may reaffirm that it is quite all right to ask people their names again.

Outcome Goals

The purposes of this 10-minute exercise are: (1) to break the ice and maximize each member's immediate involvement in the group; (2) to help the members begin to recognize those nonverbal behaviors which affect others; (3) to reduce group tension by focusing on positive feedback; and (4) to accustom the members to giving feedback.

Homework Suggestions for Participants

1. Introduce yourself three times this week. Assess what you liked about how you came across and what you liked about how the other person responded. (Do not assess what happened after the introductions, that is a separate interaction!)

2. Notice how other people introduce themselves to strangers.

3. Ask someone to repeat his name shortly after you have been introduced; assess how direct and assertive you were; if you were nervous, identify clearly what the worry was.

Homework Suggestions for Trainers

1. Practice (with tape recorder) how you would start a group, including a brief overview of the group sessions, a definition of assertiveness and assertion training, any other basic information, and a lead into the Introductions exercise; keep it to less than ten minutes (later you can give mini-lectures throughout the sessions on any point you want to reinforce).
2. Practice conducting the Introductions exercise with several friends. Afterwards evaluate the degree to which you gave clear instructions, kept the focus on positive feedback, kept the exercise moving, and made sure that all the members were introduced.

EXERCISE 2
Inane Topics

The Introductions exercise leads smoothly into "Inane Topics" which focuses on nonverbal communication. The exercise might begin by asking the participants to think of all the behaviors people respond to besides a person's words. The participants will usually cite most of them: eye contact, smiles and facial expressions, body posture, hand gestures, and voice loudness, tone, rapidity, and smoothness. Note that the content of most social conversations (particularly with strangers) is often insignificant, but that quite a bit is happening: People are checking each other out and developing impressions. Finally tell the members that the purposes of this exercise are to recognize which behaviors people react to in others and to learn what others like about how they "come across." In this exercise, one person will talk while the other two people listen. The primary learning occurs as a "listener" in this exercise.

The trainer writes "inane" topics on slips of paper (suggested topics: pegs, lint, watches, pads, pins, toilet paper, Kleenex). Members then form groups of three's and each person randomly selects an inane topic from the paper slips. Each person is then asked to talk conversationally for about a minute and a half about the topics. (The time should be shortened if the participants are likely to experience too much anxiety about talking that long.) The two listeners in each group are asked to be attentive but not to talk since this is a monolog exercise. The listeners, however, should be identifying the nonverbal behaviors that are effectively holding their attention. *After all* three persons have spoken, each receives *positive, behavioral* feedback from the listeners on what they *liked* about the speaker's nonverbal behaviors. Trainers need to check that the feedback focuses on how (nonverbal behavior) the person behaved rather than on what (content) the person said.

Feedback should be offered after all three group members have talked, rather than after each person talks. When each speaker in turn gets immediate feedback, the speakers are likely to imitate the previous speaker and feel anxious about doing as well or better than the previous speaker. When they receive positive feedback after everyone has talked, they realize that it is for their "uncoached" behavior. Members usually expect critical reactions and relax when they do not occur. Occasionally a member will report feeling silly during this exercise. In such a case a trainer may ask the participants whether they can give themselves permission to do something silly or to be imperfect.

After this exercise, without placing direct focus on ineffectual behaviors, the trainers should suggest that participants think about their own behavior and possibly select specific nonverbal behaviors they might wish to change while in the group.

Outcome Goals

The goals of this 20-minute exercise are: (1) to stimulate the group members' awareness of those nonverbal behaviors which influence their first impressions, (2) to identify the engaging behaviors which participants are currently employing, (3) to stimulate consideration of nonverbal behaviors which participants might choose to change during the group, and (4) to teach group members to give specific behavioral feedback. Lastly, some participants are surprised to learn that they can talk about "nothing" for a minute and a half. Although we are not encouraging banality, many participants report being more willing to engage in brief social conversations previously avoided for fear of having nothing to say!

Homework Suggestions for Participants

1. Observe the nonverbal behavior of three other persons during the week.

2. On three occasions, pay attention to your own nonverbal behaviors and identify clearly those engaging behaviors you like.
3. Choose one nonverbal behavior you would like to change. Engage in this nonverbal behavior on five specific occasions and assess each time if you are behaving more as you would like. Continue practicing and assessing until you are comfortable with the change.

Homework Suggestions for Trainers

1. Can you identify eight different nonverbal behaviors to use in this exercise?
2. Practice how you would make the transition from Introductions to the Inane Topics exercise.
3. Check your own nonverbal behavior and identify what you like and what you too would like to change.
4. Practice conducting the Inane Topics exercise with several friends. Afterwards evaluate the degree to which you gave clear directions, helped the participants to focus on positive feedback for nonverbal behaviors, and helped the participants identify those nonverbal behaviors they would like to change in themselves.

EXERCISE 3

Giving and Receiving Compliments*

This exercise focuses on assertively giving and receiving positive opinions and feelings. After explaining how such behaviors also require assertiveness, trainers can ask the participants to describe (or better yet, have them act out) ways in which persons *respond* to compliments that would make the giver unlikely to offer another compliment; for example, denying shyly ("Oh gosh, who me?"), returning the focus immediately ("Oh, I like *your* shirt, too!"), or rejecting ("You like this old rag, I've had it for ages and it's way out of style"). This can be followed by acting out negative ways of *giving* a compliment; for example, self-depreciating ("I'm pretty much a flop at baking, but wow, you're terrific"), sarcastic ("Those pants really do fit well, don't they!"), or crooked ("Most people don't like you, but I do"). The

* We wish to recognize Rimm & Masters' (1974) original suggestions of introductory exercises regarding giving and receiving compliments, making positive self-statements, and carrying on small talk conversations. We have created exercises focusing on these types of assertive behavior.

trainer can then demonstrate ways of giving and receiving brief, unqualified compliments.

At this point some participants express the fear that they would appear conceited if they agreed with or directly accepted a compliment. Trainers can distinguish between healthy self-pride ("Thank you. I felt good about my speech too"), and egotism (*"Of course* I did a good job on the speech. I *always* do well"), which attempts to impress or "one up" others. Trainers can also discuss how we are frequently told to not feel good about ourselves, how we listen to criticism more than praise, etc.

Then, with the group standing in a circle, one person can give a genuine compliment to the person on the right and have that person respond. The receiver then gives a compliment to the person on his right. The two participants should interact briefly, before the receiver turns to give a compliment to the next person. The compliments do not have to be deeply personal but must be sincere (even after about an hour into the first session, something complimentary can be said about each participant).

At this point, the members then go around the circle again and briefly have each "giver" express to the receiver something which she specifically *liked* about how the "receiver" responded to her compliment. Trainers should have group members give feedback directly to each other, as opposed to talking about someone to the trainer or the group. That is, participants would use the second person pronouns ("You made good eye contact and you were loud and clear"), rather than the third person ("He made good eye contact. . . "). Most participants initially use "he" or "she," but after a brief explanation that it is more direct to speak *to* someone rather than *about* him, they begin to talk with each other.

People vary in their comfort when giving or receiving compliments. Members might be encouraged to discuss their reactions during the exercise, and if they seem particularly uncomfortable with either giving or receiving compliments, they should be encouraged to work on it in future behavior rehearsal sessions.

Outcome Goals

The goals of this 20-minute exercise are: (1) to help the members learn how to give and receive compliments assertively, (2) to demonstrate that positive interactions also involve assertiveness, (3) to facilitate positive, supportive interactions in the first session, and (4) to encourage the participants to allow themselves to hear and receive compliments and to give them genuinely, thus increasing their sense of self-worth.

Homework Suggestions for Participants

1. Give three compliments each day for a week. Assess how comfortable and how direct you are.
2. When you receive compliments, notice how comfortable you are, how fully you receive them, and how assertively you respond.
3. If you recognize a specific behavior while giving or receiving compliments which you would like to change, practice changing it and look for gradual improvement.

Homework Suggestions for Trainers

1. Think of five different ways that people respond unassertively to compliments.
2. Practice conducting the exercise, particularly including an explanation of why giving and receiving compliments is an assertive behavior. Evaluate how well you helped the people feel comfortable in accepting the compliments.
3. Check out how assertive you are in giving and receiving compliments.

EXERCISE 4
Yes—No!

In pairs, participants face each other while one person says the word "yes" and the other responds with "no" *at the same* loudness level for a minute or two. The "Yes" person should vary the loudness from very quiet to as loud as possible, and the "No" person should match the loudness level each time. Nonassertive persons are often quite unaware of how quiet they are and would like to be able to increase their voice loudness at certain times, while aggressive persons might want to be able to speak more quietly at times. Group members might be encouraged to check out their voice loudness and judge whether they feel their present range of loudness is wide enough.

Furthermore, by matching the loudness level of the "Yes" person, the "No" participant can assess the amount of loudness *control* he uses. (Another variant of this exercise is to have the "No" person respond *one level lower* than the "Yes" person when the "Yes" person has reached a fairly loud level.) Those members who react uncomfortably to demanding and refusing forcefully may wish to work on this problem in behavior rehearsals. The Yes-No exercise can also naturally lead into the exercise on making and refusing requests (Exercise 15).

Outcome Goals
The primary purpose of this 10-minute exercise is to help persons become aware of the full range of loudness available to them and to contrast it with the range of loudness they are accustomed to. This exercise also enables the participants to recognize how quiet or loud they are from an experiential base rather than hearing it from others.

Homework Suggestions for Participants
1. Intentionally talk louder (or softer) than you usually do during a short interaction with someone. Begin to get a sense of how loud or quiet you generally tend to be.
2. Change the loudness of your voice in a conversation (either with a friend, in the mirror, or with a tape recorder). Assess how comfortable you are moving along the continuum of loudness.
3. Look for situations where you would like to change the loudness of your voice (higher or lower) and change your voice accordingly; do this as an experiment so that you will be changing your voice loudness in different situations. Use the beginning discussion of each session to clarify any problems and to report your results.

Homework Suggestions for Trainers
Develop brief exercises for other voice qualities such as intonation, rapidity, clarity, fluidity so that participants can assess their current behavior and try out new levels.

EXERCISE 5
Carrying on Social Conversations
This exercise focuses on some basic communication skills. We include such an exercise because nonassertive persons sometimes avoid or have difficulty carrying on conversations because these basic skills are not fully part of their response repertoire. The trainer can introduce this exercise with a brief description of the three components of communication skills: asking open-ended questions, responding to free information, and paraphrasing. A demonstration of open-ended versus closed

questioning, such as the following dialog between Janet and Mark, is often most helpful.

Closed Questioning

Janet: Hi, are you a student here?
Mark: Yes.

Janet: Are you a bio major?
Mark: No.

Janet: Are you a social ecology major?
Mark: Yes.

Janet: Do you like it?
Mark: Yes.

Pause...

Janet: Do you live here in town?
Mark: No.

Janet: Do you live at the beach?
Mark: No.

Janet: Would you like to live at the beach?
Mark: Yes.

Naturally, Mark could volunteer more information if he wanted. Asking open-ended questions, however, maximizes the other person's opportunity to respond more fully. Nonassertive persons often avoid conversations because they are anxious about what to say, the "pregnant" pauses, or being considered dull. They incorrectly feel a great deal of responsibility for carrying the conversation. Asking open-ended questions equalizes the flow of conversation and increases the likelihood of receiving more free information to respond to.

Open-ended Questioning

Janet: What do you do at the university?
Mark: I'm a student.

Janet: What are you majoring in?
Mark: Social ecology.

Janet: I've heard about that program but don't know much about it. What do you study for it?

Mark: Well, there are four different emphases, but I'm in community mental health... (and so on).

Janet: What do you like about the program?

Mark: Well, I get a lot of opportunities to work in mental health agencies and see if... (and so on).

Obviously, this conversation could be quite stilted unless both people were genuinely interested. Asking open-ended questions won't guarantee an elaborate response but does increase the *opportunity* for the other person to talk extensively. The format for this exercise is to practice separately each of the three responses introduced and then practice integrating them into a comfortable conversational style. Obviously, one would not be encouraged to carry on such a one-directional conversation, as above, even with good open-ended questions.

For the first step of the exercise, have the participants pair off with one person practicing a succession of open-ended questions and the other responding genuinely; then reverse these roles. The next step is to integrate responding to the free information elicited by the open-ended questions. Have the pairs practice asking open-ended questions *and* also responding to the free information with their own opinions, disclosures, or information. For example:

Janet: What do you study in social ecology?

Mark: Well, I'm specializing in community mental health but others are in urban planning and administration of justice.

Janet: Oh, I'm interested myself in community mental health; I'm in the med program and I've been interested in preventive medicine, including mental health. What are you studying this quarter?

Sometimes individuals really do not have anything to say in response to someone else's free information, yet they would like to continue the conversation. Therefore we also introduce "paraphrasing" as an effective response which, in effect, communicates that one is listening, is interested, and would like to hear more. For example:

Janet: What do you study in social ecology? (*open-ended question*)

Mark: Well, I'm specializing in community mental health but others are in urban planning, administration of justice ....

Janet: It sounds like social ecology is a collection of a number of different specializations. (*the paraphrase*)

Mark: Yeah, they all seem to be very different, yet they all deal with people and how we function as part of a system or a particular segment of society.

After demonstrating (modeling) paraphrases, have the pairs practice integrating open-ended questions with responses to free information and paraphrasing. Practicing may be somewhat awkward at first. Usually, however, group members report feeling relieved about being actively involved in a conversation without carrying so much responsibility for its continuance. Some people may wish to work further on the cognitive and behavioral components of this type of interaction in the behavioral rehearsal sessions. This exercise should take about 30 minutes.

Outcome Goals

The primary goals of this exercise are: (1) for participants to be able to demonstrate the three communication skills of asking open-ended questions, responding when possible to free information with personal opinions or information, and paraphrasing, and (2) for participants to feel less anxious and consequently freer to choose to engage in social conversations when desired. Again, simply having these skills does not "create" genuineness and sincere interest but, if both are present, the skills will help to facilitate communication.

Homework Suggestions for Participants

1. Carry on a conversation with someone you do not know well, consciously using the three responses. (You might also try another conversation with someone else where you do not use any of the three responses and compare the conversations.)
2. Observe the conversational styles of three other people and specifically identify what they do that is effective (also look at nonverbal behaviors).

Homework Suggestions for Trainers

1. Practice giving a brief introduction to the three communication skills, including a demonstration of each.
2. Observe your own conversational style and note your use of these skills and any others you might want to add to the exercise.

80

EXERCISE 6
Contracting for In-Group, Ongoing Behavior Changes

During the first session, the leaders can ask the participants to choose a behavior each would like to change *within* the group. Behaviors which are often chosen include: speaking louder (softer), speaking tersely without redundance, speaking more often, elaborating upon responses, making more eye contact with others, expressing genuine disagreements of opinion, speaking more crisply (especially when ending a statement).

It is generally more effective to have the participants state their changes in terms of what they want to do ("I want to speak firmer and end my sentences more clearly"), as opposed to what they want to stop doing ("I want to stop whining and trailing off to a whisper at the end of my sentences"). The behaviors should be as clear and specific as possible so the person knows when the changes are attained. If the person wants feedback from other group members, a systematic means for that person to ask for feedback should be established, rather than leaving the responsibility for feedback with the other participants. The behaviors should be ones which the person can realistically engage in as part of the ongoing process of the group (often the behaviors participants suggest are more appropriate for a specific behavior rehearsal). Brief reminders at the beginning of each session may help participants to be more systematic about the changes and to add new behaviors to change.

Outcome Goals

Through this exercise, participants (1) begin actively involving themselves in *self-help* primarily using themselves as monitors (thus strengthening their internal locus of evaluation), (2) see themselves as capable of effecting self-change and feel more potent, and (3) realize that working on one or two specific behaviors systematically is a reasonable and effective method of self-help. About 15 minutes should be allowed for this exercise.

Homework Suggestions for Participants

Periodically, but systematically, observe your own behavior outside the group in order to identify *specific* behaviors you might wish to modify within the group on an ongoing basis.

Homework Suggestions for Trainers

Identify several behaviors you would like to work on for yourself. Also be prepared to offer a half dozen examples of behaviors participants might wish to change on an ongoing basis within the group.

EXERCISE 7
Discrimination of Assertive, Aggressive, and Nonassertive Behavior

Unless group members correctly understand assertive, aggressive, and nonassertive behaviors, the training sessions are likely to run afoul; for example, the members may incorrectly perceive another member's assertion as aggression, etc.

In setting up this exercise, the trainer can select ten to twelve situations from the Discrimination Test (Chapter 2) which group members are likely to encounter in their lives. The trainer states the context of each situation and then plays the response on audio tape. The exercise may be introduced with the following remarks:

> We're going to listen to a series of statements on the tape recorder. Some of the statements will be assertive, some will be aggressive, and some will be nonassertive. As we listen to each statement, I'd like each of you to make an independent decision as to whether the statement is assertive, aggressive, or nonassertive. Afterwards, I'll ask each of you in turn to tell us what your private decision was. Don't go by majority rule in making up your mind.
>
> I'm particularly interested in those who see the statement differently from the rest of the group because this will give me a chance to clear up whatever confusion may exist about these different behaviors. This is very important because so far we've been talking about these behaviors in the abstract; when we get down to discussing real situations, it's not always so easy to make the differentiations. (Jakubowski, in press, b)

After this introduction, the trainer describes the first situation, plays the response, and the members identify whether the statement is assertive, aggressive, or nonassertive. Those individuals who misidentify the response are then questioned. It is important that the trainer does not simply say that the person was incorrect but rather that the trainer tries to discover the source of the person's misunderstanding. The following example illustrates the type of group process carried out in this exercise. The group has just heard the following audio-taped response, "I'd like to help you out but I don't feel comfortable loaning my car." One member has misidentified this statement as aggressive.

Trainer: What was it about the response that caused you to see it as aggressive?

Linda: It hurts the other person's feelings . . . It's putting her down.

Trainer: How do other people see that response?

Member: I think it's showing consideration even though she's refusing the request.

Trainer: (To Linda) So some people do not see this response as putting someone else down. Linda, is it possible that you would feel disappointed and hurt by this refusal and that's what causes you to think that others would be feeling the same way?

Linda: Well, my feelings do get hurt pretty easily.

Trainer: Is it kind of like saying to yourself that the other person must not like me because they don't want to do what I asked them.

Linda: I never thought of it that way . . . I guess that's true.

Trainer: What's important here is to be careful about assuming that other people will react the same way we do in a situation like this. Now let's play that statement over again. Listen very carefully and see whether the person is putting the other person down or whether the person is just refusing the request. (Trainer plays the tape again.)

Linda: I see what you mean. That's what you called an empathic way of saying no.

Trainer: Exactly right.

At this point, the trainer went on to briefly ask Linda whether her concern about hurting other people and losing their approval was one of the major reasons why she was having trouble being assertive. The trainer then indicated that learning how to be more assertive and reduce inappropriate guilt was one of the major things that the group would be working on in coming sessions.

Outcome Goals

The main goal of this exercise is to identify the participants' misunderstandings about assertive, aggressive, and nonassertive behavior and to help them correct their misunderstandings.

Homework Suggestions for Participants

During the week, notice different ways in which you and other people act assertively, aggressively, and nonassertively. Bring three examples of these behaviors to the next group session.

Homework Suggestions for Trainers

1. Construct an audio-discrimination tape. If you create your own situation, have at least three other people blindly rate the responses as assertive, aggressive, or nonassertive.

2. Conduct this exercise with a group of friends. Assess the degree to which you helped identify individuals' misunderstandings about these concepts. Determine whether you stayed too long with one member and caused that person to merely give up disagreeing with you.

EXERCISE 8
Identifying Personal Rights
Recognizing How
Personal Rights Can Be Violated
Discriminating Between Nonassertive,
Assertive, and Aggressive Behaviors*

This exercise incorporates several important issues for assertion training. First, a trainer gives a mini-lecture which: (1) differentiates between assertion, aggression, and nonassertion, (2) introduces the relationship between a belief system which values personal rights and assertive behavior, and (3) identifies what personal rights individuals possess. Such an introduction might be done as follows (including a lead into the first step of the exercise).

---

* This exercise is based on the use of filmed vignettes such as P. A. Jakubowski-Spector, J. Pearlman & K. Coburn. *Assertive training for women: Stimulus films.* Washington, D.C.: American Personnel and Guidance Association, 1973. And, C. Steel & J. Hochman. *Improving personal relationships: Assertive training for high school women, Stimulus films.* Washington, D.C.: American Personnel and Guidance Association, in press, b.

Many times people are not sure about how they would like to behave in a particular situation because they are unclear about what rights they have and what rights others have. Since many (maybe all) interpersonal behaviors imply certain personal rights, it's important that we recognize what those personal rights are in order to act on them. The most fundamental of these personal rights is the right to express your beliefs, opinions, needs, and feelings while not violating the personal rights of others. For example, I believe I have the right to disagree with a colleague in a staff meeting and offer my own opinion that the Center should offer more group service. I do not believe I have the right to be abusive or tell someone who has a different opinion to "shut up."

Many people do not believe they have certain personal rights and do not act on them. Identifying and accepting these rights leads to assertive behavior.

Sometimes other people attempt to violate our personal rights, put us down, or "discount" our opinions, needs, and feelings. They would like us to respond nonassertively and they violate our personal rights. Very often these "violations" are not only communicated by what the other person is saying or implying but also by their nonverbal communication.

We'll be using a series of filmed vignettes for this exercise. A person will appear on the screen and will speak to you in a way that will violate your personal rights. I'd like you to get into groups of three and after the first vignette, discuss the various ways this person was violating your rights, putting you down, or somehow discounting you *and* identify what personal rights you have in the situation.

After the participants have observed the first vignette and discussed the violations and discounts, the trainers might ask someone from each triad to share what she identified. The trainers should recognize that personal rights are usually violated by the way the person behaves and not necessarily by the issue itself. For example, during one scene (in the Jakubowski-Spector, Pearlman & Coburn film, 1973) the actress says, with condescension, "Oh, you didn't get the notes I borrowed last week? Well, no problem, I gave them to Bob and I'm sure he'll give them back." Speaking abruptly and looking at her watch, she continues, "Look, I've got to go now. You will lend me this week's notes, won't you?" The personal rights of the participant are: the right to express concern over one's property and the right to say "no" to the immediate request. The person on the screen is violating those rights by the lack of respect expressed in the tone of her voice, by brushing aside the concern for the previous notes, and by pressuring for agreement.

The trainers should also have triads develop several examples of actual responses that would be nonassertive, assertive, and aggressive. After developing these examples, participants might then share them with the whole group.

Trainers can also ask participants to share how they *would actually like to respond* in that situation, using this time to help participants clarify and discriminate particularly between assertive and aggressive responses. A relatively simple assertive statement would be an appropriate response for some of the vignettes, while others require extended complex assertive discussions involving a combination of empathic and confrontive skills. Participants may express some concern about the appropriateness or "OK-ness" of a particular response. Rather than pass judgment on a specific response, the trainers can have that person assess if it fits the criteria for assertive behavior and identify what the personal rights are in the situation.

An extended group discussion focusing on the vignettes and the issues of personal rights will stimulate questions such as: How will I know when I've acted aggressively or assertively? What can I do if there's a conflict between my rights and the rights of others? Should I be assertive if it costs me my job or a friend? How can I be assertive and yet not hurt people's feelings or make them angry? What if I do assert myself and the other person doesn't change his behavior? How can I keep from being so angry that it overwhelms me and I act aggressively? What if I do a terrible job of asserting myself? (Pearlman, Coburn & Jakubowski-Spector, 1973). These questions and others like them will occur throughout assertion training.

A second way to conduct this exercise is to work with one participant who would volunteer to work on the situation portrayed in a particular vignette. The whole group can participate and respond but the following questions might first be asked of the volunteer: What personal rights do you think you have in this situation? What makes it hard for you to respond assertively in this or a similar situation? How would you usually respond in this kind of situation? What would you like to say to this person? How would you like this person to respond? What assertive statements could you make that would achieve your goals? (Pearlman, Coburn & Jakubowski-Spector, 1973). The trainers could then do a brief behavior rehearsal. This process is a briefer version of the cognitive restructuring and behavior rehearsal procedures described in Chapters 5, 6, and 7.

A third way of using this exercise is to set up triads where one participant reacts to the film, a second participant asks the questions cited above (possibly listed on a blackboard), and a third participant observes the interactions of the other two, making suggestions when their communication is blocked and giving positive feedback at the end of the discussion on what was observed. The triadic discussions should not be allowed to lapse into simple advice-giving, which does not maximize the capacities of the person reacting to the vignette, often does not consider his feelings, and does not develop assertive responses that "fit" for the individual.

Through this two-hour exercise and all of assertion training, the trainers supportively give permission to the participants to regard themselves and others highly and to act on that regard.

Outcome Goals

The goals of this exercise are: (1) to stimulate participants to identify and to accept their personal rights, (2) to recognize how personal rights can be violated by others and by ourselves when we deny them, (3) to elicit emotional reactions to the vignettes, (4) to stimulate participants to think of similar situations with which they have had difficulty in being assertive, (5) to discriminate between nonassertive, assertive, and aggressive responses, and (6) to practice responses which the participant would like to express in such a situation. The exercise is fun and deals with the very important issue of personal rights at a comfortable level. The recognition and acceptance of personal rights and the discrimination of nonassertive, assertive, and aggressive behaviors will also greatly facilitate the process of cognitive restructuring and behavior in later sessions.

Homework Suggestions for Participants

1. Identify one personal situation similar to one of the stimulus films that you would like to work on in a role play during a later session.
2. Think of any persons you have had difficulty responding to: Identify

any personal rights you have with that person (in specific situations), recognize *how* the other person might be violating your rights, specify any catastrophizing you might be doing, think of several assertive responses you might make to this person.

Homework Suggestions for Trainers

1. Identify five stimulus situations that would be appropriate to the group you will lead. If possible, make video tapes and use them as suggested in this exercise.
2. Plan several sessions using the American Personnel and Guidance Association stimulus films as a takeoff point (see footnote, p. 84).
3. Practice giving a brief statement discriminating between assertive, nonassertive, and aggressive responses.
4. Be able to recall the personal rights covered in this exercise.

EXERCISE 9
Identifying Personal Rights
Accepting Personal Rights in Fantasy

Cathy Steel and Janice Hochman (in press, a) have created a two-part exercise which helps group members identify personal rights and experience accepting these rights (we have partially modified the exercise they present).

In the first part, the trainer gives a few examples of personal rights and instructs the participants to brainstorm all the personal rights they can think of. They are told that during this five-minute period their suggested rights will not be evaluated or criticized. During the brainstorming, the trainer notes the group's suggestions on a blackboard or a large sheet of paper.

At the end of the five-minute period, the group then clarifies, modifies, deletes, or adds to the list of personal rights. We have found that it is often beneficial to have the group discuss any limitations on these rights and the responsibilities which accompany the rights. This is particularly important when the assertion training group includes highly aggressive people. This discussion may take from 5 to 15 minutes.

The second part of the exercise involves a group fantasy. The members are instructed to look at the list of personal rights and to silently select one of the rights which they feel most uncomfortable in accepting. Afterwards the participants are given the following instructions.

Close your eyes . . . get in a comfortable position . . . take a deep breath, hold it as long as you can, and then let it out slowly. . . . Now imagine that you have the right you selected from the list . . . Imagine how life would change as you accept this right . . . How you would act . . . How you feel about yourself . . . about other people. . . .

This fantasy continues for two minutes, after which the trainer says:

Now imagine that you no longer have the right . . . Imagine how your life would change from what it was moments ago . . . How you now act . . . and feel about yourself . . . and about other people. . . .

This fantasy continues for one minute, since the participants usually find it easier to imagine the right being taken away than accepting the right.

Afterwards the group members form pairs and discuss the following questions:

1. What right did you select?
2. How did you feel when you accepted the right?
3. How did you act differently when you had the right?
4. What did you learn about yourself in this exercise?

When the pairs have finished sharing their experiences, the group may discuss how they can help themselves to accept these personal rights, and what methods they used to deny themselves these rights. Trainers can also help group members create more productive messages to counter those messages which cause them to deny themselves a particular personal right as the following example illustrates. The woman had trouble accepting her right to occasionally not cook for her family.

Trainer: How do you stop yourself from accepting that right?

Sharon: I tell myself, "I'm a homemaker and that's just one of my responsibilities."

Trainer: Is it like saying, "I'm a lazy and irresponsible woman to not want to cook all the time"?

Sharon: That's pretty close to it.

Trainer: What do you know about yourself that tells you that that thought is at least partially a lie?

Sharon: Well, I've got a full-time teaching job and I have a husband and three children to take care of. They help out, but I still do the brunt of the work.

Trainer: OK. So part of you knows that you are a hard worker. But it's also like part of the message goes "I must not be weak. I must not need help with household responsibilities."

Sharon: That is true of me. You know as matter of fact I enjoy cooking most of the time. It's just when I get really hassled from teaching once in a while that I'd rather not cook and instead go to a restaurant, or have the family cook. But I feel guilty when I even think of doing that.

Trainer: Tell me, when your husband or the kids are hassled, tired, or under pressure, do you make allowances for them?

Sharon: Yes (laughs).

Trainer: When you feel hassled and don't want to cook, would it help if you said to yourself, "I'm just asking them to make allowances for me for right now, just like when they're hassled I make allowances for them."

Sharon: That would help a lot . . . I like that!

Outcome Goals

The goals of this 45-minute exercise are: (1) to help the participants become aware of how much freer they feel when they accept the assertive right, (2) to increase their awareness of how they deny themselves the right, and (3) to use the resulting group discussion to identify specific counter-messages they could use to help themselves accept the right.

Homework Suggestions for Participants

Carry out the fantasy exercise in which you accept the personal right, once a day for a week. Notice how you feel. Discuss any trouble you had carrying out this exercise in the training group.

Homework Suggestions for Trainers

Carry out this exercise with a group of friends. Assess the degree to

90

which your instructions were clear and you were able to help the group members resolve any disagreement about the rights, and to develop messages for helping them to accept these rights.

EXERCISE 10
Identifying Human Rights
Accepting These Rights

An alternative group exercise which can be used to achieve the same goals as those in Exercise 8 has been created by Dianne Jones Freeman and Barbara Gray (personal communication, 1975). In this exercise, which takes approximately two and a half hours, the trainer presents large sheets of paper which are titled the Rights of Children, the Rights of Parents, the Rights of Employers, the Rights of Employees, etc. The particular group of rights which are selected by the trainer would obviously depend on the type of people in the assertion training group.

The participants are asked to list various rights that belong to each of these groups. After all the lists are completed, group members compare them and identify rights that cut across various groups. The trainer then asks the members whether they would agree that one group of people has the same rights as another group. For example, "I see here where we've said that children have the right to act silly. But that right doesn't appear on our list of parental rights. Do parents have the right to be silly? What do you think?" During this process it becomes gradually clear to the participants that all the groups of people have the same or similar rights. The trainer then points out that the group has really been talking about *human rights* and since everyone in the group is *human*, they are entitled to all the rights which they have identified.

At this point, members are asked to select the five rights that they feel comfortable accepting. Each of them, in turn, then says to the group "I have the right to . . ." while maintaining eye contact with the group members and speaking confidently. They are then given positive feedback from the group. After the entire group has done this, each member takes a turn standing up and facing each member of the group and once again repeats, "I have the right to . . . ." Finally, the members select five human rights that other people have said they were entitled to, but which they felt less sure of accepting for themselves, and they say "I have the right to . . ." as assertively as possible to the rest of the group members, who may then give various "permission" messages such as "Yes, you have permission not to laugh at jokes. As a matter of fact, I'd feel closer to you if you didn't laugh at jokes that didn't strike you as funny."

At the next group session, the trainer then writes a fantasy trip for each person, which describes accepting these personal rights and how the person would act and feel. During this fantasy trip, various relaxation suggestions are also made by the trainer.

Outcome Goals

This exercise is designed to achieve similar goals as those in Exercise 9. The method in achieving these goals is simply different. Although this exercise takes more time, it may be more appropriate for group members who deny themselves crucial rights simply because they have a particular role in society.

Homework Suggestions for Participants

Every day in the next week, repeat the statement "I have a right to. . ." and recall the permission message you were given in the group.

Homework Suggestions for Trainers

Practice conducting this exercise with a group of friends or members of the target population. Assess the degree to which you helped the members see how various assertive rights belong to different groups of people. Assess the degree to which you facilitated the group giving "permission" messages.

EXERCISE 11
A Brief Introduction
to Rational-Emotive Principles*

The trainer can begin with a brief introduction to rational-emotive principles regarding human behavior (Ellis, 1962, 1971, 1973; Ellis & Harper, 1975; see also Chapter 5). The following is an example of such an introduction:

> Nonassertiveness often arises from irrational and incorrect thinking, emotional under- and overreactions to stimuli, and habitually dysfunctional behavior patterns. What we tend to label

* We wish to recognize the original work of Albert Ellis to the theory and practice of rational-emotive principles.

our emotional reactions to situations are mainly caused by our conscious and unconscious evaluations and assumptions. We feel anxious or depressed because we convince ourselves that it is not only unfortunate and inconvenient, but that it is *terrible* and *catastrophic* when we fail at a major task or are rejected by a significant person. We also may feel *hostile* because we believe that others who act unfairly *absolutely should not* act the way they do.

The rational-emotive philosophy holds that there are no legitimate reasons for people *to make themselves* hysterical or overly agitated. It does support the expression of strong, appropriate feelings like sorrow, regret, displeasure, or annoyance. Experiencing self-defeating emotions like guilt, depression, rage, or worthlessness adds a magical hypothesis that things *ought* to be different, rather than the more reasonable notion that things would be better if they were different.

Ellis (1973) offers two excellent examples to explain his A-B-C theory of human behavior. These two examples or others more appropriate to the group members might be used. The trainers should briefly describe the A-B-C theory using specific examples (and a blackboard, if available).

Point A is a particular stimulus activity, action, or situation, such as an interview for an important job or an argument during which one's mate yells unfairly. At point B the person either has a *rational belief* (RB) such as: "It would be unfortunate if I were rejected at the job interview" or "It is annoying to have my mate scream at me unfairly." The person may, however, go from point A to an *irrational belief* (iB) like: "It would be *awful* if I do not get this job" or "My mate is horrible for screaming at me." Such irrational beliefs state or imply a should, ought, or demand that the person get what he wants.

If the man moves from Point A to point RB, he experiences the rational consequences (RC) of his rational beliefs. He might feel concerned about the job interview, plan for expected questions, and, if he does not get the job, feel disappointed, sad, frustrated, or displeased.

If he moved from point A to point iB, the next step is point iC (irrational consequences). He will then likely feel anxious, self-hating, self-pitying, depressed, and enraged. He may develop psychosomatic ailments; he will become defensive and, if rejected, is likely to rationalize the rejection by blaming external factors. He may then spend much time preoccupied with the hopelessness of it all and do nothing about changing his situation.

The trainer, at this point, might ask group members to cite possible rational (RC) and irrational (iC) consequences to the second example of the mate screaming unfairly. Then, the trainers might pass out a list of the basic irrational beliefs developed by Ellis (Ellis & Harper, 1975; see also Chapter 5).

After the participants read the irrational beliefs and their rational alternatives, the trainer should offer two or three specific situations (point A's) and have the group follow them through possible rational and irrational sequences either as a whole group or in triads. Then have each participant (in groups of three) share a real-life personal situation which elicited irrational beliefs. At this point, the trainer can either simply have each person think of alternative rational beliefs and consequences, or the trainer can use the rational self-analysis method (Exercise 12).

This exercise might be conducted in 30 to 45 minutes depending on how much discussion and clarification takes place.

Outcome Goals

Participants will: (1) learn some of the relationships between thinking, feeling, and behavior, (2) be able to discriminate between irrational and rational thinking, (3) learn several of the basic, underlying irrational beliefs, (4) learn how to develop more rational thoughts in specific situations, and (5) be able to use the A-B-C's as a way to conceptualize in later sessions.

Homework Suggestions for Participants

1. Think of any other irrational beliefs which might be more common today.

2. Go through the A-iB-iC sequence for at least two real-life situations and substitute rational beliefs and consequences.

3. Read several of the references on rational-emotive theory.

4. Write down the A-B-C's of several situations to share with the group next session.

Homework Suggestions for Trainers

Complete items 1, 2, and 3 from above.

EXERCISE 12
Rational Self-Analysis*

This is another exercise in which members learn to analyze their irrational thoughts and develop more rational ways of thinking. The exercise is introduced by the following satements:

> The rational self-analysis exercise is designed to help you learn to identify and change irrational self-messages which cause you to feel extremely anxious, angry, depressed, or hopeless about acting assertively in a particular situation. This exercise first involves your describing a specific situation in which you'd like to act assertively but have been unable to because fear or other strong emotions prevent you. The situation you choose to work on should be a specific one, as the following example illustrates:
>
>> At meetings where people are very competitive, and everyone tries to outdo everyone else and come out on top, I become totally quiet and fearful of speaking up, even when I have a relevant comment to make.
>
> Here's another situation which is not sufficiently specific:
>
>> Feeling anxious and scared; want to run away and let somebody else take care of the problem for me.

The trainer then instructs the group to write a specific situation in which they'd like to be more assertive but in which their emotions cause them to act aggressively or nonassertively. Afterwards the trainer can say:

> The next step in this method is to write down the negative thoughts that come to your mind as you think about acting assertively in the situation. Each of these thoughts will usually contain an irrational catastrophizing sentence in it. Remember that these thoughts would be ones which would produce negative feelings in you, for example:
>
> 1. People will think what I have to say isn't very bright or that I don't really understand the situation and that means I must be stupid.

---

* We wish to recognize Albert Ellis as the originator of the process of rational self-analysis and Maxie Maultsby (Goodman & Maultsby, 1974) for the creation of the self-analysis form.

2. People will expect me to explain my views and I won't be able to. I'll be a complete failure.

Are the following examples of self-defeating irrational thoughts?

1. I feel guilty that I don't write to my parents more often.
2. My boss is awful. She had no right to criticize me. She should have liked my work.
3. I'm going to fail a test and that makes me a failure.

In the group discussion that follows, the trainer may note that the first statement does not describe thoughts; it simply describes a feeling. The last two statements are thoughts which are likely to produce negative emotions. Then the group members write their own self-defeating irrational thoughts. Afterwards the members are instructed how to challenge and thus change their internal messages. The trainer can introduce this segment of the exercise by making the following statements:

The next step is to develop challenges to these thoughts. Look at each of the thoughts you've written. They'll be challenged in two ways. The *first* challenge is to identify the flaw in the self-message. Asking yourself, "Is this 100 percent true?" "Is the consequence I fear definitely going to happen?" "What do I know about myself or other people that says this may not happen?" will help pinpoint these flaws.

For example, take the statement: "People will think what I have to say isn't very bright or that I don't really understand the situation and that means I must be stupid." First of all is this true? Is it definitely a *fact* that people will think this? Is there a possibility that they will think different thoughts? Here's what a challenge would sound like:

Challenge: It is possible that they will think what I have to say is bright. In the past, when I've said something, people have sometimes responded favorably. Some people may even like what I say. Generally it's only one or two people who are likely to respond negatively. The rest of the people may have a neutral reaction.

The *second* challenge involves asking yourself two questions: (1) Even if this bad event happened, is it a catastrophy? Could I handle it? and (2) What implications does this bad event have for me? Does it make me a bad or worthless person? Does it make the other person bad? If not, what does it realistically make you or the other person? Here's how the second challenge would sound:

> *Challenge:* Even if people think that what I have to say isn't very bright, everyone is entitled to make a mistake. It's inconvenient and disappointing if they don't all think my thoughts are brilliant, but it's not the end of the world. I won't fall apart although I don't like it and may feel uncomfortable. Just because I say something that isn't bright according to their standards doesn't automatically make me stupid. I don't have to say something bright 100 percent of the time in order to be bright. Better to offer my ideas than say nothing. If I never said anything then they'd have real reason to believe that I have nothing to offer.

Effective challenges do not include unrealistic pep talks ("Everything will turn out perfectly OK, cheer up") or should statements ("I should just relax and not be a chicken) or rationalizations ("I don't really care what they think of me"). Rational challenges accurately assess a situation and reasonably recognize the possible outcomes.

After this discussion, the group participants are instructed to develop written challenges to their irrational, emotion-producing thoughts. When members discover effective challenges, they will usually experience a gut reaction. If their challenges only make intellectual sense and don't emotionally affect them, the rational self-analysis was done incorrectly.

Outcome Goals

This 45-minute exercise helps the participants to identify and challenge their irrational thinking which leads to excessive anxiety, anger, or guilt—feelings which may cause the members to react nonassertively or aggressively. When members become skilled with this method, they can use these skills outside of the group to cope with emotions which interfere with their acting assertively.

Homework Suggestions for Participants

1. Use the rational self-analysis procedure in three situations during the week.

2. Look for other situations to which you might like to apply the procedure later.

Homework Suggestions for Trainers

1. Try the procedure yourself. Also, think of as many simple challenges as you can to some of the most common self-defeating statements.
2. Practice how you would introduce this exercise and how you would involve the participants in identifying their own situations, irrational thoughts, and challenges.

EXERCISE 13
Rational-Emotive Imagery

This procedure was developed by Maultsby & Ellis (1974). Its purposes are: (1) to demonstrate the relationship between thinking-imagining and feelings, and (2) to demonstrate how feelings can be controlled by altering thinking.

First, the participants should imagine an unpleasant experience or activating event. The participants are told to pay very close attention to the details of the situation so that it will seem as realistic as possible. The trainer might guide the participants (with their eyes closed) through various aspects of their imagined event: the feelings and behaviors of others, the context, their own behavior, any physical tenseness, and especially their feelings. As the participants imagine their situations, they will tend to feel upset and uncomfortable. The trainer should instruct them to experience these feelings fully rather than to try avoiding them. The participants should feel increasingly anxious, hostile, depressed, or embarrassed. The trainer then instructs the participants to force aside the strong negative emotions so that only mild disappointment or irritation is felt. Trainers should continually encourage participants to force themselves to change their strong feelings.

After allowing the participants a brief time to change their feelings, the trainers should make the following point:

> When you have let yourself go through this procedure and pushed yourself to a point where you feel only disappointed or irritated, look at the thought processes that have produced these new, appropriate feelings. Notice exactly what words you repeated to yourself to change the feeling. If you observe yourself clearly, you will note that you have in some manner changed your belief system

and consequently changed your emotions. Let yourself clearly see what you have done and what important changes in your thinking you have made. Become fully aware of the new beliefs. You can use these internal messages in situations which occur in everyday life.

A variation of this procedure is to focus on and dispute the bad feelings and self-defeating thoughts once the participants have gotten in touch with them. The participants attack the negative, irrational thoughts and substitute more appropriate beliefs. Then they vigorously and strongly fantasize how they would feel and behave after they started giving the old ideas up. The trainer instructs the participants to picture themselves disbelieving these ideas and feeling and acting in accordance with their new rational challenges, and to imagine, in detail, their new thinking, feeling, and behavior.

In some cases, participants are unable to imagine themselves handling the situation assertively, but are able to picture someone else doing so. We believe that is an acceptable first step if the participant eventually imagines himself handling the situation as well.

In order to become proficient at these cognitive-emotive tasks, the participants should become familiar with the basic irrational ideas (see Chapter 5) either through the trainer or through reading cognitive-behavior modification and especially rational-emotive books and pamphlets (see References).

This exercise can take about 30 minutes. Often, however, participants raise stimulating questions which the trainer may wish to discuss. Cognitive control is often a new and powerful idea for participants and it is worthy of extended discussion.

Outcome Goals

Participants should realize how they can exercise cognitive control and thereby alter feelings and behaviors. They should also be able to distinguish between "power of positive thinking" statements, rationalizations, irrational thinking, and rational thinking.

Homework Suggestions for Participants

1. Practice this technique systematically on a specific situation for ten minutes each day.
2. When you are feeling intensely angry or excessively anxious, look for the thoughts you are saying to yourself. Challenge their irrationality

and force yourself to substitute more rational thoughts. Then check your resulting feelings and behaviors.

Homework Suggestions for Trainers

1. Practice guiding several persons through the imagery steps.

2. Become completely familiar with the irrational beliefs (see Chapter 5).

3. Have someone guide you through the imagery steps as you think of a situation that is disturbing to you. Note any changes in thinking and feelings and any difficulties you might have with imagery.

EXERCISE 14
Emotive Imagery*

This exercise presents a method whereby group members can reduce their anxiety about acting assertively. Trainers may introduce the exercise by saying:

> We use our imagination to scare ourselves about acting assertively. We imagine the worst thing that the other person could say and our own difficulty in responding. Thus we create anxiety with our imagination. We can also, however, use imagination to reduce our anxiety. We all know that when we feel more confident and good about ourselves, it is easier to act assertively. The procedure which uses imagination in this way is called emotive imagery. The technique requires certain kinds of imaginary scenes which produce positive feelings like mirth, happiness, self-pride, and confidence.
>
> For example, just before asserting herself with her lover who was often critical, a woman imagined a time with him when they had a particularly open and honest discussion together. The remembered scene brought back feelings of security and acceptance and reduced her anxiety to a more manageable level so that she could more easily be assertive with him (Jakubowski-Spector, 1973a).
>
> It is important to note that the purpose of emotive imagery is *not* to lull one into a false sense of self-confidence. Rather,

---

* Arnold Lazarus and Arnold Abramovitz (1965) are credited with the development of this procedure.

emotive imagery helps one to utilize the same faculty (imagination), which has previously generated anxiety, to now elicit calm and confident feelings. The goal of such imagery is to reduce anxiety to a point where other cognitive and behavioral skills can be employed toward assessing and handling the situation itself more assertively.

The trainer should encourage members to discuss previous scenes which could generate positive feelings. Some participants report that emotive imagery of quite unrelated scenes, such as a day in the woods during which the person felt serene and calm, have also worked to reduce anxiety. The scene should be a real experience in the person's past. Above all, the scene should truly elicit positive *feelings*. Participants should be encouraged to identify *what* positive feeling is likely to work for them, for example, security, safety, pride, happiness, confidence. One might feel potent and competent when remembering making an excellent point at an important meeting, or feel safe and accepted when thinking of an intimate moment with someone.

The trainers should then have the participants think of a situation in which they'd like to act assertively and then use the positive emotive imagery to reduce the anxiety generated. This exercise should take about 30 minutes.

Not all group members will be able to use this procedure, since not everyone can imagine scenes which produce positive feelings. Moreover, not everyone has easy access to their capacities for visual and emotive imagery. Nevertheless, the procedure has been a powerful intervention for many participants as they approach stressful situations.

Outcome Goals
Through this exercise participants learn how to use imagery to reduce anxiety instead of using that same imaginative capacity to increase their agitation.

Homework Suggestions for Participants
Practice this technique systematically on a specific situation for ten minutes each day.

Homework Suggestions for Trainers
Practice guiding several persons through the imagery steps.

EXERCISE 15
Making and Refusing Requests

Nonassertive persons often avoid making reasonable requests of others. When they do make requests, they seem to be apologetic or do not expect them to be accepted. Some nonassertive persons have trouble saying no and instead give excuses for not being able to comply with another's request when the real issue is that they do not want to comply. In contrast, aggressive persons can sound demanding, coercive, and hostile in requesting and resentful and hostile in refusing.

After briefly explaining that making and refusing requests effectively is another form of assertive behavior, the trainer should have the members form pairs. Let the pairs create their own role play situations (fellow workers, roommates, friends) and have one person make a reasonable request and the other just respond with "No"; then switch roles.

A brief discussion with the whole group usually reveals that saying "No" is not all they wish to communicate. The members should then begin to clarify what else they wish the requester to know (possibly why they are refusing, or a willingness to comply in a different way or at a different time). This is an appropriate time to note again that we all have certain personal rights as to how we spend our time and what we do with our property and our bodies. Essentially, we emphasize that it is OK for people to make reasonable requests and it is also OK to refuse them.

Have the pairs then make and refuse requests, intentionally offering excuses that avoid the real issues. For example, in response to a request to borrow the stereo for a party, a person might say, "Gee I can't because when my parents gave it to me, they made me promise not to loan it out" (when this is untrue). Or when asked for a date to say, "I really don't know what my plans will be for Friday night" (when this is untrue and you actually do not want to date the person). The "requesters" should persist and confront the "I can't" responses either with solutions or alternatives that still include a request. Participants find their "I can't" responses unsatisfactory although easier to give. The fear of being selfish or hurtful to others may need to be clarified. Usually, several participants raise a number of questions about how to deal with the person who might feel hurt by a refusal, especially if the request is for a date. Participants also want to know how to deal with the person who persists or the person who asks why he is refused ("Why? Don't you like me?"). In the former case, they can practice changing the issue from accepting or refusing the date to confronting the person with his persistence in the face of clear refusal. In the latter instance, participants need to know that they are free to answer such a question as fully as they wish; they also have the right to choose not to answer at all, saying that they prefer not to go into an explanation.

The behavior of making or refusing requests can be heavily influenced by the meaning attributed to such behaviors. Trainers might invite participants to discuss the thoughts or beliefs which would lead to avoiding *making* requests. The following beliefs might emerge: "The other person might not be able to refuse; The person might refuse and that would mean that person doesn't like me and I must be no good; My needs are not so important that I should infringe on another person; If I ask, then I'll be obligated to that person." In regard to *refusing* requests one might think: "I can't hurt the person like that; my needs aren't as important as others'; They won't like me any more; If the person asked, it must be really important since I wouldn't ask unless it were essential." In most cases, participants can recognize the personal rights and faulty beliefs they engage in and are willing to try out alternatives. If anyone is not comfortable making or refusing requests *and wishes to work on that*, trainers should have those persons identify specific situations for the cognitive restructuring-behavior rehearsal sessions.

Lastly, have the pairs make and refuse requests, attempting to be honest and direct, particularly emphasizing "I don't want to" or "I won't" messages, rather than "I can't." Explanations and expressions of concern for the requester's reaction are appropriate if stated in a forthright, honest manner and do not put the participant in a "one-down" position.

The focus can also shift to any discomfort people experience in *making* requests effectively. Members can practice and receive feedback on the directness of their requests without apology or low expectation of compliance. Frequently, when people learn to refuse requests, they become more comfortable in making requests.

Outcome Goals
The purposes of this exercise are: (1) to recognize how beliefs regarding personal rights influence behaviors, (2) to have the members

assess their comfort and effectiveness in making and refusing requests, (3) to provide some information regarding the *direct* expression of a request or a refusal, (4) to practice discriminating between effective and ineffective refusals and requests, and (5) to offer a belief system which highly regards personal rights and to demonstrate its positive influence on actual behaviors. About 30 minutes should be allowed for this exercise.

Homework Suggestions for Participants

1. Make three reasonable assertive requests that are somewhat difficult for you; then, assess what you liked about how you made them.
2. Every day restate any personal rights you have been avoiding which you now wish to act upon.
3. Assertively refuse any requests you would like to turn down.

Homework Suggestions for Trainers

1. Practice discriminating between refusals which state essentially "I won't" or "I don't want to " from those which state "I can't" when that is not the case. Be able to give several examples of each.
2. Know the personal rights at issue when refusing requests. Also know the irrational fears or catastrophizing which often support not acting on those personal rights. Be sure that the participant actually wants to say no! Practice dealing with participant ambivalences, such as "I want to say no but I feel like I shouldn't (couldn't)."

EXERCISE 16
Making Statements Without Explanation

Nonassertive persons often avoid taking action in a variety of situations because they fear they do not have a good enough explanation for their behavior. Moreover, when they do take action, it is only after having given a lengthy explanation (sometimes untrue) to justify their behavior. The focus of this exercise is on practicing making any type of statement without explaining.

The trainer can begin by describing the dynamics cited above and giving an example: Two couples were waiting to be seated in a restaurant. They had also put their names on a list at a better restaurant next door and after one person checked, found that they could be seated there in a few more minutes. Upon returning to his group, the person who checked at the better restaurant found his party already being seated. He informed them that they could have a table next door in just a few minutes. Two persons in the group were uncomfortable leaving (even though they both preferred the other restaurant). The group did leave and one member of the group simply informed the hostess that they decided not to stay, whereupon she thanked him for telling her. The two persons who were uncomfortable later discussed the situation and realized that they both felt they had to explain, even justify, their leaving. One also believed they were probably causing great inconvenience and the other worried that the hostess and others might be offended. Both were struck by how comfortably their friend had stated their decision without explanation.

After citing such an example, the trainer can suggest a number of other situations where this dynamic can occur and ask the group to think of their own examples. The group might also identify what worries they would have and practice a variety of situations making statements *with* and *without* explanation.

The following are examples of situations which might be used in the group:

1. Leaving a shop without buying anything after a salesperson has taken a great deal of time to show you a variety of products and their features (this can be even more difficult if it's a craft store and the salesperson is the creator).
2. Dealing with door-to-door salespersons who try to put on a "hard sell" by asking a series of questions: Do you have children? Are you concerned with their educational and cultural development? Do you have educational materials for them? Are they written for children or for adults? Finally, they will hit on a "no" answer and there's the opening.
3. Calling a travel agency and canceling travel arrangements which have already been made.
4. Going into a coffee shop and asking for a glass of water or asking for a hanger in a cleaners.

In any of these situations, participants may wish to provide elaborate explanations. The issue raised here is that one does not *have* to do so, nor does the explanation have to be a good one by others' standards. It is important to make the point that this exercise does not suggest that persons *never* offer explanations.

Outcome Goals

The goals for this exercise are: (1) to help participants discriminate between their *wanting* to explain their behavior and their *having* to explain their behavior, (2) to suggest that people have a right to make statements without explaining them, (3) to identify a frequently occurring behavior pattern where persons avoid taking action or making statements for fear that their explanations will not be well received, and (4) to practice making statements with and without explanation and assessing how each feels and what thoughts are generated.

This exercise can take from 20 to 40 minutes depending on the reactions of the participants and the situations they identify.

Homework Suggestions for Participants

Observe your own behavior to determine how inclined you are to explain your behavior. You might also wish to try out various degrees of explanation in different situations and assess your own reactions.

Homework Suggestions for Trainers

Identify several good examples of situations to use in the group where participants might be inclined to over-explain. Develop explanations for such issues as responding differently in different situations and with different persons. Be prepared to avoid having participants overgeneralize this exercise to all situations and persons.

EXERCISE 17
Dealing with Persistent Persons

The focus of this exercise is on the frequently occurring type of situation where someone makes a request which a group participant might assertively reject, whereupon the person persists with greater efforts to change the participant's mind. Essentially, this exercise is an extension of the Making and Refusing Requests exercise with particular attention given to changing any irrational thinking and unassertive behaviors which arise in response to another's persistence.

After briefly explaining the focus of the exercise, the trainers might cite one or two examples of this type of situation. For example, a therapist phoned a colleague to request that her client be admitted into a monthly therapy-training group. Her request was made in a direct, assertive fashion but the colleague refused, explaining that there already was a pool of persons from which he admitted participants, that he felt they had priority, and would surely fill the group. At this point both persons were behaving assertively. The therapist, however, began a second effort to convince her colleague to admit her client: "Yes, but my client is *really* ready to work. She needs this experience and the group would get a great deal from her." Her third effort: "Surely many of the people on your list are just going but aren't putting much into the group." Her fourth try: "I don't want to try to use any influence since I am a good friend of Dr. X, but . . . ."

After offering this example, the trainers might then ask how the participants might respond to each statement. This could be followed by a discussion of the irrational thinking or discounting of personal rights which prompt nonassertive or aggressive behavior. The most common dynamic is that the person who refuses and finds the request renewed with greater strength irrationally believes that the explanation truly is not good enough; he therefore must think hard for even better justifications for refusing. This thinking usually leads to anxious scrambling and flimsy excuses which are then disputed by the "requester," leaving the "refuser" in a one-down position. Others might worry that the requester will not like them or that continuing to refuse might create "an unpleasant scene" which would be awful. This discussion usually should be brief (about ten minutes).

The trainers can then introduce a variety of responses which participants might wish to use in such situations; for example, progressively moving from empathic assertions to simple assertions or to confrontive assertions. For example, the colleague could begin with an empathic assertion: "I know you really would like Ms. A to be in the group, but I am committed to the others first." As the therapist persisted, the colleague could progressively drop the empathic component (content and tonality) and move to simple, direct assertions: "I'm going to honor my commitment to give these people priority."

Another possible response after the requester has persisted for some time is to shift from the request—the *content*—to a confrontation regarding what the person is doing—the *process* ("As you continue to persist I am getting more uncomfortable and irritated since you don't seem to be respecting my decision"). If all else fails, one might practice a request that the person change her behavior ("I'd really like you to stop persisting, will you?"). Another response might be to define clearly what one *is* willing to do (especially if it be persistent demands on one's time) thereby gaining control and setting clear limits on what one is willing to do and what one is not willing to do. For example, one participant worked on responding assertively to her grandmother who made constant, guilt-eliciting demands on her time. She established certain specific times that she really was willing to be with her grandmother and made it clear that this was the limit. After expressing understanding of her grandmother's desires to see her, she clearly stated her offer. (See also Exercise 19 on defining one's own behavior.)

In triads, the participants then can practice their own specific situations.

Outcome Goals
Participants should: (1) learn how to use empathic, simple, and confrontive assertions as someone continues to persist with them, (2) be able to determine when their answers or explanations are adequate even when the persistent person acts as though they are not, and (3) be able to recognize the personal rights and thinking going on when someone is persistent with them.

Homework Suggestions for Participants
Homework for participants is difficult since they may not interact with a persistent person. They might, however, particularly observe others, looking for this type of interaction and imagine how they would handle it.

Homework Suggestions for Trainers
1. Think of several situations which might be more appropriate for your group when a person inappropriately persists. Practice how you would present this exercise.
2. Think of three possible objections that group members might raise and plan how you would respond to those reservations.

EXERCISE 18
Small Group Behavior
Rehearsal Exercise: The Line
This exercise is an excellent introduction to the behavior rehearsal components of assertion training. Participants are placed into two groups of five participants each and each group forms a shoulder-to-shoulder line. Each subgroup works separately with one trainer; if there is only one trainer, the trainer can move between the two groups. The first person

in the line identifies a specific situation to work on. The trainers should suggest specific types of interactions like refusing requests, asking someone to change his behavior, or responding to demeaning remarks. The first person (A) steps off the line, faces the second person (B), and *briefly* defines the situation. For example, person A wants to say no to a student who requests her to be his professor of record for a special readings and research course when person A has unquestionably overcommitted her teaching time already for the semester. Person B would initiate the interaction, playing the role of the student by making the request and person A would refuse. The participants (A and B) would stop after that single interaction and the other members in line (C, D, and E as well as B) would give person A specific, *positive*, behavioral feedback on her behavior. Person A would then add anything else that she liked and then specify any changes she would like to make in her content or manner of responding.

It is extremely important that the person working have no more than two, or at most three, changes to work on at a time. As with the behavior rehearsal procedures described in the next chapter, it is crucial to work on small segments of behavior (one or two interactions) and a manageable number of changes. If person A does not identify two changes to make, the other participants can make *suggestions* for person A's consideration. The trainers should help the participants to make suggestions ("I think you would come across more assertively if you dropped the 'you know' at the end. What do you think?") and get a decision from person A, rather than making "should" statements ("You should stop saying 'you know' at the end of your response"). By making suggestions, rather than commands, the person working assumes greater responsibility for choosing what she would like to do.

Let us assume that person A's first response was "Well, uh, gee, uh, I don't know; I'm awfully busy this semester, you know." Persons B, C, D, and E tell person A that her eye contact was good, her voice was clear and loud enough, and she did state that she was very busy this semester. (Trainers should be sure that participants give feedback to each other *directly* saying "You . . ." instead of "She . . ." as though talking about the person to the rest of the group.) Person A then identifies what she liked about her refusal and decides what changes she will make. Person A then moves to person C in the line and practices the situation again with person C initiating the same request. The role play stops after the initial interaction.

Persons B, C, D, and E cite any improvements (without repeating those cited the first time), particularly focusing on the changes person A chose to make.

As person A moves to person D, the trainer explains that she has an option to continue working on that first interaction or to go beyond the first response and practice dealing with continued persistence, in which the requester uses guilt, anger, or ignoring tactics in an attempt to get her to change her position. In the following example, person A chose to practice empathic assertion and also to go beyond the first interaction with person D.

D: Dr. Loxley, I would like to do a special readings and research course on assertion training with you this semester. Would you sign my special credit card?

A: John, I'm really pleased that you are interested in assertion training but I won't be able to work with you this semester since I've already overcommitted myself to other teaching duties.

D: But Dr. Loxley, I'm expecting to graduate at the end of this semester and I'll never get to learn how you do it.

A: I can see that you'd really like me to do this, but right now I do not want to take on any more time commitments; I won't do justice to any of them at that point.

D: Well, damn, what am I supposed to do now?

A: I don't know. You might talk with Dr. Parker or Dr. Voss who also know a good deal about assertion training and might be willing to work with you this semester.

The trainer should not let the role play go beyond three or four interactions, particularly if person A gets stuck or anxious. The process of giving positive feedback and identifying changes should be repeated. Person A then practices an extended interaction with Person E. Even if everything about the interaction is not changed to Person A's satisfaction, the responses with person E are likely to be much more assertive. The group would then work in the same fashion with each person in the group. Usually, four or five persons can work in each line in about one hour.

The role of the trainer is to observe and reinforce participants, give good behavioral feedback, and to help people focus on the task.

Outcome Goals

The goals of this exercise are: (1) to practice brief interactions which are real to the participants, (2) to maximize participant involvement, (3) to learn several fundamental procedures of behavior rehearsal, (4) to facilitate the transition from structured exercises to the complex behavior rehearsals in later sessions.

Homework Suggestions for Participants

If possible, go out and do what you practiced in the exercise!

Homework Suggestions for Trainers

1. Practice giving a brief explanation of the exercise including a demonstration of how to do it.
2. Think of three more types of interactions you might use in this exercise format.

EXERCISE 19
Defining One's Own Behavior or
"I Love You But I Won't Buy You a Jaguar"*

The purposes of this exercise are to increase the participants' awareness of ways in which others have redefined the meaning of their behavior and to practice assertively responding.

One typical redefinement situation begins with a friend asking a person for a favor. If the person refuses, the friend begins to define the refusal as a personal insult or rejection. Naturally, since friends do help each other, there is a relationship between friendship and helping. This exercise, however, focuses on interactions where others imply or assume a perfect correlation between friendship and meeting every request regardless of one's personal rights or the degree of inconvenience. The trainer should clearly suggest that while one may often wish to help others or meet their requests, one has a personal right to refuse such requests without feeling guilty.

In another typical example of redefinition, a couple who were friends of one group member indirectly expressed hurt and jealousy when the participant and her husband went out for an evening with a

---

* We thank Dr. Rita Whiteley for this creative phrase which we adapted to this exercise.

111

third couple. The friends inquired if she had a good time "with *them*" and if they were as much fun. The group member responded half-heartedly and tried to change the subject several times. After the incident, she knew something "unusual" was going on but didn't know how to respond. She brought it up in the group since she did not believe she handled the situation as well as she would have liked.

Other people will sometimes be more direct in their inaccurate accusations. For example, a group member, upon arriving late at an important meeting, was met with, "The least you could have done was inform the group you would be late!" The group member immediately offered a variety of explanations yet, in retrospect, felt he sounded defensive.

In all three of these examples, the person's behavior was re-defined by someone else and in a negative manner. The process of reclarifying one's own behavior involves two steps: (1) admitting, in a factual manner, the behavior that occurred, and (2) stating what that behavior does *or* does not mean, also in a direct and honest manner. The group member whose friends were jealous practiced responding in a direct yet empathic manner: "We did have a good time with Joan and Paul and I enjoy being with you, too." The participant who was late to the meeting practiced responses like "I am late for the meeting and I do believe it is an important one." Both participants also practiced responding when other people denied that the second part of the state-ment was at all an issue.

In this exercise, the group may form pairs or triads and practice responding to another's redefining their behavior.

Several escalations could also be added to this exercise where the participants might practice: (1) expressing irritation or concern toward the person who has redefined their behavior, or (2) dealing with a person who persists in redefining their behavior.

Outcome Goals

From this exercise, participants should be able to recognize when their behavior is misperceived or misinterpreted and when incorrect motives or meanings are attributed to their behavior. In addition, participants will have learned a direct and nondefensive way to respond to such redefinitions.

Homework Suggestions for Participants

Observe yourself and others in situations where someone else is at-

112

tempting to redefine your behavior. Notice what kinds of thoughts you have; do you readily agree, get angry, get anxious? If you do not handle such a situation as well as you would like, write it down and bring it to the group.

Homework Suggestions for Trainers

Think of examples where others might redefine behaviors that are more appropriate for your group than those cited above. Be prepared to describe this dynamic and elicit ideas from the group as to how to respond assertively.

EXERCISE 20
Beginning and Ending Sessions

After the first session begins with "introductions," succeeding sessions might start with a report of behaviors that members have chosen to work on between sessions (homework) and specific situations that occurred during the week in which the participants believe they behaved assertively or did not behave as effectively as they would have liked. Successes should be genuinely rewarded. Discussion might lead to clarification of basic issues, but should be brief. (Focus on the participants' ability to evaluate their assertiveness as opposed to judging their behavior.) When participants cite situations they did not handle as well as they would have liked, a brief discussion in which the members clarify their personal rights, what kept them from being assertive, and what they would like to do would be appropriate.

To close a session, after making homework plans (see Chapter 6), the group might do a "whip" where each person in turn gets to make a brief statement. The other members might respond attentively but no discussion takes place. Participants simply make their statements. The trainer or a participant might suggest sentences such as: "Today I learned that . . ."; "Right now I feel . . ."; "This session helped me to . . ."; "What I like about myself is . . . ." The whip provides an opportunity for everyone to participate briefly in the close of the session. It takes about 5 minutes.

SUMMARY

The process goals for conducting exercises are: (1) to help create a supportive, positive atmosphere where participants experience success and are rewarded for it, and (2) to utilize maximally the cognitive, affective, and behavioral contributions of the participants as opposed to an over-focus on the leaders' contributions. The outcome goals are: (1) to learn separately some of the procedural components of behavior rehearsal and cognitive restructuring, (2) to learn some fundamental communication skills to facilitate assertive behavior, (3) to feel more confidence and less anxiety with assertion, and (4) to begin recognizing some areas for further work in the behavior rehearsal sessions.

In using these structured exercises, we believe it is crucial to give participants an opportunity to strengthen their own evaluative capabilities. This means that the participants are trained to use and strengthen their own judgment about their behaviors. They should not become despondent or dependent upon the evaluations of others.

OTHER EXERCISES

Refusing Requests

The exercise on making and refusing requests might be supplemented by the following exercise created by Dr. Rita Whiteley (personal communication, 1975). The trainers ask each person to identify a personal belonging that is important or precious to them. The trainer then attempts to borrow that object using all conceivable manipulations (flattery, crisis, guilt, pressure, condescension, helplessness). Each participant gets to practice refusing assertively and to persist in that refusal. The trainer might also request something that the participant agrees to lend and then introduce new information, making the agreement progressively more demanding or unreasonable than the original request. For example, a participant agreed to loan his ten-speed bike to enable the trainer to get home. By the end of the interaction the trainer asked to keep the bike for an unspecified period of time, and to have the participant drop it off at an inconvenient time at his office across the campus. An important caution is in order for this type of exercise: Trainers should be very careful that these interactions do not lead to a self-depreciating, negative experience for the participant. The trainer should stop the interaction before the participant experiences considerable difficulty in responding assertively. The purpose is not to push the participant until he gets anxious but rather to raise some important issues regarding refusals and to develop and practice assertive responses.

Expressing Feelings Spontaneously

Salter (1949) suggested that clients should begin to express their feelings more spontaneously. Although he was somewhat indiscriminate in his exhortations, direct expression of feelings is an assertive behavior worthy of specific attention. The trainers should raise the important issue of recognizing that expression of all one's feelings all the time is not the suggested goal. Rather, the goal is to help persons who hold back appropriate feelings to express them more directly, while not supporting aggressive expressions under the guise of "just being honest."

The trainer can help the participants to express their feelings more directly and appropriately by having them assess feelings they really wish to share and the possible consequences of sharing these feelings. The participants might form pairs and practice sharing the feelings (both positive and negative) they experienced in specific situations in their immediate lives. For example, "I'm angry with my roommate," "I feel really great today," "I'm anxious about student teaching," "I love a wonderful person."

The trainers might then ask the participants to make homework contracts to use "feeling-talk" systematically each day. In addition, asking for a "feeling-talk" statement is an excellent "whip" at the end of a session.

Using Protective Skills

There is some disagreement in the literature regarding the use of techniques which have been labeled "gamesmanship" (Potter, 1970; Wolpe, 1973a; Cotler, 1975; Lazarus, 1975). This collection of responses may, at times, differ from other assertive responses in that the other person is more likely to feel "one-down." Our position is that almost all situations can be handled with more direct, assertive statements. Nevertheless, some persistent persons continue to nag, perservere, rage on, and annoy to the point where certain of these responses may be appropriate. Some of these protective exercises can be integrated into other exercises, such as using the "broken record" (continually restating the initial statement) after giving a good I-message which is discounted. "Fogging" (responding to repeated nagging with "I probably am" or "It probably will" and then explaining what one is doing, why, and that one will continue until the nagging stops) might also be integrated into other exercises or practiced in separate exercises (see Chapter 2 for a discussion of these exercises).

Using Implosive Procedures

An interesting procedure has been described by Wolpin (1975) in which group participants identify a specific situation that they would like to handle more assertively. After an agreement to work on it is made, the trainer and the participant act out the situation, going far beyond the appropriate expressions of feeling. The trainer and participant end up yelling and screaming at each other and may even get into pushing, shoving, and wrestling. This technique is especially appropriate for the expression of anger. Doing this overreaction seems to have a cathartic (and possibly desensitizing) effect. The lack of negative consequences and the realization that outbursts can be controlled seem to have a relieving effect on some participants. Moreover, participants often report having a greater sense of control to engage in the more *assertive behaviors which are then practiced* after the shouting match. This type of exercise, in the hands of a competent trainer, can be a valuable technique to free a participant to practice the less intense assertive behaviors which, heretofore, may have been too bold for the participant to attempt.

Some people may find such an "implosive" exercise to be too threatening. Trainers should only invite persons to use this technique and respect their decisions. We believe that trainers with little clinical practice should be careful when using this procedure since such intense expressions can have fearful and guilt-laden repercussions for more disturbed participants.

Other situations which fit this structured exercise format are: expressing disagreement with another's opinion, speaking to a group, asking for clarification of a statement (especially in a class or seminar), asking *why* someone is doing something or is asking for something from you, joining a conversation already in progress, persisting in a request which seemed to be refused with little justification or explanation, asking and being asked for a date or any invitation, establishing agreements regarding dividing work (both at home and on the job). The list could be endless. The exercises simply should be appropriate to the concerns of the group members, otherwise the situation or type of response is probably better approached during the cognitive restructuring and behavior rehearsal sections to come.

Lastly, when selecting exercises, trainers should give primary consideration to the strengths and concerns of the participants. For example, a group of graduate student women identified as a primary concern their assertive expression of legitimate anger. The trainers, therefore, devised some exercises for discriminating between assertive expressions of anger and a variety of aggressive and nonassertive, yet angry, responses to the same situations. (They also fought with batacas which enabled physical expressions of anger without the danger of hurting someone.) Another group of professional women worked more on nonverbal components of assertive behavior and responding to others who violated their personal rights, as opposed to developing verbal skills which were already evident. The selection and amount of time devoted to specific exercises for each group should be modified according to their strengths, needs, concerns, and level of assertiveness.

REVIEW QUESTIONS

1. Cite three purposes for using structured exercises during the first few sessions.

2. Explain why it would *not* be effective to utilize structured exercises as the sole procedure for every session.

3. Identify and describe five *process* goals that you would use as guidelines for creating your own exercises, i.e., provide for specific behavioral feedback, start with positive feedback, involve all participants maximally.

5
Cognitive Restructuring Procedures

Cognitive restructuring is the process by which individuals become aware of their own thinking patterns which lead to ineffectual behaviors and change these thought processes to more productive ones. Since both nonassertive and aggressive persons become frustrated easily— nonassertive persons acquiescing in order to reduce their own frustration, and aggressive persons attacking (Ellis, personal communication, 1975)—group members can learn to use cognitive restructuring procedures to slow down and modify such abrupt behavior. There are three basic steps to the cognitive restructuring process (overlapping in time): (1) identifying the specific assertion situation clearly, determining its appropriateness for assertion training, and helping group members set their own goals for that situation, (2) using cognitive-behavioral intervention techniques, and (3) identifying one's personal rights in the situation.

The outcome goals of the cognitive restructuring and behavior rehearsal sessions are: (1) to reduce the anxiety participants experience in the specified situation, (2) to increase the person's repertoire of effective responses for that situation, (3) to help participants develop a belief system which highly values their personal rights and those of others,* (4) to teach members how to recognize irrational assumptions and catastrophizing and to replace these with rational assumptions and expectations of how they will act in the situation and how other people

---

* Since Chapter 3 has already discussed the importance of this belief system and Chapter 4 presents exercises which can be used to develop these beliefs, we shall not cover these issues in this chapter.

might act, (5) to help participants develop their own cognitive capabilities to behave more assertively. Ideally, participants experience an internally based sense of confidence and competence as a result of the cognitive restructuring and behavior rehearsal procedures.

The following sections describe in detail each component of the cognitive restructuring model.

THE COGNITIVE RESTRUCTURING MODEL

Part 1—Identifying the Situation Clearly

The cognitive restructuring and behavior rehearsal sessions focus on concerns brought to the group by the participants. Having done several exercises in previous group sessions which focus on specific contexts structured by the trainers (e.g., the exercises in Chapter 4), at this point in the group the participants are usually thinking about their own unique problems. In order to stimulate their recall of *specific* problem situations, trainers should encourage members to think about the places, groups, and individuals they spend time with and the events of the past week.

Some participants, however, express a vague or abstract concern ("I don't have any confidence"). Almost all of these vague concerns can be conceptualized in terms of specific behaviors. For example, lacking confidence can be nonassertively manifested by avoiding conversations with members of the opposite sex at parties, not asking for a date with a fellow classmate, ineffectively giving a presentation to a group, or not confronting a fellow worker who is making unreasonable work demands. Lack of confidence can be aggressively manifested by being continually critical and accusing of others, as a means of keeping criticism off oneself.

We do not encourage trainers to spend time focusing on manipulative behaviors designed to avoid working on changes. For those people who consistently and strongly avoid clarifying problem situations, an open-ended therapy group might be more appropriate. We do believe, however, that some people are not accustomed to thinking behaviorally, particularly about themselves. Taking the time to shape their concerns to specific situations is quite appropriate.

A word of caution is important at this point. In describing their concerns and the people involved, participants sometimes place inordinate attention, with implied blame, on those other persons. Even when

120

there is obvious truth to how inappropriately these others are behaving, the trainer should focus *on how the participant wishes to deal* with the situation more assertively, possibly including confrontation of the other person's inappropriate behavior. Otherwise, it is easy for the group to complain about and bemoan the behavior of others while losing the focus on changing their own behavior.

As a general guideline it is particularly important, especially with participants who tend to avoid focusing on themselves, to get a verbal commitment that they want to work on changing the specified behavior. Moreover, with some nonassertive persons, trainers may find themselves actively working toward clarifying a target situation while the participant is withdrawing more and more from the interaction. In both cases the trainer should regularly determine in a nonjudgmental way if the person actually wants to work on the emerging target behaviors. Below are two examples of this initial step of clearly identifying the specific situation and participant behaviors which will be the target of the cognitive and behavior rehearsal procedures.

In the first example, the participant (P) initially places considerable focus on the professor's behavior and how she would like him to act, but smoothly moves toward clarifying, with the trainer (Tr), what she wishes to work on.

Tr: Who would like to work on something?

P: I would. I've got this problem with the professor I'm a teaching assistant for. He keeps giving me all this extra work that doesn't have anything to do with the class.

Tr: That seems like an appropriate situation for our group. What do you want to work on?

P: Well, I wish he'd stop giving me all that work. He's so inconsiderate and he just leaves all this work in my box in the morning. Anyway, he's such a fast talker. I can hardly get a word in edgewise.

Tr: It sounds like you almost believe the situation is impossible to resolve. What is it you want to work on?

P: Yeah, you're right. Sometimes I do think it's impossible, but maybe it's really not. What I really want to work on is how I can say something to him about it so he'll stop and won't hold it against me.

121

Tr: There's no guarantee what his response will be, but you can practice how *you* might approach him with the issue until you believe you're expressing what you want and in a way that minimizes the chances of his being offended.

P: That's what I'd like.

In the second example, the participant begins with a more vague concern but quickly moves to a clearer specification of several workable situations.

Tr: Who wants to work on something?

P: I guess I do . . . I don't seem to have any confidence.

Tr: Bill, how does your lack of confidence get in the way of your being effective?

P: Oh, I don't know, I just don't do a lot of things cause I guess I'll just mess it up, or if I try, I expect to screw up and I usually do.

Tr: What are some of the things that you avoid that you would like to be able to do effectively?

P: Well, like getting along with people.

Tr: What are some specific things you'd like to do?

P: Well, I'd like to be able to talk with women and not get scared and stumble around . . . and I'd like to talk up more in class . . . and I guess I'd like to go out more.

Tr: OK. Those are really good examples because they're clear and specific behaviors. One way to approach an abstract concern like lack of confidence is to focus on specific situations like the ones you mentioned. What situation would you like to work on now?

P: I think I'd like to start with just talking with one woman for a little while.

Part 1, cont. — Determining the Appropriateness of the Situation for Training and Setting Goals

As the problem becomes more specific, trainers, as in the above examples, should have the participants clearly define their goals for the interaction. For example, in refusing requests, a participant may merely wish to communicate a brief and definite refusal to a vagrant's request for loose change. Whereas, when asked for a date, the participant may wish to say "no" but also explain to that person why she does not wish to have a dating relationship. As group members begin to work on specific situations, the clarification of goals is crucial. The goals may also change as the cognitive restructuring and behavior rehearsal proceeds. Moreover, some goals will be out of the participant's full control, e.g., being treated fairly or with respect, or securing cooperation in the resolution of a problem. The participant can practice behaving in ways that would likely maximize the accomplishment of such goals, but their occurrence cannot be guaranteed even with the most assertive behavior. Trainers should regularly help participants clarify their goals and identify how much control they have over their accomplishment.

Sometimes members are undecided about their goals. For example, a participant may be undecided about staying in a relationship and working on improving it. If his only concern is to engage the group in a lengthy discussion of the relative merits of his alternatives, that is not appropriately part of assertion training. If, however, he is excluding some of his alternatives (e.g., staying in the relationship and discussing his concerns with the other person or ending the relationship) because he doesn't know how to accomplish them or fears the consequences of his choice, assertion training can be helpful. By increasing options, assertion training facilitates decision-making.

Occasionally, a member's situation is clear but is not appropriate for assertion training. For example, a woman was working on asking her mother to be more expressive of her caring and to listen to her without immediately giving advice. As the role play progressed, it became clear that she did not believe that her mother was willing to meet either of her requests, whereupon she became genuinely sad and upset. The trainer responded empathically to her immediate distress and then suggested that she might wish to work with a counselor individually on her relationship with her mother. The group members were comfortable with the intensity of feeling stimulated by the role play and with the way the trainers recognized her sadness without turning the session into a therapy group.

Part 2 — Using Cognitive-Behavioral Interventions: Rational-Emotive Procedures

After specifying the situation and goals clearly and determining their appropriateness for assertion training, but before beginning the behavior rehearsals, we explore the cognitive components with the participant.

123

Most psychological problems involving assertion have cognitive, affective, and behavioral components. Therefore, a combination of a cognitive, affective, and behavioral approach to assertion training seems most appropriate. People do make assumptions about themselves and others which sometimes are irrational and lead to anxiety, intense anger, guilt, avoidance, and/or unassertive behaviors. The cognitive restructuring component of assertion training can help participants develop a framework to assess their thinking and its relation to their resultant feelings and behaviors.* In our approach, part of the cognitive restructuring involves a highly focused version of Albert Ellis' rational-emotive therapy (Ellis, 1962, 1971, 1973; Ellis & Harper, 1975).

In brief, it is Ellis' conviction that people do not have direct "emotional" reactions to most situations but rather that they think first. Thus, people feel anxious, depressed, and guilty because they believe that it is "awful" and "catastrophic" to fail to accomplish a major goal or to be rejected by a significant person. Moreover, people feel intense anger when others behave unfairly toward them. They believe they should never be treated unfairly, it is terrible when they are, and others should be severely punished for doing so. What people label as their emotional reactions are mainly caused by their conscious and preconscious assumptions, evaluations, and interpretations of situations.

The A-B-C Paradigm
Ellis' approach to the relationship between thinking, feelings, and behaviors follows an A-B-C paradigm. Point A represents an *activity* or situation which an individual finds upsetting, e.g., asking for a raise. At point B the person might irrationally *believe*: "If I ask for a raise and my boss doesn't give it to me, I must be incompetent and a failure at everything and that's intolerable." At point C the person *consequently* feels anxious, depressed, and therefore might avoid asking for a raise or ask in a nonassertive manner. "The primary distinction between an irrational idea and the rational alternative is that with the former belief one convinces oneself that things are *unbearable* which leads to intense anger while the latter alternative leads to frustration, irritation, and, usually positive action. The distinction is not merely semantic. The

---

* Wolfe (1975) and Linehan & Goldfried (1975) have found a partial support for this position.

resultant feelings are qualitatively different. *Sadness, frustration,* and *irritation* result from strong preferences, desires, or wants. However, *depression, despair, excessive guilt,* and *rage* arise from the belief that 'I *must* . . . and if I do not, it is *awful* and I can't stand myself (or 'it')!' " (Ellis & Harper, 1975).

Ellis (1973) suggests that the A-B-C theory can be extended to points D and E. These points constitute the interventions which can be employed in an assertion group. At point D, the trainer and the participant work to *determine* the irrational beliefs connected to the unassertive behaviors. The critical distinction between rational and irrational thinking is that when one is rejected, fails at a major task, or is treated unfairly, it is (1) rational and appropriate to think it is unfortunate and an inconvenience and to feel sad, frustrated, or irritated, and (2) irrational to catastrophize by convincing oneself that it is awful and terrible and to think absolutistically that one *must* be accepted or successful or to *demand* unswervingly that one be treated fairly. At point D, the irrational beliefs are then *disputed* and challenged: What would be so *awful* if I asked in an ineffectual manner? How would my boss' displeasure be *terrible?* How could his rejection destroy me? What if I didn't get the raise?

At point E, the participant *substitutes* more rational ideas for the irrational beliefs previously held. For example, before asking his boss for a raise, the participant might think: "I would like my boss to agree with my reasons for getting a raise." The participant would then feel concerned and begin planning his presentation in a thoughtful manner. If he is turned down by his boss, he might rationally think: "It does not mean that I am incompetent. It is inconvenient that I did not get the raise, but I can handle it." Such thinking would reduce his anxiety before seeing his boss. Afterwards, if he did not receive the raise, he would then likely feel disappointed, displeased, frustrated, and sad. If he thought irrationally at this point (My boss doesn't think I can do anything right! How dare he treat me this way! It's unfair!), he would more likely feel enraged, he might become defensive and blame others, rationalize his mistakes, develop psychosomatic reactions, or become preoccupied with the hopelessness of the situation and do nothing about it. Such a person usually feels quite insecure and may have brief periods of self-doubt and depression which are quickly covered up again by aggressive behaviors. Such self-defeating thoughts are based on a magical belief that things *ought* to be different, rather than the more reasonable conviction that things would be *better* if they were different.

125

Many people dichotomize their thinking and their feelings instead of conceptualizing the A-B-C-D-E steps. Participants often incorrectly describe themselves as being in a state of conflict between "my head and my gut." In the group, they might say: "Intellectually, I know I want to ask for a date, but emotionally, every time I have a chance I get scared to death" or "I feel excited like I have something really worthwhile to say and then I think to myself that it probably isn't that important." In either case the conflict *appears* to be between thoughts and feelings, yet neither is always reliable. Consequently, such generalizations as "always trust your gut" or "think before you act" are not always valid. In actuality, there is always thinking *and* feeling going on, some of which is rational and appropriate and some irrational and excessive. Thus the earlier dichotomized conceptualizations of dating might be restated as follows, to include both the thinking and feeling: "If I think that I want to ask for a date and believe it would be nice if the person accepted and unfortunate if not, I would then feel calm and relaxed in asking and if turned down feel disappointed. However, if I think about asking someone for a date and I believe that if I do it badly or I am rejected, then I must be a boob and a failure, I will feel awful and berate myself and become severely depressed." Thus the dichotomy between thinking and feeling disintegrates when participants recognize the A-B-C's wherein thinking and feeling occur together.

A case example / The relationship between underlying irrational thinking and unassertiveness can best be explained by an example. One participant was concerned about her inability to tell a man her desire to have their relationship become something more than a friendship. She identified the problem quite clearly, yet experienced considerable difficulty imagining herself saying what she knew she wanted to say to him. As she began to look for irrational assumptions, she realized that her fears were: (1) This man might not want the more romantic sexual relationship she wanted; he might reject her (she is a failure as a woman) and that would be awful; (2) Since she was not experienced in such conversations, she might appear foolish in bringing it up and that would be terrible, because "I must be perfect, I'm not any fool"; and, most importantly, (3) If he did reject her, she would be all alone and not have any relationship at all and that would be unbearable. Her resultant behavior with him was to avoid intimacy and to hope that he would bring up the subject. While away from him, she was anxious, irritable, worried, and sometimes angry with herself and with him.

In the group, she identified and challenged each of these irrational assumptions, substituting more reasonable thoughts for each. She then practiced the conversation. In the real situation she did express her interests to the man, who had also been holding back hoping for a more intimate relationship. In this case, the participant was greatly rewarded for her assertiveness. If, however, the man was not responsive to her wishes, she might have done further work on the irrational fears of being alone forever and being a worthless, undesirable person. This participant was better able to profit from behavior rehearsals after having identified and challenged the underlying irrational beliefs supporting her nonassertive behavior.

We have often found that the more participants think rationally, the greater the likelihood of their acting assertively. This cognitive approach to personal growth and therapeutic change focuses heavily on helping participants to utilize their own internal capabilities to assess and challenge their over- and under-reactions to situations and problems. It is a process of de-awfulizing and de-absolutizing thinking and of recognizing the internal resources available to meet problems and conflicts.

Ten Irrational Ideas

Ellis (1975) cites ten irrational beliefs which are commonly learned and which lead to disturbing emotions.* We believe (along with Ellis and others) that three of these beliefs are the basic irrational assumptions upon which most persons function ineffectively. The remaining seven beliefs are also irrational and can lead to unassertive behaviors; however, they are probably "second order" cognitive reactions after one of the three basic beliefs is operating. Since we have regrouped the ideas,[†] they will be numbered in a different order from the listing in Ellis & Harper's *A New Guide to Rational Living* (1975). Each irrational idea is stated below along with examples of how such thoughts can result in unassertive behaviors. More rational beliefs are also presented.

* Readers are encouraged to read Ellis' *Reason and Emotion in Psychotherapy* (1962), and the more recent, *A New Guide to Rational Living* (Ellis & Harper, 1975) for a fuller elaboration of rational-emotive principles and an analysis of the irrationality of each irrational idea. Ellis' *Humanistic Psychotherapy* (1973) offers an excellent explanation of rational therapy principles and procedures.

[†] We thank Dr. Ellis for providing us with his latest version of these ideas (Ellis, personal communication, November 1975).

The three most basic irrational ideas deal with the issues of personal rejection, personal competence, and fairness.

Irrational Idea Number One: You must—yes, must—have sincere love and approval almost all the time from all the people you find significant / If a person thinks that assertiveness will result in disapproval, then that person will likely engage in nonassertive behaviors which might include (1) never expressing opinions, (2) avoiding conflict even when others violate personal rights, (3) never expressing personal desires, (4) holding back feelings (both positive and negative), and (5) withdrawing from social interaction or intimate relationships even though desired.

One group participant was unable to confront her neighbor with the fact that his dogs regularly strewed her garbage over the street; another avoided restricting or disciplining his children's misbehavior; while a third was unwilling to deal with a neighbor who made unreasonable demands on her time; and a fourth participant was not informing his lover about what he wanted and what he enjoyed in their sexual relationship. Each of these group members came to recognize that the fear of rejection or disapproval was the basis for their nonassertive behaviors.

Some general rational alternatives to Irrational Idea Number One are: (1) I would *like* to be approved of by every significant person, but I do not *need* such approval; (2) If I am not approved of by someone I would like to have like me, I can attempt to determine what it is that person does not like *about the way I behave* and decide whether I want to change it; (3) If I decide that this rejection is not based on any inappropriate behavior on my part, I can find others I can enjoy being with; (4) I can determine what I want to do rather than adapting or reacting to what I think others want.

Irrational Idea Number Two: You must *prove yourself thoroughly competent, adequate, and achieving, or you* must *at least have real competence or talent at something important* / This form of absolutistic thinking has resulted in such nonassertive behaviors as: (1) being extremely anxious, to the point of being unwilling to deliver a presentation at a professional conference; (2) worrying excessively (with resultant behavioral dysfunctions) over upcoming student teaching; (3) prefacing almost every task which requires some skill with profuse criticism of external influences which make the accomplishment of the task less likely (and thereby not one's own "fault"); (4) avoiding social interactions for fear of having nothing worthwhile to say; (5) avoiding trying out for enjoyable athletic activities for fear of failure; (6) being extremely anxious, as a new member, of expressing opinions at Board of Education meetings.

The critical ingredients of this irrational assumption are its *perfectionistic* expectation, the *absolutistic* quality of the perfectionistic expectation (I *must* do perfectly well), and the assumed *tragedy* if perfection is not attained. Consequently, general rational messages could be: (1) I would like to be perfect or best at this task but I do not *need* to be; (2) I'm still successful when I do things imperfectly; (3) What I do doesn't have to be perfect in order to be good; (4) I may be happier if I am successful, but success does not determine my worth as a person, unless I let it; (5) I will be happier if I attempt to achieve at a realistic level rather than a perfect level; (6) I still want to achieve and to be successful and if I am, I will likely be happier. If I am not successful, I will likely be unhappy but not depressed and miserable; (7) It is impossible for anyone to be perfectly competent, achieving, etc.; (8) Above all, if I *demand* that I be perfect, I will always be pushing or worrying when I'll slip; instead, if I do what I want and what I enjoy as well as I can, I'll feel happier and perform better.

Irrational Idea Number Three: You have to view life as awful, terrible, horrible, or catastrophic when things do not go the way you would like them to go / Some people act on this irrational assumption by whining, complaining about, or bemoaning their "tragedy." Often they will withdraw into isolation, or speak extremely bitterly about others (especially certain groups of people such as men, women, bosses, children, or mothers-in-law), or act helpless and destroyed. Essentially, they feel and act victimized.

One group member who was an undergraduate student was unfairly accused of cheating on a test by a teaching assistant. The student immediately agitated to the point of yelling disruptively and making idle threats. When the T.A. walked away, the student rushed to the course professor and launched into another hysterical outburst about how unfairly the T.A. had treated him. Although the professor agreed to look into the matter, several days passed and the student launched another outburst with the dean of the college, loudly charging he was being railroaded by the "system." The dean responded by directing him back to the professor (and out of his office as quickly as possible).

129

The point here is that each step taken by the student was probably a reasonable one; however, the overly emotional manner in which he presented himself (vacillating between fear and anger) and his inordinate focus on how unfairly he was treated led only to his being treated with even more avoidance. Moreover, he expended a great deal of time and energy ruminating over this situation. Had he expressed serious concern and irritation toward the teaching assistant and primarily focused on how to resolve such an accusation, he would likely have received a more responsive audience at least in the professor and the dean.

Another participant's wife left him after twelve years of marriage. In the limited interactions he did engage in with others, he referred ad nauseam to how unfairly she treated him after he had given her the best years of his life. In social conversations he was inclined to rant and rave about what a louse his wife has been, hoping to enlist others' sympathy. His presenting concern to the group was his inability to engage in conversations where he made friends. This case is a good example of a situation where role playing social conversations is not enough; the person also needs to change the self-statements and cognitions which prompt the present dysfunctional behavior. The problem was presented as a behavioral deficit (poor social skills), but it had cognitive components as well.

More rational substitutes for this illogical idea might be: This person has really treated me badly and I don't like the situation or that person's behavior. What can I do to change either? If I can't change either, it is frustrating but not dreadful and awful. I can begin to make plans for making my life as desirable and enjoyable as I can.

The next three irrational ideas pertain to aggressive, blaming behaviors; nonassertive, phobic responses; and denial of realities which do not yield perfect solutions.

Irrational Idea Number Four: People who harm you or commit misdeeds rate as generally bad, wicked, or villainous individuals and you should severely blame, damn, and punish them for their sins / Persons who are operating under this irrational idea usually are behaving aggressively toward others. The aggression might be quite overt where the person is constantly criticizing others for their incompetence, lack of sensitivity, ignorance, or evilness. Constantly questioning the motives of others or excessively berating persons who actually have been unfair are the typical manifestations of this belief. In our groups, people often raise situations where someone else truly is behaving in a manner that is obnoxious or unfair. Because they have been believing the irrational idea that if someone acts badly they should be blamed, they often behave aggressively. Aggressive participants often treat others as worthless individuals deserving of damnation because they have made mistakes raising their children, they drink too much, they have not succeeded in their careers or education, they do not do their work efficiently or effectively, they have been insensitive, and a host of even more foolish expectations.

People not only turn this severely critical thinking on others but also turn it in on themselves. When they fail at a task, are rejected by a significant other person, or treat someone else unfairly, they then damn themselves for being such bad or wicked persons. For example, a group member cited a situation where he punished himself by resigning from an important civic committee he truly enjoyed when he realized he had made a mistake that seriously held up the committee's work. Not only was he catastrophizing over being incompetent, but he actually told himself that he should be punished for his misdeed by leaving the work he so much enjoyed. In another case, a woman who was recently divorced decided that she was a failure as a person since she could not keep her marriage together and therefore deserved to be punished. Consequently, she was determined to work herself nearly to death to make it up to her children and to meet any of their needs to the denial of her own. Again, the basic idea of failure comes into play first and then the accompanying belief emerges that one is thereby deserving of punishment.

The more rational alternatives are: (1) I can tell people firmly and directly what they are doing that has negative consequences for me, and I don't have to go so far as to punish them for their behavior; I may feel irritated or hurt and I don't have to berate that person; (2) When I do punish someone, it costs me, too, in energy and seldom does it facilitate correction or change; (3) Just because I think something is wrong, doesn't mean it *is* wrong; (4) I (or others) may have behaved obnoxiously, unfairly, or incompetently, but that does not mean that I (or others) always will; (5) I can recognize and admit my own (or others') wrong acts and I can work hard to correct or have others correct this misdeed or its future occurrence.

Irrational Idea Number Five: If something seems dangerous or fearsome, you must become terribly occupied with and upset about it /

This irrational idea results in unrealistic anxiety as opposed to reasonable concern and fear, which keep us from playing on the freeways and exposing ourselves to other real dangers. Anxiety leads to preoccupation, which actually interferes with the clear thinking that would lead to control of the dangerous or fearsome situation. Any of the assertion situations cited under previous irrational ideas might also include the preoccupation presented here. Inappropriate fears of interacting with others, either individually or in group contexts, are typical situations where participants have responded with such debilitating anxiety.

In one case, a student who was about to begin student teaching found himself unable to sleep worrying over this impending trauma. Another person agitated so much over her first date that she became physically ill.

More rational alternative beliefs would be: (1) If I am not as good (a speaker) as I (or others) would like, I can handle it; or (2) It's impossible to prevent a bad event from occurring by worrying about it; instead of worrying, I can think constructively and problem solve; (3) In all likelihood that event will not be as bad as I fear. Even if it is bad, I won't crumble, I can stand it though it will be uncomfortable. With such rational beliefs, participants can begin to practice more assertive behaviors which, heretofore, they have avoided.

Irrational Idea Number Six: People and things should turn out better than they do and you have to view it as awful and horrible if you do not quickly find good solutions to life's hassles / Essentially the issue here is that many times people find themselves in circumstances where none of their options is desirable. When thinking irrationally, one would then bemoan with absolutistic catastrophizing that things *should* not be that way and that it is awful that they are, rather than accept the reality. For example, one woman was so highly disturbed that her professors and her family were both making demands on her time that she could not do anything. She convinced herself that the situation was unbearable, that a *perfect solution to accomplishing everything existed somewhere* and that she was woefully inadequate as a mother and student. She felt guilty, angry, and depressed and was less effective in both roles. Before working on the behavioral components of being assertive, she and the trainers explored and challenged her thinking which unearthed the irrational belief. She substituted the following more rational assumptions which helped her to use the behavior rehearsals more fully: I do not need to overreact to these pressures. It doesn't appear that a "perfect" solution exists. I will accept that reality and do the best I can. I will determine my priorities and accomplish what I can in assertively communicating my limits to others. If others are not satisfied, that is unfortunate. I can work toward improving this situation.

The final four irrational ideas represent four distinctly different beliefs. Although the cognitions differ, the behavioral results are all likely to be passive or avoidant. Persons holding these irrational beliefs also tend to take less responsibility for themselves and their behavior. Consequently, these assumptions should be challenged so that participants can begin to utilize their cognitive, affective, and behavioral capacities to modify their own behavior.

Irrational Idea Number Seven: Emotional misery comes from external pressures and you have little ability to control your feelings or rid yourself of depression and hostility / As participants begin to work on situations, they realize that this idea often plays a part in their unassertiveness. Some group members believe that they simply have a bad temper, or are "high strung" or are just always depressed. (Trainers, however, should not disregard the possibility of primary physiological disturbances which might contribute to pervasive mood states.) Behavior rehearsals which are directed at change through the use of the participant's own capacities are unlikely to be effective until this irrational idea is challenged and discarded, at least tentatively. People who operate under this irrational idea may be more listless and inactive in the group. They are not "pouters" or "whiners" who are looking for a rescuer, but rather have come to a genuine conviction that they can do little to change. Statements such as "I can't stand it when things start piling up, I just go to pieces" or "I guess that's just the way I am" or "He *made* me so angry" all imply some external cause for their behavior and feelings.

Interestingly, participants who erroneously believe that other people cause them to feel hurt, angry, or miserable often hold the reciprocal belief that they can cause others to feel upset, angry, hurt, or miserable. Consequently, they hold back the expression of their opinions, feelings, or needs for fear of *causing* disturbance to others. They fail to recognize that people have some choice in how they will respond. One person was unwilling to say no to an invitation to a date which she did not want to accept for fear she might hurt the other person severely. Another person did not answer his phone for three days for fear his parents would call and ask about his new living arrangement and be terribly upset and angry. Although he was also anxious about how he would handle their call, he was *extremely* upset about what his decision "would do to them." Nonassertive people seem, first, to worry inordinately about the impact they might have, erroneously believing that their opinions, feelings, and needs *cause* others to feel and behave in highly disturbed ways. Then, they decide to protect these others from their terrible powers by holding back, which often leads to their own frustrations and tensions.

Although we believe that one cannot *make* someone else angry, upset, or hurt, one can certainly behave in ways that make it very likely that others will respond with such feelings. We are not supporting the idea that people should say anything and everything, regardless of how hostile or harmful, and pass it off as the other person's total responsibility when he feels bad ("That's his problem!"). Although we do not control others, we can have some influence on them. Thus, we support the concept of responsible assertiveness where people behave in a way which takes others' feelings into consideration. One guideline we suggest is that participants first determine how the other person is reacting to their behavior and then think about whether that truly seems to be an appropriate and reasonable response. If the person is hurt, angry, upset, or critical, check your own perception of *your* behavior. Try not to agree too fast or to deny defensively. If you agree that you may have been wrong or done something that did violate another's rights, you can admit that. If you disagree about the degree of impact of your behavior, you might express regret that the person chose to respond in that way but you still stand by what you said.

More rational alternatives to Irrational Idea Number Seven are: (1) I *can* stand it when things go wrong; I can choose to stand it if I want to; (2) I do have quite a bit of control over how I react to situations; (3) Others also have choices in how they react to me. I am responsible for my own behaviors and can accept the reasonable consequences; as long as I respect the rights of others, I do not have to take 100 percent responsibility for their reactions to me.

Irrational Idea Number Eight: You will find it easier to avoid facing many of life's difficulties and self-responsibilities than to undertake more rewarding forms of self-discipline / People who hold this belief sometimes react aggressively. One such person frequently blew up, partially because he felt he "must" have immediate relief from his irritations and worries and "could not tolerate" controlling these feelings. Nonassertive persons frequently believe that the immediate relief of discomfort is more important than the longer range displeasures resulting from avoidance and the discounting of their personal rights. With such individuals, we often develop contracts which not only establish systematic schedules for making specific changes, but also include immediate reinforcers for improvements (Malott, 1972). Participants work on such avoidances as not going to parties, not taking seminars which require open discussions, not making job interviews, not talking with their spouse about their needs, not confronting others with their behaviors.

More rational beliefs include: (1) Even though I get immediate relief when I avoid a disturbing situation or blow up, I feel unfulfilled and that is often as frustrating; (2) What I am avoiding will probably not be as awful as I convince myself it is; (3) Avoidance does not ultimately lead to pleasure.

Irrational Idea Number Nine: Your past remains all-impotant and because something once strongly influenced your life, it has to keep determining your feelings and behavior today / This belief also supports behavioral patterns that are passive and deny the individual's potency. Group members often believe that *they* cannot change because the way they are happened *to* them long ago. They ignore some important facts: (1) in addition to *learning* ineffective behaviors, they actually, at some level, *decided* that these behaviors were necessary for survival; (2) these behaviors may no longer be necessary for survival or a more effective behavior may now be an even better option; and (3) it is possible to learn more effective behaviors just as ineffective behaviors were learned in the past.

More rational thinking would support the conviction that: Although my past does exercise considerable influence, I am not *fixed* cognitively, affectively, or behaviorally, and I can change.

Irrational Idea Number Ten: You can achieve happiness by inertia and inaction or by passively and uncommittedly "enjoying yourself" / Essentially, this form of irrational thinking is a "rationalization" to cover fear of some activity. Unfortunately, such inactivity breeds greater passivity to the point where an individual can become highly withdrawn and almost blunted to stimulation. One group member

135

created a dull, routinzed daily pattern which avoided contact with others and left the person bored and passive. A fairly obvious rational alternative might be: I can decide to involve myself in other people, in feelings, in creating things, or in ideas.

Many people, upon reading these ten irrational ideas, would not readily perceive themselves as operating under any of them. In the relatively short duration of most groups not everyone is willing to accept the fact that he is operating under irrational beliefs. Nor are some willing to believe that they can change their irrational beliefs and subsequent feelings and behaviors. We have, however, had considerable success in brief group training with many persons who have not only altered their thinking, but have generalized their rational ideas to many other situations not practiced or discussed in the group.

We believe it is critical for trainers to appreciate that irrational thinking has served an important function (often at a survival level) for individuals espousing them. Although these beliefs have led to great discomfort, they have been the best the individual has had available. Trainers should, therefore, challenge these irrational beliefs in an informative and supportive manner, *not* from a critical position. They should help develop more rational alternative beliefs and provide the permission and protection which can facilitate movement toward significant changes. People often do not eliminate their irrational ideas entirely. Challenging them is an ongoing process.

Case examples / The following shows how a trainer (Tr) might quickly but precisely clarify the irrational thinking connected to non-assertive behavior, challenge that thinking, and substitute more rational assumptions from which the participant (P) might feel and behave assertively. The participant is a university professor who had great difficulty speaking up in departmental meetings, even when decisions important to her work were being discussed.

Tr: What is happening with you when you're in the meeting and an important discussion is going on?

P: I think of what I'd like to see happen, but then I change my mind when someone prefers some other way and I jump back and forth and get confused.

Tr: So you think of your own opinions but get confused when others offer contradicting opinions. How do you feel during this time?

P: Well, I get tense and frustrated and I guess I'm scared to speak up and take a side.

Tr: Imagine being scared in that situation for a second and put into words what you are scared about.

P: Well, I'm afraid to speak up.

Tr: OK, go with it a little further; if you speak up, what might happen?

P: (Pause) Well, some people will disagree with me . . . or I might say something very stupid.

Tr: And if people disagree with you. . . .

P: Then they'll be angry with me and not like me.

Tr: So, you have been thinking that if you do offer your opinion in the meeting, some of your colleagues might not like you any more, or you might say something stupid and they would think less of you.

P: Yes, that sounds silly but it's true.

Tr: It also seems that if some of your colleagues didn't like you or thought you were stupid that that would be really awful.

P: Yes, it feels terrible.

Tr: OK, there are several places where your thinking really doesn't make any sense. First, you are afraid that people might not like you if you disagree with them and that's just not necessarily true. It's also not true that you are likely to say something dumb.

P: Yes, when I really think about it, like now, I know that that's not necessarily so, but I worry that both might happen.

Tr: And that's where you really start catastrophizing. "What if they don't like me . . . what if I say something stupid . . . it would be awful!"

P: That's right, it really seems like that would be terrible.

Tr: What's so terrible about the possibility that some of your colleagues might not like you or that you might say something stupid?

P: Well, I don't really think it's so awful when I really think about it, but I still feel scared when it happens.

Tr: Yes, when you hold onto the irrational thoughts and catastrophize over them, you still experience the fear. If you gave up the irrational assumptions, what rational thoughts might you say to yourself instead?

P: Well, I'd say that it's unlikely that people will dislike me just because I disagree with them and that it's unlikely that I would say stupid things.

Tr: Right, those are much more reasonable assumptions. What others might you say?

P: That even if one of my colleagues didn't like me or if I really did say something that didn't make sense, it doesn't mean I'm a bad person nor is it the end of the world.

Tr: That's excellent. Those really are rational, reasonable assumptions that make a great deal more sense to be acting on than what you've been assuming.

P: Thank you.

Tr: If you put these more rational statements into positive statements about yourself, how might you phrase them?

P: Well, I'd say "I can disagree with people and still get along with them" . . . and "I can focus on my own opinions and they are often valuable contributions" . . . and I'd say "If someone does get angry, or likes me less, or thinks I'm stupid, I can determine if that seems legitimate. If it isn't, I can trust my judgment and deal with them. If I believe it is legitimate, it's not the end of the world and I can choose to change my behavior."

Tr: Wow, that sounds great. You're really able to identify what thinking gets in your way and to specify the more rational assumptions clearly. You might say these positive statements to yourself as we continue and get into practicing how you might behave in response to these more reasonable beliefs.

P: OK (smiling).

Tr: How did you feel when you were saying the rational thoughts?

P: I felt good, sort of strong and confident and calm.

Tr: Great

138

The most critical point of this cognitive analysis is to identify the basic, underlying irrational thinking (fear of not being liked by significant others; fear of not being competent at all times) as opposed to dealing only with the overt fear of speaking in the group. In this example, notice that the trainer gave the participant maximum opportunity to think about her own irrational and rational thinking and specifically rewarded her clear thinking.

The following example illustrates clarifying the situation and identifying the irrational beliefs with a "twist" which is not uncommon.

Tr: Who would like to work?

P: I would. I've been having a difficult time dealing with my apartment mate who agrees to do half the cleaning and dishes and then he doesn't do it.

Tr: What is it that you'd like to do?

P: I'd like to confront him with what he's doing and get him to do his share.

Tr: OK. That seems to be a reasonable goal. What keeps you from making this confrontation?

P: Well, actually I have brought it up a number of times. He just sits there and agrees but then it never happens.

Tr: It sounds like you have been assertive in bringing up the issue and now you want to deal with his behavior in response to your assertion. Is that right?

P: Yes, actually now that I think of it, that's when I get all tied up and I don't know what to do.

Tr: OK. Let's try to sort out what happens. When he agrees but doesn't do it, how do you feel?

P: I'm angry . . . resentful . . . (pause) . . . and I feel put down . . . discounted.

Tr: What irrational beliefs might you be thinking that lead to these feelings?

P: Well, that it's awful and catastrophic that he is behaving so irresponsibly and that he does not respect our agreement and is treating me unfairly.

Tr: And what do you do when you irrationally think that it is awful and catastrophic?

P: First I get angry but I don't share it. Then I've been telling myself that I'm overly sensitive and I'm not being rational and that I'm catastrophizing about how he's treating me so I go away. But then I feel lousy because I still feel discounted.

Tr: It sounds like you may be discounting your own *legitimate* feelings and rights and you've *tried to rationalize away* what seem to be legitimate feelings. What personal rights *do you* have in this situation?

P: (After some pause) The right to state my opinion that he should do his share as agreed . . . and the right to confront him when he doesn't respond with action (pause). I realize now that I've been worried about being too picky and that I was making too much out of this. Actually, I was overreacting, but I don't have to withdraw completely. I can put the situation in proper perspective and act on my reasonable rights. Even as I say it now, it seems clear and feels right. I don't have to blow up but I don't have to withdraw either.

Tr: That's really great. You did some fine thinking just then. What would you like to practice doing as you act on your personal rights?

P: Two things come first to mind. I'd like to work on confronting him with his unresponsiveness to our agreement and I want him to know that I don't like it when he discounts me like that.

Three important points are raised by this example: (1) the nature of the situation on which the participant worked progressively changed as she thought about it, (2) the irrational beliefs and personal rights came to the fore clearly, and, most importantly, (3) the trainer helped her recognize her overreaction to her irrational thinking, which left her not acting on her legitimate personal rights. Persons who worry about being too critical sometimes only go part way in assessing their irrational thinking. They identify the irrational beliefs and then attempt to stifle any reactions at all to the situation. The second part, of course, is to identify reasonable and legitimate rights and to act on those convictions. The woman began to realize that she had a pattern of rationalizing away her personal rights. She made many significant changes, mostly on her own, with her new perspective. This case also demonstrates how a relatively small conflict can lead to important insights and behavior changes.

Helping one person assess her irrational beliefs often causes the observing group members to become more aware of their own irrational cognitions as well. When a participant starts recognizing other members' irrational thinking, it is important that the trainers very carefully prevent participants from becoming interpretive and playing "pseudoshrinks" by telling the person what they think she is probably thinking ("You're probably so worried about keeping somebody else from getting his way, that you forget what you want"). Such a statement is presumptuous, possibly critical, and puts the person in a one-down position ("I know you better than you know yourself"). For many unassertive people, this is a familiar place that triggers withdrawing from the group.

Part 2, cont. — Using Cognitive-Behavioral Interventions: Cognitive Coping Skills

Another type of cognitive-behavioral intervention involves identifying faulty "internal dialogs" and developing coping skills. The assumption is that *what a person says to himself* (e.g. self-statements, images, self-evaluations, attributions) just before, during, and after an incident is an important determinant of how he will act. Meichenbaum (1975a) has demonstrated that there is an important relationship between a person's behavior and what he says to himself. Schwartz and Gottman's (1974) research also supports this position. They found that both high assertive and low assertive college students were able to say what an assertive response would be in a specific situation. Both groups could act assertively in a hypothetical "safe" situation. However, when the same situation was changed slightly to increase the threat level, the low assertive students made a poorer performance. A questionnaire revealed that the low assertive students made more negative and fewer positive self-statements than did the high assertive students. Thus it was the nature of their internal dialogs (what they said to themselves) which differentiated the two groups. A substantial body of research now demonstrates that cognitions can influence behavior (for reviews, see Mahoney, 1974; Meichenbaum, 1974). Although space does not permit such a review here, it is accurate to conclude from these studies that what a *person says, or fails to say, to herself can and does influence behavior.* Such internal dialogs are, therefore, appropriately a focus in assertion training.

141

In contrast to Ellis, Meichenbaum (1975a) suggests that the difference between highly anxious (or angry) persons and others is not the presence or absence of irrational ideas, but rather, the presence or absence of adequate coping skills to deal with the irrational ideas and subsequent feelings. In other words, highly depressed people and occasionally sad individuals may both hold irrational ideas; the former have not learned to cope with these, while the latter have.

Meichenbaum (1975a) offers a model for helping participants learn to deal with their faulty internal dialogs. The focus we've adapted to assertion training involves helping the participants to (1) recognize their faulty internal dialogs, (2) develop coping skills to respond to their faulty dialogs, and (3) practice coping skills in situations which gradually approximate real-life stressful situations.

Before helping group members recognize their faulty internal dialogs, it is first necessary that they understand how thoughts and feelings can effect behavior. The rational-emotive exercises described in Chapter 4 provide trainers with one way of accomplishing this initial objective.

Recognizing faulty internal dialogs / Trainers can help participants recognize their internal dialogs by having the group members in turn close their eyes, vividly recall a real-life, anxiety- or anger-producing situation, and report the sequence of thoughts, feelings, and images (e.g., visual image of crying uncontrollably and running away) as they occur before, during, and after the fantasy (Meichenbaum, 1975a).

Very importantly, as the participants share their thoughts, the trainer helps them to recognize their faulty thinking styles. Ellis' use of basic irrational ideas and his attack through logical arguments is one approach. However, we agree with Meichenbaum's (1975a) suggestion that the participants and trainers do this labeling together and less directively so that the members not only recognize their faulty thinking styles but also begin to make sense of their behavior, receive assurances that they are not irreparably lost to ineffectual behaviors, and begin to have hope and expectations of change. Beck (1970) has identified several additional faulty cognitions to which trainers can alert participants: (1) drawing conclusions when evidence is lacking or even contradictory, (2) exaggerating the meaning of an event, (3) disregarding important aspects of a situation, (4) oversimplifying events as good/bad, right/wrong, (5) overgeneralizing from a single incident. During this discussion the trainer and group members focus on looking for *types* of faulty thinking as well as specific self-defeating thoughts. This enables the participant to recognize faulty thinking patterns that may occur across different situations in their lives. Essentially, this process of cognitive assessment takes what were automatic, habitual cognitive responses and brings them to awareness.

Developing and practicing coping skills in response to faulty dialogs | As the following example by Meichenbaum (1975a) illustrates, a participant uses cognitive coping skills at the point he becomes aware of his faulty internal dialog cognitions. Thus, recognition of this faulty cognition becomes a cue to cope and change his thinking. In this example, the coping skills mainly involve instructing himself to focus on the constructive steps he needs to take to meet the task at hand, e.g., confronting his roommate.

Faulty What if he gets real angry? I know I'll just blow the whole
Dialog: thing. I always do!

Coping Wait a minute! This is just the kind of thinking I should be
Thoughts: looking out for. I knew it was coming. Now what do I need
to do? I can take one step at a time. I can relax and take a
deep breath. I can think of what I want to say.

Tables 4 and 5 (pp. 150-153) illustrate other types of self-statements participants could use when they become aware that their thoughts and feelings are dysfunctional and interfering with their approaching or handling a situation. As the tables show, it is important that individuals also develop ways of coping with dysfunctional thoughts and feelings which occur after an unsatisfactory encounter with another person. It is equally as important, after a satisfying encounter, that individuals also develop the internal capacity to reinforce themselves for coping in the situation. What the persons say to themselves about these new thoughts and behaviors determines whether the behavior change will perist and if it will generalize to other situations (Meichenbaum, 1976).

As Meichenbaum (1975a) notes, accepting and relabeling one's anxiety can be an effective coping skill. Instead of saying to himself, "I'm really anxious. I'll never be able to think with all this anxiety," a person could instead relabel his physical arousal as, "This tenseness can be an ally, a cue to cope." Needless to say, it is important that trainers help participants find their own ways of relabeling anxiety and not just give them pat formulas.

Self-induced relaxation can be another coping skill. When the person becomes aware of her anxiety or excessive anger, she could remind herself to tense and relax certain muscles, take deep slow breaths, think of a relaxing scene (e.g., getting a back rub), or use words which elicit relaxation (calm, relax). Chapter 6 describes relaxation procedures in greater detail.

Trainers may teach the participants thought-stopping (Wolpe, 1958, 1969, 1973a) as a coping skill. The trainer starts by instructing the members to silently ruminate about some disturbing experience. Without warning, the trainer suddenly shouts "Stop!" and asks the members what happened to their thoughts. When participants report that their thoughts went away, the trainer can note how it is possible for them to influence their own thoughts. We follow this with a discussion of more realistic, rational, or strongly self-affirming (e.g., *I* can say no) statements the individuals could use to substitute for the stream of negative thoughts. Afterwards, the individuals start their stream of negative thoughts, say "Stop" out loud, and then make their coping self-statements (also out loud). Finally, they repeat the entire sequence and this time they yell "Stop!" internally. This procedure is similar to Rimm's (1973) covert assertion.

Finally, statements which assess the reality of the situation (e.g., Just because he's frowning doesn't automatically mean he's going to reject me) or which dispute irrational ideas may be used as coping skills.

When teaching coping skills, trainers may use modeling films which demonstrate people using coping strategies in stressful situations. The model first demonstrates fearful behaviors, then coping behaviors. The model is first shown as fearful, then coping, and finally mastering the particular situation. (Chapter 7 discusses how such modeling films may be developed.) An alternative is to have the members practice these coping skills in short exercises during which the trainer describes the particular coping skill, gives examples, and has the participants first practice the coping skills out loud until they are satisfied with their degree of success. Afterwards, the members move on to practice the skill internally. Participants may also use covert modeling (e.g., Kazdin, 1974) in which they imagine a model using coping skills and behaving assertively.

After the members acquire the coping skills, they need to experience using these skills in stressful situations which gradually approximate real life. The behavior rehearsal procedures described in the following chapter are an excellent way of providing such experiences. Afterwards, the members could be given a homework assignment to apply these skills in their daily lives, keep a diary of their experiences (the coping statements they used, the degree of success achieved, the results) and report on their experiences in the group.

Part 2, cont. – Using Cognitive-Behavioral Interventions: Self-Assessment Skills

Another cognitive approach to behavior change suggests that maladaptive behaviors may result from a lack of problem-solving skills, particularly skills which involve assessing the situation and oneself (Meichenbaum, 1975a; D'Zurilla & Goldfried, 1971; Goldfried & Goldfried, 1975). In terms of assertion training, developing such skills would involve helping the participant use a set of assessment questions in assertion encounters.

SUDS

Before participants use assessment questions, they must first be able to recognize their anxiety levels in assertive encounters. Trainers can teach participants the concept of "Subjective Units of Disturbance Scale" (SUDS) developed by Wolpe & Lazarus (1966). Dr. John Flowers is credited with the following method of teaching participants how to determine their SUDS levels. After explaining that this scale ranges from 0 (as comfortable as possible), to 100 (an unbearable feeling), one participant is asked to estimate her SUDS level at the moment (e.g., 25). Then the trainer unexpectedly yells loudly and directly at that person: "What is it now! This very minute!" The participant usually responds with a much higher SUDS level. The trainer can then explain that people can discriminate easily between high and low SUDS levels, as just demonstrated. Trainers should demonstrate SUDS with just one participant. Since the process can be a bit startling, the trainer might then respond supportively ("I know I surprised you, but I wanted you to see how your SUDS level changes in different situations. What's your SUDS level now?"). Most importantly, the trainer should keep the atmosphere light hearted (yet not at the participant's expense). Some trainers may not be comfortable with startling a participant in order to demonstrate the principle. An alternative might be to explain the SUDS scale and simply ask all of the participants to rate their SUDS levels.

145

Self-Assessment Questions

After learning the concept of SUDS, trainers could distribute the following self-assessment questions to the participants. Participants are encouraged to phrase a series of assessment questions in a manner comfortable for them. The following are examples of questions in a recommended sequence:

> What is my SUDS level?
> What am I doing (verbally and nonverbally)?
> What am I feeling?
> What am I thinking?
> What do I want to be thinking, feeling, and doing?
> What thoughts, opinions, needs, feelings do I want to express in this situation?
> What do I want the other person to know?
> What thoughts are keeping me from doing what I want?
> What do I think is appropriate to express?
> How can I go ahead and express what I want?

Clearly, some interactions do not allow for such lengthy analysis. However, all of these questions need not be asked and answered in every situation. Their purpose is to identify whatever is blocking the desired responses and to facilitate clear thinking although anxiety is present. Participants report that they can think through the sequence in a few seconds, particularly if it is a recurring situation to which they have given some prior thought.

This self-questioning procedure is emphasized so that participants can learn to assess their thinking, feeling, and behaviors in specific situations. We teach participants to ask themselves these questions because they are more likely to learn and use the procedure than if trainers merely asked those questions of the participants and hoped they would model the behavior. During the behavior rehearsals, the trainers will initially ask these questions, but whenever possible they should ask the individuals working to determine what questions they might ask themselves. In this way, the trainer is introducing a series of helpful questions and the participants are determining experientially when and how to use them.

A case example / The following is a demonstration of how the trainers might introduce this questioning process. (Note: Assume that

146

the situation has been specified; any irrational thinking challenged; the personal rights clarified; and SUDS level explained.)

A participant, who is an apartment manager, wants to ask her employer for a greater reduction in her rent. In fact, she had already approached her employer once, and came away feeling she did not handle the situation as well as she would have liked.

Tr: What was your SUDS level as you were about to meet with your employer?

P: About 85! . . . really high.

Tr: Before we practice this scene, I'd like to ask you a series of questions which we can all use in any situation when we recognize that we are more uncomfortable than we'd like to be. I'll ask you the questions now, but later and outside the group you can ask them of yourself. (Trainer gives the woman the list of self-assessment questions.) You might ask them in the sequence I use or just use some of them. They should help you to gain some understanding of your own thinking, feeling, and behaviors, get some control over what you do, and reduce some of your anxiety. *You can think even when you are anxious and afraid.*

P: OK.

Tr: As you approached the meeting, what were you doing?

P: Well, I know I was scared. I went into his outer office and I was shaking and my voice cracked and I sounded apologetic when I told the secretary who I was. I'm also pretty sure I didn't look at her.

Tr: OK, you have a good sense of how you communicate your hesitation. And you said you were feeling scared?

P: Yes.

Tr: And what were you thinking?

P: Well, I was thinking the irrational things we discussed before, like it's awful if he gets angry with me and the situation is really out of my control.

Tr: What do you want to be thinking, feeling, and doing?

P: I'd like to think rationally that I can handle his anger if it comes and that I can influence what happens in the conversation a great

147

deal. I want to feel confident and in control of my thinking, my feelings, and how I behave. And I want to ask for the reduction in rent and stick to it assertively even if he gets angry or starts questioning me suspiciously like before.

Tr: That's really excellent; you have a clear sense of what you would like to be like in this situation. What would it take for you to do that?

P: First, I want to say the rational assumptions to myself and the rights I have like "that I have a right to *ask* for a raise and to justify my request." Then I'd like to practice some of the assertive ways I might actually ask him *and* stick to my request if he starts pressuring me.

Tr: That sounds great. (To the group: When you're in a situation where it's hard for you to be assertive, you can also use the questions I just asked. Using these questions will help you get a more effective hold on the situation.) OK, let's go on and practice this situation with your employer.

Not everyone will be able to respond as clearly and concisely as the participant in this example. The trainer may have to work for greater clarity if the participant responds vaguely. Notice that the trainer genuinely rewards the clear thinking done by the participant. Also, all the questions were covered in a brief time. Not all these questions need be asked by the trainer in all situations since some of the answers overlap with the issues raised in the consideration of irrational thinking and personal rights. However, the first time the questions are used, all of them should be asked.

These cognitive-behavioral techniques have been presented as a collection of interventions that can be offered prior to and during behavior rehearsal procedures. In addition, one or two entire sessions could be devoted to teaching group members how to conceptualize their thinking and how to use the specific interventions themselves. We do not offer a preferred format. Rather, we suggest that trainers try those interventions which seem to be most appropriate and feasible for the group, individual, or situation until further research can be more definite in differentiating the relative efficacy of these interventions with specific assertion issues.

SUMMARY

The three-step process of the cognitive restructuring process includes: (1) identifying specific assertion situations clearly and setting goals for that interaction, (2) using a variety of cognitive intervention techniques, most notably those developed by Ellis and by Meichenbaum, and (3) identifying the personal rights in the specific situation. Not all the cognitive interventions are employed at one time. A participant would likely become bogged down if lengthy training in all the interventions were attempted by the trainer. We recommend that initial group sessions deal with some total group training in recognizing and changing irrational beliefs (Ellis) and identifying and coping with faulty internal dialogs (Meichenbaum). Other cognitive interventions might be employed intermittently as deemed appropriate. Suffice it to say that we have found that cognitive techniques can enhance behavioral procedures and ultimately the process of behavior change. As Meichenbaum (1975a) so cogently notes, how trainers will implement the cognitive restructuring process will be influenced by their own personal styles. Meichenbaum suggests that trainers imagine Carl Rogers using rational-emotive principles to appreciate how a trainer's personal style can influence the treatment method!

REVIEW QUESTIONS AND EXERCISES

1. Describe the three stages in the cognitive restructuring process.

2. Explain Ellis' A-B-C theory of behavior, citing one original example.

3. What are Ellis' three basic irrational ideas?

4. How does Meichenbaum's approach to cognitive restructuring differ from Ellis' approach? How are they similar?

5a. How can faulty internal dialogs be used as cues to cope?

   Explain how these types of imagery can be used in assertion training.

6. Describe how cognitive restructuring procedures can be integrated with behavior rehearsal techniques in assertion training. Why is this integration recommended?

7. Identify a personal situation which arouses excessive anger or anxiety, and apply one of the cognitive-behavioral interventions.

Table 4
Examples of Self-Statements for Dealing with Anger

Preparing for Provocation

This is going to upset me, but I know how to deal with it.
What is it that I have to do?
I can work out a plan to handle this.
I can manage the situation. I know how to regulate my anger.
If I find myself getting upset, I'll know what to do.
There won't be any need for an argument.
Try not to take this too seriously.
This could be a testy situation, but I believe in myself.
Time for a few deep breaths of relaxation. Feel comfortable, relaxed, and at ease.
Easy does it. Remember to keep your sense of humor.

Reacting during the Confrontation

Stay calm. Just continue to relax.
As long as I keep my cool, I'm in control.
Just roll with the punches; don't get bent out of shape.
Think of what you want to get out of this.
You don't need to prove yourself.
There is no point in getting mad.
Don't make more out of this than you have to.
I'm not going to let him get to me.
Look for the positives. Don't assume the worst or jump to conclusions.
It's really a shame that she has to act like this.
For someone to be that irritable, he must be awfully unhappy.
If I start to get mad, I'll just be banging my head against the wall. So I might as well just relax.
There is no need to doubt myself. What he says doesn't matter.
I'm on top of this situation and it's under control.

Coping with Arousal

My muscles are starting to feel tight. Time to relax and slow things down.
Getting upset won't help.
It's just not worth it to get so angry.
I'll let him make a fool of himself.
I have a right to be annoyed, but let's keep the lid on.

150

Time to take a deep breath.

Let's take the issue point by point.

My anger is a signal of what I need to do. Time to instruct myself.

I'm not going to get pushed around, but I'm not going haywire either.

Try to reason it out. Treat each other with respect.

Let's try a cooperative approach. Maybe we are both right.

Negatives lead to more negatives. Work constructively.

He'd probably like me to get really angry. Well I'm going to disappoint him.

I can't expect people to act the way I want them to.

Take it easy, don't get pushy.

Reflecting on the Experience

a. When conflict is unresolved:

Forget about the aggravation. Thinking about it only makes you upset.

These are difficult situations, and they take time to straighten out.

Try to shake it off. Don't let it interfere with your job.

I'll get better at this as I get more practice.

Remember relaxation. It's a lot better than anger.

Can you laugh about it? It's probably not so serious.

Don't take it personally.

Take a deep breath and think positive thoughts.

b. When conflict is resolved or coping is successful:

I handled that one pretty well. It worked!

That wasn't as hard as I thought.

It could have been a lot worse.

I could have gotten more upset than it was worth.

I actually got through that without getting angry.

My pride can sure get me into trouble, but when I don't take things too seriously, I'm better off.

I guess I've been getting upset for too long when it wasn't even necessary.

I'm doing better at this all the time.

Reprinted by permission from R. W. Novaco. *Anger control: The development and evaluation of an experimental treatment.* Lexington, MA: D. C. Heath and Co., Lexington Books, 1975.

Table 5
Examples of Self-Statements for Coping with Stress

Preparing for a Stressor
What is it you have to do?
You can develop a plan to deal with it.
Just think about what you can do about it. That's better than getting anxious.
No negative self-statements; just think rationally.
Don't worry; worry won't help anything.
Maybe what you think is anxiety, is eagerness to confront the stressor.

Reacting during the Stress-Producing Situation
Just "psych" yourself up—you can meet this challenge.
You can convince yourself to do it. You can reason your fear away.
One step at a time; you can handle the situation.
Don't think about fear; just think about what you have to do. Stay relevant.
This anxiety is what the doctor said you would feel. It's a reminder to use your coping exercises.
This tenseness can be an ally; a cue to cope.
Relax; you're in control. Take a slow, deep breath.
Ah, good.

Coping with the Feeling of Being Overwhelmed
When fear comes, just pause.
Keep the focus on the present; what is it you have to do? Label your fear from 0 to 10 and watch it change.
You should expect your fear to rise.
Don't try to eliminate fear totally; just keep it manageable.

Reflecting on the Experience

It worked; you did it.
Wait until you tell your therapist (or group) about this.
It wasn't as bad as you expected.
You made more out of your fear that it was worth.
Your damn ideas—that's the problem. When you control them, you control your fear.
It's getting better each time you use the procedures.
You can be pleased with the progress you're making.
You did it!

Reprinted by permission from D. Meichenbaum. Self-instuctional methods (How to do it). In A. Goldstein & F. Kanfer (Eds.), *Helping people change: Methods and materials.* New York: Pergamon Press, 1975.

6
Behavior Rehearsal Procedures

Although considerable attention has been given to the cognitive components of our assertion training model, the process of behaviorally rehearsing the situation is equally critical. Behavior rehearsal procedures may seem to be simple at first glance. In one sense they are, since none of the components of behavior rehearsal is beyond our intellectual abilities to comprehend. The art of effective behavior rehearsal is, however, very complex. The issues considered in this chapter include: (1) the varied components of behavior rehearsal, (2) the combination of components that can be used, and (3) case examples of behavior rehearsal. Chapter 7 describes modeling and behavior rehearsal.

THE COMPONENTS OF BEHAVIOR REHEARSAL
The components of behavior rehearsal which have been reported in the literature on assertion training are:

1. *Modeling* / The participant observes the trainer, a coached actor, another participant, or an audio or video tape demonstrating assertive behavior and vicariously learns the assertive behavior.
2. *Covert modeling* / The participant imagines someone else behaving assertively in a situation that is personally difficult for him.
3. *Rehearsal* / The participant practices assertively responding in the problem situation with the trainer or other participants role playing others in the scene. The participant repeatedly practices responding until she behaves assertively.
4. *Covert rehearsal* / The participant imagines himself behaving assertively in the problem situation, which possibly has been previously modeled by the trainer.

5. *Role reversal* / Role reversal requires the participant to take the role of the receiver of the assertive behavior and thereby potentially gain some insights. The trainer or another participant takes the participant's part and models assertive behavior.
6. *Reinforcement* / The trainers and other participants give positive reactions to specific assertive behaviors practiced by another group member. *Improvement* is rewarded rather than only the final behaviors.
7. *Coaching* / The trainers and other participants offer "explicit descriptions of what constitutes an appropriately assertive response" (McFall & Twentyman, 1973).

A RECOMMENDED COMBINATION OF COMPONENTS AND A RATIONALE

Considerable research effort has been directed toward identifying the specific components of effective behavior rehearsal (McFall & Marston, 1970; McFall & Lillesand, 1971; Friedman, 1971a, 1971b; McFall & Twentyman, 1973; Young, Rimm & Kennedy, 1973; Kazdin, 1973; Eisler, Hersen & Miller, 1973; Rimm & Masters, 1974). Unfortunately, the research literature does not point conclusively to a particular *combination* of components as being more effective than other combinations, particularly for complex human interaction.

The behavior rehearsal components recommended in this chapter have all been individually substantiated as having contributed to behavior change. In addition to research support, an additional critical question in choosing these components was: How can we maximize the participants' use of their own capacities in the group? We believe that the format suggested below allows participants to take a greater role in determining what and how they wish to communicate. They learn primarily through their own discovery, and consequently formulate comfortable assertive behaviors, congruent with their own styles of relating.

Our emphasis is mainly on rehearsal, reinforcement, self-assessment (see Chapter 5), and coaching. Our coaching typically takes the form of suggestions, rather than imposed descriptions of what constitutes an "appropriately assertive response." Modeling by the trainer or other participants may be used when the person working has limited responses which are appropriate to the particular concern. In addition, a number of cognitive techniques are integrated into the behavior rehearsal procedures as described in Chapter 5.

156

A General Behavior Rehearsal Format

The person rehearses the situation with other participants playing the other roles in the scene. Using participants (as opposed to the trainers) to play the other people in the scene facilitates greater involvement on their part, helps take the focus off the trainers for a brief period, and frees the trainers to more fully observe the person working. The worker may find that one of the participants in the group reminds him of someone in the scene. Having this person play the role can make the role play more realistic. In addition, when participants play people they consider to be "unlike themselves," they often realize that their behavioral repertoire is larger than they had thought.

The total situation is broken into small workable segments which the person practices. Lengthy rehearsals leave the participant with too many things to think about. In addition, lengthy interactions tend to arouse increasing anxiety and often are terminated at a point where the participant is not functioning effectively at all. Consequently, the trainers stop the rehearsal after one or two brief transactions and ask the participants observing to tell the worker specifically what they thought *was assertive* about what and how he communicated. The worker is encouraged to determine if he agrees with the feedback given. Thus, the process is one of giving positive reinforcement *and* placing the final judgment with the person working.

The worker is then asked what else he believes was assertive. Trainers can reverse these two steps, if they wish. The "trade off" seems to be between maximizing the observers' involvement and utilizing the self-assessment capabilities of the person working. The feedback and self-assessment should be clear and behaviorally specific: "Your voice was loud enough for me to hear easily and you ended your sentences with a firm voice and a nod of your head" versus "You were strong and I knew you meant what you said."

The worker is then asked to identify one or two specific things to be improved. These changes might be in nonverbal behaviors or content. If the worker wishes to stop doing something (e.g., prefacing a small request with an abundance of apologies), the trainer should have the worker clarify what the more assertive behaviors would entail.

The worker then practices this segment of the scene again. The feedback and self-assessment should follow and focus primarily on the specific changes the worker chose to make. It would be redundant to renew all the positive feedback received after the first attempt; however, increased assertiveness in the behaviors role played in the first rehearsal should be pointed out. After the second practice of a small segment, the trainer and other participants suggest additional changes the worker might wish to try out. This process of offering coaching suggestions is extremely important because the locus of judgment can easily change from the worker to others. The trainers model and explain that suggestions are to be offered as *suggestions for the worker's consideration* ("How about if you tried stating your response more briefly?") rather than as critical "shoulds" ("You really should speak up, I couldn't hear you at all!"). The trainers should also emphasize that the worker has the final responsibility to accept, modify, or reject all suggestions. This procedure is consistent with our experience that participants usually have the discriminatory capabilities to make such judgments and that part of being assertive is to use them. Trainers should always respect a participant's decision to stop working. At the same time, trainers can clearly explain what they believe is still unassertive.

When the participant is able to behave assertively with little or no anxiety in one small segment of the situation, the scene is then extended. As each segment is successfully accomplished, the participant moves on. The final rehearsal runs through the entire scene.

The most important characteristic of this rehearsal procedure is the focus on successive improvements. The person is reinforced for progressive movement toward the final goal rather than only when the assertive behavior is fully completed.

Participants are often concerned about the reactions they might get to their assertion and wish to practice how to handle others' negative reactions. The group can role play various negative reactions that the worker might receive. In some cases the negative reaction might not be realistic, but rather just what the worker *fears* most. When participants learn that they can handle the feared response, they feel more at ease and can be more assertive. Needless to say, trainers need to be sensitive that the participants do not become overwhelmed with negative respones during the role plays. The process of assertion training should be a successful experience.

If the worker is uncertain about the effect of her assertive statement, reversing roles (where someone else makes that statement to the worker) enables her to experience it as the recipient. The worker, as recipient, may have no negative reaction, thereby becoming less afraid of acting assertively. If, however, the participant does experience a negative reaction to an assertive response, the trainers may need to clarify the irrational beliefs and personal rights at issue.

When the person working is genuinely having difficulty expressing a thought or feeling, the trainers or other participants may model assertive behavior for the worker. When persons are very anxious about practicing an assertive behavior, the trainers might then utilize the cognitive restructuring procedures suggested in Chapter 5 or the relaxation techniques in this chapter.

After completing the rehearsals, participants are encouraged to try out the newly acquired assertive behaviors in the actual situation. At the same time, we avoid making the individual feel that he *must* now assert himself. The participants are also reminded to realistically assess the consequences of their assertion.

Demonstrations of Behavior Rehearsal

The following detailed example of the rehearsal procedure is a continuation of the situation developed in Chapter 5 on self-assessment questions: A female resident manager of an apartment complex (Judy) wishes to ask her employer (Mr. Brown) for a greater reduction in her rent in view of the amount of time she is working as manager. (Note: Assume that the situation has been specified, the irrational thinking challenged, the personal rights clarified, and that she is ready to practice the scene with another participant whom she has coached to act like the manager.) The trainer (Tr) has set up the physical scene as realistically as possible with Judy knocking on the door to enter her employer's (E) office.

Tr: Come in and say what you want and see how it goes. You're not supposed to be perfect, so just give it a try.

E: Come in!

Judy: Hello, uh, Mr. Brown, uh, how are you? It's uh, been a long time since I've uh, met with you.

E: Yes, Judy, what can I do for you?

Judy: Well, uh, I don't know, uh, I know you're very busy and everything, but I wanted to ask you something about my apartment manager's job.

E: Yes, what is it?

Judy: Well, I was wondering if you realized how much time it took to do all the things the job requires?

E: I should think I do, after all it's what I'm paying you for, isn't it!

Tr: OK, let's stop here since it's easier to take the situation a little bit at a time and focus on it closely. What can you all tell Judy that you thought was assertive about what she's said and how she's behaved so far?

P_3: Your voice was loud and clear.

P_4: Your tone sounded genuinely interested when you asked how he was doing and yet you were brief.

P_5: You walked right in and sat down facing him directly.

Tr: Those were good specific observations of your nonverbal behavior. What else did you like, Judy?

Judy: I was pleased that I did speak up right away and that I got to the issue quickly.

Tr: Those are both true. What would you like to do differently?

Judy: Well, I'd like to stop saying "uh" when I speak so that my voice flows more smoothly. . . and I didn't like the way I raised the issue of the job. It seemed too indirect and I put too much responsibility on Mr. Brown to continue the issue.

Tr: Those are both excellent points. How would you raise the issue of job time differently so that you are really expressing what you want to say?

Judy: I would tell him how much time I actually put into the job and express my wanting a greater reduction in rent.

Tr: That sounds much more like what you said you wanted to communicate earlier. Try it again and we'll particularly look for your dropping the "uh's" and stating your concerns more directly.

E: Come in!

Judy: Hello Mr. Brown, how are you?

E: Fine, Judy, what can I do for you?

Judy: Well, I've been concerned for some time now that I have been working about 20 hours a week as apartment manager and I would like you to consider increasing my rent deduction to $200 per month.

Tr: OK. Stop. Will people give Judy some specific feedback about what you think she just did that was assertive?

P_3: You definitely dropped the "uh's" and your words flowed much more smoothly.

P_4: I thought you were just as clear and direct as can be in stating your information and making your request. It was great!

P_5: You also eliminated stating your great concern over interrupting his busy day so that your concerns were stated more directly.

Judy: Yeah, I really liked the way that sounded, too. I also felt that I was more in control of the conversation when I expressed my request directly.

Tr: That's great, you did make the changes you wanted. Is there anything else you'd like to do differently?

Judy: Well, yeah, I was aware that I had a sort of shy or sheepish grin while I was talking and I'd like my face to express my serious concern.

Tr: OK. And does anyone else have any changes you might suggest to Judy?

P_6: Yeah, Judy, would you want to make more eye contact with Mr. Brown?

Judy: Oh, yes, that's a good point; I was looking away a lot.

Tr: OK. Try it again and this time focus on your facial expression and eye contact.

Judy then practiced several more interactions. At first the employer was encouraged to be cooperative and support the request. When Judy successfully completed the entire scene to her satisfaction, the trainer then asked her to practice the scene with the employer responding negatively (e.g., anger, threat, indifference, guilt, or whatever "hooks" her). The situation was then practiced until *Judy was satisfied* with how she assertively handled the employer's uncooperative response. Below is an example of such an *extended practice.*

Tr: Judy, when we talked earlier about the catastrophies you worried over before going in to see Mr. Brown, you mentioned that he might get angry with you and yell or berate or accuse you somehow. Would you like to practice an extension of this situation where Mr. Brown is not as cooperative as before?

Judy: Yes, I really would because that's what ties me up most inside. If I knew I could handle that, I would be more confident.

Tr: OK. Tell Bill (the participant role playing Mr. Brown) what he should be like.

Judy: Well, you would first act real busy and then when I bring up the issue of how much time I spend as manager, you would begin asking me in an accusing manner how I do spend my time, as though you believe I don't really do anything. Then when I talk about getting a greater reduction in rent, you get angry and accuse me of trying to put something over on you.

E: That's really clear. I'll give it a good try.

Tr: Try it from the beginning and I'll stop you after a few interactions.
(knock, knock)

E: Come in, come in!

Judy: Hello Mr. Brown, how are you?

E: All right; what do you want to see me about?

Judy: Well, I want to talk with you about how much time I'm putting into the apartment manager's job. It's over 20 hours a week, and—

E: Twenty hours a week! What could you possibly do that takes 20 hours a week! Just what *are* you doing that supposedly takes so much of your time?

Judy: Well, uh, lately a lot of people are losing their keys and I have to let them in and—

E: Surely, *that* doesn't take 20 hours now does it?

162

Judy: Well, no, I guess you're right. But I have had to check a lot of damage and repair work and make arrangements to have it fixed. That takes a lot of time, right?

Tr: OK, let's stop here. Tell Judy what you liked about the way she behaved.

P$_4$: Your voice was calm and pleasant when you greeted him. And when you began explaining your business, you sounded appropriately serious.

P$_6$: You had good eye contact most of the time.

P$_7$: You got to the point very quickly and clearly.

Tr: Those are good points. What did you like, Judy?

Judy: Well, I liked everything about the way I entered and got to the point. I felt calm. My facial expression and my voice matched my words. I also liked that I was willing to answer his question about how I spend my time even though he cut me off to ask it. At another time I might have been so flustered with his breaking my train of thought that I would not be able to respond at all.

Tr: That's an excellent observation, Judy. Really insightful. Is there anything you would like to do differently?

Judy: Yes, when he interrupted me I was still anxious. What I wanted to do was think a bit so that I might give him a more complete answer. I responded quickly with something that really doesn't take a whole lot of time, although it is an inconvenience, but that's a different issue. So what I'd like to do is pause briefly, collect my thoughts, and answer calmly. I also could hear myself sounding apologetic or defensive like I was talking to a strict parent. So I'd also like to sound more "informational" and less intimidated.

Tr: Those are good, clear changes. It does sound like Mr. Brown keeps people off guard by challenging and questioning, which puts him in a sort of judgmental position and pulls for you to be adaptive and seek his approval.

Judy: Yes, that's the way I see him and how he'd like me to be. And I do have a right to my opinions.

Tr: That's an excellent point. Do you have some ideas how you could help yourself to take the time you need to collect your thoughts?

Judy: Like we discussed before, when I notice my anxiety going up, I could remind myself to take a deep breath and focus on what I want to tell him.

Tr: Very good. Let's try it again. Focus on pausing to think and stating your answer in an informational manner without seeking his approval. Let's pick it up where he says, "What do you want?"

E: What are you here to see me about?

Judy: I want to talk with you about how much time I'm putting into the manager's job. It's over 20 hours a week, and I—

E: What? How could you possibly be working 20 hours a week? Are you kidding; just what *are* you doing that supposedly takes so much of your time?

Judy: (Pauses briefly) Most of that time has gone into checking damage or malfunction reports from tenants and making the appropriate arrangements for repairs. I also have to check each repair job and verify its completion. Then there's the regular administrative work required for rent collection. I also spend several hours a week showing apartments to prospective tenants. As a matter of fact, I have kept a rough record the past three weeks of how much time is spent doing what.

E: OK, so you do put in those hours. You're getting a rent reduction, aren't you?

Judy: Yes, that's what I want to discuss with you. I would like to have the rent reduction increased to $200 per month which amounts to about $2.50 an hour.

Tr: OK. Stop. That was really excellent! Will people tell Judy what you really liked?

P_3: Yeah. You were really hanging right in there; you did pause when he interrupted you and your response was firm and you sure gave him some excellent facts. Your voice changed most of all; you sounded confident.

P_5: I really liked the way you stayed calm and informational instead of falling for his pressure tactics.

P_6: You didn't say "uh" when he interrupted you, like you did last time and your facial expression was serious but not harsh.

Judy: That's good to hear. It felt really good to me, too. I was in control of my thoughts and although I got a little anxious, I was able to realize what I wanted to say and how I wanted to say it and I did it!

In both of the above examples, the situation was segmented into workable units, considerable reinforcement was given and focused on improvements, participant involvement was solicited for positive feedback and suggestions for change, and Judy was given ample opportunity for self-assessment. The feedback and assessment were behaviorally specific, attending to what Judy said, as well as the way in which she communicated. Little attention was given to the irrational fears or personal rights during this practice since they seemed to be adequately resolved. Other persons may profit from periodic clarification of these cognitive aspects during the rehearsal process.

One last point merits consideration. In the above example, emphasis was placed on evaluating Judy's behavior, rather than on the employer's reactions to her behavior. This was done deliberately since nonassertive persons tend to give less attention to realistically evaluating their own behavior, and instead overly focus on the other person's reactions. Naturally, we do not recommend that participants totally disregard how others respond to them. In some situations, it is important that the other person's reaction is examined, especially if that person holds power or significant reinforcers for the individual. It is important, however, that such an examination involve thinking rationally about the other person's reaction, as opposed to catastrophizing. In these situations, the trainer and group members may help identify ways in which the participant could be assertive and yet minimize the chances of a negative reaction from the other person.

AN ANATOMY OF A CONFLICT

In the following passage, we will present a fairly complex interaction between a mother and daughter and the internal dialogs of both persons. We offer this vignette to clarify how a trainer can take a fairly extended, complex interaction and approach it utilizing assertion training procedures.

Kathy Craig is in her senior year of college and returns home for a visit with her parents. She has decided to live with a man she has been dating and she is planning to inform her mother and seek her approval and support. Both mother and daughter enter this conversation with predispositions, not only about the issue of men and women living together, but also about themselves, each other, their roles toward each other, and the meaning of such a decision. Some of the thinking in this vignette is irrational and will lead to distortions and disturbance. Other thoughts will be rational and lead to appropriate feelings and assertive behaviors.

> While Kathy and her mother are together one evening watching television, Kathy quite casually mentions, during a commercial break at a highly dramatic moment in an excellent movie, that she is planning to live with Joe in the fall.

> *Kathy is anxious about what her mother's reaction will be and also is angry that the conversation may be a real hassle. Consequently, she plays down the significance of the matter well below what she really would like to communicate; that is, she is serious about this decision, has given it considerable thought, and she, too, is somewhat uncertain about the outcome.*

> As Kathy's message sinks in, her mother shrieks, "What! My God, you're joking!"

> *Partly because Kathy is giving a mixed message verbally and nonverbally and because her mother comes to the immediate conviction that such a decision would be disastrous, her mother opts for the magical hope that this was a joke.*

> Kathy responds defensively saying, "See, I knew it would be like this. You *never* take me seriously! Well, I'm serious now and we *are* going to live together!"

> *Kathy helps to set her mother up for this attack and then lets her have it. The basic irrational belief here is: My mother will probably not agree and she will not treat me as an adult; that is so unfair that I can't stand it and she is awful! One outcome of this belief is that Kathy exercises power in a way which can be punishing.*

166

Mrs. Craig then responds in a sincere manner, "Well, I see you are really serious about this. But have you considered the consequences?"

At this point Mrs. Craig breaks out of the power game and responds in an empathic, yet direct, manner. Her second sentence could have sounded similar, yet communicated a totally different message had she said in a distressed voice, "But haven't you got any idea of the consequences?"

Kathy's response is, "Yes, Joe and I have talked a great deal about the consequences for us and how you and Dad and Joe's parents would react. We really care about you and want your approval and support for our decision."

Kathy's response is an honest, assertive expression of her opinions and feelings.

Mrs. Craig says, "But what do you think our neighbors will think ... and your father's business associates ... and grandmother?"

Mrs. Craig is catastrophizing over her own conviction that this decision is awful, *welling up others who would agree,* and *is also catastrophizing over how she will not be able to stand the judgments of others.*

Kathy angrily retorts, "I don't give a damn about them!! I care about me! What about me, damn you!"

Kathy is operating under the faulty belief that just because her mother is concerned with the opinions of others she doesn't care about her (which may or may not be true). She has decided that her mother is a mean and awful person deserving of verbal punishment. In fact, Kathy does care about her grandmother and is even somewhat sensitive to affecting her father's business relations. None of these issues, however, is great enough to change her decision. Her intense anger reaction, however, is the result of the irrational belief that it is unbearably unfair that her mother is concerned about others' opinions. She could communicate her opinions about the impact of her decision on others in an assertive manner if the irrational thinking was eliminated. Kathy may be right that her mother thought of the family image first. To decide that her mother is therefore unloving and thereby deserving of her intense anger does not necessarily follow. A more rational response might be to decide "It is unfortunate and frustrating that my mother thinks of others' opinions before she thinks of my desires; she may even care about them more than she cares about my welfare. That is sad and irritating but it is not unbearably unfair and does not warrant intense anger and hostility from me." In fact, Kathy's mother does care a great deal about her although she also cares about social image.

Mrs. Craig responds to Kathy's outburst saying, "Kathy, I do care about you very much. You are my primary concern. I am also concerned about what others will think. But I just realized that, really, I am afraid you have made a harmful decision and I've been trying to pressure you to change it. What I really am afraid of is that you will be hurt."

Mrs. Craig comes through again with a perceptive and genuine expression of her own thinking, feeling, and behavior.

Kathy says, "I really do know you care but it's important for me to know that you respect my judgment and my thinking. I'd like you to know what issues I have considered and how Joe and I arrived at our decision. I'd also like to know your reactions to our thinking. I know you think it is a bad decision and I'd like to know what you think is bad about it and not get super-agitated as we talk about it."

Kathy again states clearly and assertively her opinions and how she wants the conversation to proceed.

This interaction could continue with both Kathy and Mrs. Craig periodically slipping back into irrational thinking, emotional overreactions, and unassertive behaviors. Mrs. Craig might have gone on to attack Joe's selfish motives, to catastrophize over the fear of pregnancy out of wedlock, to invoke the sinfulness of premarital sex, to agonize over where she went wrong (to thereby induce guilt), to attack Kathy as being immature and insensitive to her parents. Kathy might also have persisted in ranting at her mother for not caring and for not respecting her right to make her own decisions. She might even be outraged that her mother doesn't *agree* with her decisions. After raging for some time, she might also convince herself that she has been ungrateful and uncaring, and become depressed and guilt-ridden.

Either Kathy or Mrs. Craig could work in a group on any of the transactions cited above by challenging the irrational thinking *and* practicing assertive responses. Some therapists might also theorize that both Kathy and Mrs. Craig are seeking some type of "gamey payoff" for the way they are behaving and that this must be identified and given up before change will occur. We believe that such may be the case for some people, but many people do not have such a strong investment in holding on to their dysfunctional thinking and behaving, and will give them up with understanding and practice for more effective options. It is also important for trainers to recognize that the irrational thinking, its origins, and its emotional and behavioral consequences are not always readily apparent to those who maintain them. That is, people are often not *intentional* in their nonassertiveness, nor are they conscious of their thinking, feeling, and behavior. Rather, they are functioning at a preconscious level which becomes conscious only when they stop and pay attention to their thinking, feeling, and behaving, as in the group. Such insight coupled with behavior rehearsal procedures can be a powerful change agent.

This interaction between Kathy and Mrs. Craig is a typical example of situations brought to assertion training groups. Trainers should be prepared to break down such extended interactions into manageable parts and conduct the cognitive restructuring and behavior rehearsal procedures described in Chapters 5, 6, and 7. Even with such a complex and changing dialog, clarification of thinking along with practice of more assertive responses can be accomplished at each interaction.

RELAXATION TO REDUCE ANXIETY

Some participants become so extremely anxious when thinking about or approaching certain situations that many of the cognitive and behavioral interventions which could be available are blocked. Trainers can teach group members several different approaches to relaxation which are designed to reduce anxiety to a level where other cognitive and behavioral interventions can be employed. Participants can learn these relaxation procedures in the group and then utilize them either before their role playing or before and during real-life situations.

The first approach focuses on deep muscle relaxation (Jacobson, 1938; Wolpe, 1958). Essentially, the process is one of tensing (for about 10 seconds) and relaxing (for about 20 seconds) specific muscle groups, usually starting with the lower extremities and moving up to the face, although the original relaxation procedure varies somewhat. Some lengthy relaxation procedures focus on very small muscle groupings like the toes, ankles, calves, thighs, buttocks, and so on. The directions for deep muscle relaxation presented below offer a briefer procedure where several muscle groups are tensed at one time.

A second approach to relaxation focuses on letting go of tensions, using imagery, and breathing deeply. Lazarus (1971) describes a relaxation procedure where the therapist has the client (1) do deep breathing, (2) focus on bodily feelings of calmness, (3) tense the whole body at once to feel the contrast with relaxation, (4) note the difference between tensions which develop when the eyes are open vs. when they are closed, (5) imagine the feeling of being calm, and (6) repeatedly say internally to oneself the words "calm," "relax," or "serene," while exhaling deep breath.

Meichenbaum (1975a) suggests that the major contribution of relaxation is a matter of mental, rather than physical, relaxation. Consequently, trainers can have group members (1) think to themselves such words as "relax" or "calm" (Rachman, 1967), (2) imagine a pleasant or peaceful image like a landscape (Yates, 1946), or (3) say soothing phrases to themselves like "I am calm and relaxed" (Cautela, 1966), while doing either Jacobson's deep muscle relaxation or Lazarus' breathing and releasing of tension procedures.

The following directions are a suggested format for a brief relaxation procedure including deep muscle tension, breathing, and several imagery techniques. This procedure can be employed in the group and trainers might also wish to audio tape these instructions for the participants' use. After participants have used a tape three or four times, they can then go through the procedure without the taped directions and use the relaxation procedures when approaching or during actual anxiety situations.

> Make yourself as comfortable as possible, loosen any tight clothing that you can, and get relaxed in your chair. Just focus on your body and feel the tension flow out as you relax more and more. Now, stretch out your legs, lift them slightly off the floor, point your feet back toward your face as much as you can. Tighten your toes, your ankles, your calves, and your thighs—tighten and tighten, as tense as you can (tighten about 10 seconds). Now, *relax* . . . feel the warmth of relaxation in your

legs and feet as you relax. Feel how pleasant it is to feel that warmth as it flows through your legs even to your toes (relaxation should be 15 to 20 seconds).

Now tighten your buttocks and stomach as hard as you can. Tighten and tighten. Hold it a bit more (again 10 seconds total). Now, *relax* . . . and let yourself feel the warmth flow into your buttocks and stomach. Notice the pleasant contrast between the relaxed feeling you experience now and the tightness you experienced a moment ago. Take a deep breath now. As you slowly let it out, also let out the remaining tension in your feet, legs, buttocks, and stomach. Continue to take deep breaths and let them out slowly as we go on (again 15 to 20 seconds of relaxation).

Now tighten your back muscles, your chest, and the muscles just under your armpits. Harder. Harder. Hold it a little bit longer (10 seconds). Now relax. Let yourself feel the tranquil flow of relaxation as it moves up your body into your back and chest. Imagine the word "calm" or the word "relax" and think that word to yourself slowly about ten times. Take a deep breath and let it out slowly as the tension drains away (45 seconds of relaxation).

Extend your arms and make two fists, tighten your triceps, your forearms, and your fists. Hard. Really hard. When I say relax, let your arms fall to your lap with the pull of gravity (10 seconds). *Relax.* Notice the tingling sensation of relaxation in your fingers and hands. Feel the warmth in your arms. Enjoy this beautiful relaxation. Imagine a peaceful, tranquil scene that is really relaxing. Picture that scene and how warm and comfortable that image is for you (45 seconds of relaxation).

Now, hunch up your shoulders as though you are trying to touch them to your ears. Tighten your neck, too. Tighter and tighter. Hold it just a bit more so that you neck actually shakes (10 seconds). Now, *relax.* Feel the heaviness in your shoulders and the warm feeling of relaxation. Take a deep breath and slowly let it out. Imagine saying to yourself, "I am calm and relaxed." Enjoy the comforting feeling of being tension free (45 seconds).

Now, open your mouth as wide as you can. Wider. Hold it a bit more (10 seconds). Now, *relax.* Feel the warm, tingling sense in your face. Let your mouth hang open as it relaxes. Breathe deeply (15-20 seconds). Now, furrow your brow and tighten your cheek and face muscles into a tight grimace (people with contact lenses should remove them before beginning the entire relaxation exercise). Tighter. Hold it (10 seconds). Now, *relax*. Feel the flow of warm relaxation enter your face and eyes. Enjoy the wonderful feeling of relaxation through your entire body.

Now take a deep breath and hold it (hold it for 10 seconds). As you let it out fully, let any tension drain from your whole body. Imagine that your body is being immersed in a warm fluid which absorbs any remaining tension. Feel your body little by little sink into this pleasant fluid and the tension seep from your body. First your feet and legs, then your torso, your arms, your neck, and your head. Breathe deeply and enjoy this relaxed feeling. (Pause a few seconds.) I will count to three. On three you will open your eyes and be refreshed and relaxed—one, two, three.

As an alternative to the above procedure, trainers might have participants tense their whole bodies only once or twice and primarily do more imagery, breathing, and focusing on already tight body parts, letting go of the tension.

HOMEWORK

Homework in assertion training groups involves the systematic planning and carrying out of specific cognitive, affective, and behavioral changes outside the group. It is extremely important that trainers provide opportunities for participants to make the transition from learning in the group to application outside the group. The emphasis in the group on specific situations and actual behavior change leads naturally to carrying out these changes between sessions.

Several approaches to making this transition are possible. *First,* during the initial session, trainers might ask the participants to identify several specific situations (speaking to parents) or types of assertive behavior (refusing requests) which they would like to work on over the course of the group. Each participant should specify the behavior changes as clearly as possible (i.e., "I'd like to be able to talk with my parents about my future without getting real upset and then blowing up in anger"). Each week, then, participants would write down the progress they have made toward achieving their goals, and assess their present behavior in that situation. They would then report at the next session on their progress, self-assessment, and their next plans for achieving the goal.

Second, trainers should be prepared to teach participants the basic principles of contingency management and contracting to help them accomplish their behavioral goals (Malott, 1972; Homme, 1970). The basic principles of planning in small segments, rewarding oneself for each small improvement, being behaviorally specific, and recognizing the competing short- and long-term rewards for assertive vs. unassertive behavior can be invaluable to participants in their efforts to change. Trainers can devote group time to helping members develop contracts for carrying out homework assignments. Some goals may be more efficiently accomplished in progressive stages using systematic rewards at each step.

One participant in his early twenties developed a contract to help him get to the point where he could comfortably initiate conversations with women his own age whom he saw on the beach and found attractive. He created a series of steps which, for him, would be progressively more difficult and would get him to his goal. Step one was to simply say hello to little children on the beach as he walked by them. Step two involved his saying hello to older adults whom he found working in their front yards along a walking path adjacent to the beach. Step three required that he stop very briefly and remark on the gardening, staying only long enough to be comfortable. Step four involved saying hello to women his own age as he passed them on this walking path. Step five was the biggest jump and required that he stop and talk briefly with a woman he found attractive.

The participant once decided he would walk along eating grapes and offer some to the woman. He would then attempt to continue the conversation. In another instance, he ran on the beach for exercise and, if he saw someone he found attractive, he would walk back after his run and say, "Hi, I saw you here when I was running by and I thought you were really attractive and that I'd like to meet you. My name's Ken."

After each step was successfully accomplished, he rewarded himself, often with the grapes. (In some cases, other people might be asked to provide or deprive the participant of the rewards contingent upon accomplishing the assertive goal.) In addition, he did not go on to the next goal until he was comfortable doing the previous step. In the group, he practiced making several different initial comments and then practiced continuing conversations with women his age. This is also a good example of contracting because each step was clearly and behaviorally specified; thus, the participant was able to determine when each step was completed, when rewards were appropriate, and when the contract was completed. It took about two weeks to complete this entire contract, a short time to accomplish something fearfully avoided for years.

Third, at the end of each session, we encourage the participants to choose some specific behavior change, which they will systematically work on during the week. The structured exercises in Chapter 4 provide a number of possibilities: giving a certain number of compliments each day, making positive self-statements each day, modifying a particular nonverbal quality (eye contact, loudness or tone of voice, facial expression), carrying on a conversation with a stranger, confronting a friend about something he does that has negative consequences for the participant. Members may choose anything at all to work on that can be considered a change toward greater personal effectiveness. We encourage people to choose small and clearly definable behaviors (from saying "hello" to three new people each day to giving a good "I-message" to someone) in order to increase the probability of success and to easily recognize when the homework is accomplished.

In addition, members are encouraged to write down during the week any situations which they believed they handled assertively or did not deal with as effectively as they would like. Specific situations are brief and easily forgotten (especially when negative). Writing them down enables participants to recall these moments and to work on them in the group. Very often, unassertive persons do not give much attention to their behaviors. Homework focuses their attention on themselves and stimulates their thinking in a descriptive, noncritical, constructive manner.

Trainers should provide a systematic method for group members to assess themselves in specific situations during the week. We have used a written form with a series of questions which participants carry with them. Participants can either ask themselves these questions as part of their self-assessment or they can respond to these questions in a daily assertion diary. The five questions are: (1) What were the positive, assertive aspects of my thinking, feeling, and behavior in this situation? (2) What areas could use improvement? (3) What was the outcome of the situation and how did it match my goals for the situation? (4) How

174

was I feeling? (5) What plans might I make for the future in dealing with this person or situation again? For example, one group member answered these questions regarding asking for a date as follows: (1) I told myself that it would not be awful if this woman refused; I liked the way I carried on a brief casual conversation before asking; I asked in a direct and positive manner without putting myself down. (2) I would like to make better eye contact, I'd like to be more physically relaxed, I'd like to practice what to say and do when she accepted. (3) She accepted! Just asking was my first goal. Her acceptance was my second goal. My third goal was to talk with her in an assertive manner and that was mostly accomplished, but I still want to work on that more. (4) I was nervous but not overwhelmed and then I was excited and really pleased with myself. (5) If we have a good time on the date, I'll ask her out again; I'll also tell her next time I see her how easy it is to talk with her.

If the situation had not gone as well, the form provides a valuable self-assessment tool. This systematic assessment thereby helps the person who has not attained the specified goals to approach that fact from a problem-solving perspective, as opposed to becoming deeply depressed or angry. Responses to the questions on the self-assessment form can be brief, even abbreviated. Its primary purpose is to facilitate thinking and to enable recall of thinking, feelings, and behaviors when the participant discusses the situation in the group.

Fourth, when participants have had an unsatisfactory assertion experience during the week, some trainers (Gloria Lewis, personal communication) have the person role play the situation again with another member or friend outside the group. These role plays are tape recorded and the participants frequently ask to have the tapes played at the next group session.

The primary purpose for doing homework is to help participants transfer their group learning to their lives outside the group. Group members begin to see the group as an experience from which they can take newly acquired cognitive and behavioral skills and apply them to their everyday lives. Homework plans are best made just before the end of each session to facilitate the connections between in-group and out-of-group behavior. At least ten minutes of every session should be devoted to homework plans.

SUMMARY

Behavior rehearsal components—modeling, role playing, reinforcement, and coaching—were defined and demonstrated. In addition, such behavioral procedures as successive improvements, providing behavioral feedback, role reversal, the use of small behavioral segments, and homework follow up were described. Extended behavior rehearsals demonstrated how to practice situations involving others who are behaving aggressively toward the participant. A particular conversation between a mother and daughter was analyzed for possible assertion problems. Lastly, relaxation and homework procedures were described in detail.

Behavior rehearsal procedures were presented as a most critical stage in the assertion training process. These procedures have proven to be effective in facilitating behavior change, especially when used in conjunction with cognitive restructuring procedures and systematic, out-of-group practice toward clearly specifiable goals.

REVIEW QUESTIONS AND EXERCISES

1. Describe the following procedural terms or phrases *and* explain why they are employed in assertion training:

   a. positive reinforcement
   b. behavioral feedback
   c. practicing *small* segments of a situation
   d. successive improvements
   e. making coaching *suggestions* for change

2. What is the rationale for having role players first respond cooperatively to the participant who is working on being more assertive? Describe a specific role play situation and add three different ways a role player might respond that is uncooperative or resistive.

3. How can cognitive restructuring procedures be integrated with behavior rehearsal?

4. Practice conducting as many role plays as possible with friends, each time attending to a different component of the process: getting suggestive feedback, facilitating movement along the rehearsal, positively reinforcing improvement, involving the group, keeping the segments short, keeping the locus of final judgment regarding changes with the participant.

7
Modeling and Behavior Rehearsal Procedures

In addition to cognitive restructuring and behavior rehearsal procedures, modeling is another important instructional component in which live or taped models are used to demonstrate various assertive behaviors or parts of one specific assertive behavior. It is assumed that by observing the model's assertion and the consequences for such behavior, group members can vicariously learn the assertive behavior in much the same way that they would acquire it from direct experience (Bandura, 1969; 1971).

Modeling procedures provide a short-cut method for giving information about various assertive behaviors, especially complex assertive behavior. Very importantly, modeling may also provide "permission" for group members to engage in similar assertive behavior. Thus, it may reduce observers' apprehensions about their own potential assertion. Finally, modeling procedures may reinforce the group members' existing assertive skills. It should be noted, however, that although modeling may benefit group members, if used crudely and in an authoritarian manner, it may hinder the members' progress. In such cases, the observers may learn to simply mimic and memorize, rather than integrate the modeling. Members may then become overly dependent on modeling experiences and not develop the skills and patience to look inside of themselves and discover what their own assertive goals would be in the particular modeled situation and how *they* would like to respond assertively.

MODELING RESEARCH
The general modeling research of Bandura (1969) and his col-

leagues (e.g., Bandura, Grusec & Menlove, 1967; Lovaas et al., 1967; Blanchard, 1970) have consistently demonstrated modeling to be an "effective, reliable and, relative to other procedures, rapid technique for both the development of new responses and the strengthening or weakening of previously acquired response" (Goldstein et al., 1973, p. 31). It is rather difficult to assess the precise contribution that modeling makes to the assertion training process since, as McFall & Twentyman (1973) have so cogently noted, the modeling research usually includes not just simple modeling, but also narratives similar to coaching or instructions. Such narratives may play an important, previously underestimated role in producing the experimental outcomes in the literature. Also, as Lacks & Jakubowski (1975) have noted, one researcher's modeling may be another researcher's modeling plus reinforcement. Bearing these cautions in mind, the assertion training literature indicates that modeling can be an effective procedure (Eisler, Hersen & Miller, 1973; Goldstein et al., 1973; Hersen et al., 1973). More specifically, modeling has been found to be better than practice alone (Eisler, Hersen & Miller, 1973). Research has generally established that modeling with rehearsal and feedback is certainly more effective than no treatment (Gutride, Goldstein & Hunter, 1973; Gormally et al., 1975), although the additive effects of these three variables are not as yet clearly understood. Furthermore, some researchers have found that combining modeling with other procedures such as focused instructions (Hersen et al., 1973) or role playing (Friedman, 1971) may enhance the effectiveness of assertion training. It should be noted, however, that McFall & Twentyman (1973) found that modeling added little to behavior rehearsal and coaching in training subjects to assertively refuse requests. As they note, the failure to obtain significant modeling effects may have been due to their studying a relatively simple assertive behavior which was probably already in the subjects' repertoire, namely the ability to say "no." Modeling may play a more important role in training complex assertive responses.

In most assertion training groups, modeling is done on an informal, unsystematic basis, that is, the trainer and/or group participants serve as live models and demonstrate alternative assertive behaviors for another group member. Such informal modeling is often used in the behavior rehearsal role reversal sequence, in which the trainer or one group member takes the role of another person in the group and demonstrates how that person could act assertively in a given situation. Assertion trainers may also use formal, systematic modeling procedures involving highly structured video or audio modeling tapes.

FORMAL MODELING PROCEDURES

In using formal modeling procedures, trainers need to decide whether they will use audio or video modeling tapes. Unfortunately, the relative effectiveness of these two modeling procedures is not yet known. McFall & Twentyman (1973) found no difference between audio and video modeling tapes (both were insignificant in their study); while Goldstein et al. (1973) found that simply telling their chronic, psychotic patients to respond independently and providing them with two detailed, verbal descriptions of such behavior was as effective as more elaborate audio tape modeling procedures. However, many trainers believe that video modeling is superior to audio modeling.

Video modeling permits group members to observe certain non-verbal behaviors, such as facial expression and hand gestures—nonverbal behaviors which play an important role in assertion and which cannot be presented on audio tape. Moreover, video tape may hold the viewers' attention more than audio tape. On the negative side, video modeling may present too many distracting stimuli which increase the likelihood of the viewers' focusing on nonrelevant features of the model's assertion. Also, we have found that viewers are often critical of video modeling, perhaps because they expect these video tapes to be as technically sophisticated as television productions. At any rate, as Eisler, Hersen & Miller (1973) note, whether trainers choose to use video or audio modeling, modeling tapes allow group members to focus on one component of the model's behavior at a time and to be repeatedly exposed to a model until they have assimilated the material. The modeling tapes also have a research advantage in that all group members are presented with identical stimuli which remain constant for all subjects.

Bandura's Four Subsystems

Before discussing some considerations which should be kept in mind in constructing modeling tapes, it is important that trainers are at least minimally acquainted with what Bandura (1971) believes are the four basic subsystems involved in modeling. These subsystems are:

1. *Attention* processes which determine whether the observers will attend to and register the appropriate modeling stimuli. Here certain characteristics of the observer (e.g., racial status), of the

model (e.g., competence, status, age, sex), and properties of the modeling cues (e.g., complexity of the modeling stimuli, discriminability of modeling stimuli) are important.

2. *Retention* processes which determine whether the viewers will retain what they have observed. Retention may be increased by having the observers symbolically code the modeled events or overtly or covertly rehearse the model's behavior. It is thought that during their exposure to the modeling, observers are inclined to code, classify, and reorganize the modeling sequence into familiar and more easily remembered schemes.

3. *Reproduction* processes which determine the observer's ability to enact the modeling once it has been retained. In this subsystem, considerations such as the viewer's physical ability to carry out the modeled behavior may become important.

4. *Motivation* processes which determine whether the viewers will enact the modeled behavior. Incentive variables also determine which modeling cues a person will attend to and remember.

Constructing Modeling Tapes*

In terms of constructing modeling tapes, considerations involving the first two subsystems will be dealt with here. *First,* generally speaking, the models should be the same sex as and similar in key ways to the observing group members. A key factor may be whether the modeling is seen by the observers as being appropriate to their own social status, sex, or social role. However, we have had some group members report becoming more assertive upon seeing children act assertively in situations which were also uncomfortable for the observing adult group member! Some of the complex interactions between the observers and the model's sex and status have been discussed by Freiberg (1974).

Second, besides demonstrating an assertive behavior, the modeling tapes generally show the model's assertion resulting in a reinforcing outcome.

---

* In addition to the considerations discussed here, trainers may find other details about constructing modeling tapes in Goldstein, Sprafkin & Gershaw (in press). Many professionals have constructed modeling tapes. Trainers may wish to write to Drs. John and Merna Galassi (University of North Carolina, Education Department, Chapel Hill), Dr. Arnold Goldstein (Syracuse University, Psychology Department), and Dr. Richard McFall (University of Wisconsin, Psychology Department, Madison) for information about their modeling sequences.

Third, the modeling scenes should be reasonably short, from one to three minutes in length.

Fourth, complex assertive behaviors, such as negotiating a change in job status, should be broken down into smaller parts which observers can more easily assimilate during the modeling and remember afterwards.

Fifth, key aspects of the modeled assertive behavior should be highlighted. This may be done by either simplifying the modeling scenes so that the key aspects of the assertion clearly stand out or by including a narrative which directs the observer's attention to salient characteristics of the model's behavior. For example, "In the following scene, notice how the employee gets to the subject immediately, and in a firm but nonhostile voice briefly states what she wants and then cites a few pertinent facts as to why she deserves a raise. Notice how she relies on reason rather than pure emotion in justifying her request." Frequently such orienting narrations also function as coaching instructions, that is, "explicit descriptions of what constitutes an appropriately assertive response" (McFall & Twentyman, 1973, p. 314). Some studies have suggested that such coaching may play an important role in increasing the desired behavior, with some researchers finding coaching to be as effective as modeling (Green & Marlatt, 1972; Goldstein et al., 1973; Rappaport et al., 1973), others that coaching plus modeling is more effective than coaching alone (Whalen, 1969), and yet others that coaching alone may be effective in increasing certain assertive behaviors while other assertive behaviors require coaching plus modeling (Hersen et al., 1973).

Sixth, when trainers develop modeling tapes for more complex assertive behaviors, we recommend that they include methods for helping group members to develop codes or covert symbolic labels for the modeling sequence of behaviors. For example, when group members observe a modeling film of a person expressing an opinion in a business meeting, coaching instructions may be "Notice how the person makes a stroking statement which notes the other's point and then makes her own point. When the other person disagrees with her, notice how she strokes again in the process of her assertion and finally asks for more information from her opposer." In the process of observing this model, viewers may devise the following code to .help them recall the modeling: Stroke and express opinion; Blocked: stroke and assert; Blocked: get more information. Although such coding activities have not as yet been studied in assertion training, studies on observational learning have demonstrated the importance of codes in helping subjects improve their immediate and, most importantly, their delayed recall of the modeled behavior (Bandura, Grusec & Menlove, 1966; Gerst, 1971; Bandura & Jeffery, 1973).

Seventh, in clinical (as opposed to experimental) assertion training, the modeling tapes are followed by group discussion and directed behavior rehearsal activities in which the group members identify personal situations similar to those presented on the tapes. These personal situations are ones for which the modeled assertive behavior would be appropriate. The participants then practice personal adaptations of the modeled behavior, typically through overt behavior rehearsals. It should be noted that a few researchers (e.g., Kazdin, 1973, 1974) have found covert practice to be effective also.

Illustrations of Formal Modeling Tapes

Examples of complex modeling sequences developed by Leon Ashford and Janice Van Buren are shown in Figure 1, Modeling Sequence for Making Requests (p. 191) and Figure 2, Modeling Sequence for Expressing Disagreement (p. 193).

As Mahoney (1974) and Meichenbaum (1975a) have noted, it would be beneficial if trainers would develop several modeling tapes which show a model using cognitive coping strategies while in an assertive encounter. Goodwin & Mahoney (1975), for example, have developed such tapes for hyperactive aggressive children. One such video tape shows a young boy participating in a verbal taunting game. In addition to being calm, looking at his taunters and remaining in the center of the circle, the model is portrayed as coping with verbal assaults through a series of covert self-instructions. These thoughts, which were dubbed on the tape, consist of statements such as "I'm not going to let them bug me."

Our following example depicts a model using cognitive coping strategies when she is returning shoes to a store and does not have a sales receipt. The customer's dubbed self-talk is italicized.

> *That looks like the manager of the department. Oh he looks fierce . . . That's OK . . . take a deep breath . . . You have a right to exchange these shoes . . . But what if he says no . . . Stop it! . . . Don't jump to conclusions . . . First just say that you'd like to talk to him about the shoes . . . Remember you just bought them two weeks ago.*

Customer: Excuse me, are you the manager? I'd like to talk to you about these shoes I bought two weeks ago. The heel's starting to come off.

Oh, he's frowning. What if he gets mad? Take a deep breath . . . because he's frowning doesn't automatically mean that he's going to refuse to take back the shoes. . . He's probably just as upset as I am that these expensive shoes are breaking down. He's probably embarrassed too. I didn't do anything wrong to cause him to get mad. If he gets mad, he's maybe mostly mad at himself or the manufacturer. All I have to do is not act snotty and just stick to the facts and what I want.

Manager: Say, lady, just how long have you been wearing these shoes anyway? These really look beat up.

Wow, how rude of him! He must really have some problems to be that nasty. Even though I don't like what he said, I don't have to lower myself to his level. Just cool it and stick to the facts. That's it, take a deep breath. Good girl!

Customer: I've had the shoes two weeks and worn them a couple of times. I do like the style of the shoes and would like to exchange them for another pair.

Very good! You deserve a good pat on the back. Sticking to the facts like that. Gee it feels good to hold your own and not retaliate!

Manager: (Frowning) Well, we'll take care of having the shoes repaired. That's the best we can do under the circumstances, with no sales receipt.

He's just got no right to talk to me that way! I'll just show him a thing or two! Hold it! Cool down . . . Getting nasty isn't going to prove a thing here. Just take a deep breath . . . You can get through. Don't give up yet. This guy's really tough . . . but hey, kid, remember you've already won half a concession. Just hang in there. Keep it cool.

Customer: I appreciate your offer to have these shoes repaired. However, I would like to exchange them for another pair. I spent a lot of money on these shoes and I want a pair that's in good shape—not a pair that have been repaired already.

You did it! It feels good to keep your cool and yet hang in there!

Manager: But the shoes will be just as good with the heel repaired and besides you don't have a sales receipt.

I'd just like to punch him in the mouth! Who does he think I am anyway, some thief? . . . I can't stand it when he thinks of me like that. I'll show him who's a thief here . . . Stop it! Take hold of yourself. Don't let this guy get your goat! The fact that he keeps making those innuendoes does have to be dealt with but you don't have to use a sledge hammer to do it. Keeping cool will show him you've got real power.

Customer: I bet you have some customers who wear shoes for ages and then claim to have gotten them just a short time ago, and it puts a lot of pressure on you to pick out these people from people who really just happen to get a pair of shoes that were not as well made. Without a sales receipt, I don't know how to prove that I bought these shoes two weeks ago, but I did. I'm a regular customer in this store and I often buy shoes in this department and this is the first pair I've asked to have exchanged.

Manager: Well . . . in this case I'll make an exception, but next time hold on to the receipt.

Hurrah for you! You did it! You deserve a good pat on the back!

After viewing each part of a cognitive coping model, group participants can stop and discuss particular coping statements that they could use for themselves. Practice in cognitive coping and assertion could occur after viewing the entire modeling sequence, or at each discussion point.

INFORMAL MODELING PROCEDURES

As indicated earlier, informal modeling procedures involve the trainer and/or group members serving as live models for another group member and demonstrating alternative assertive behaviors. Informal modeling may occur in a number of ways.

Mini-Modeling

Mini-modeling refers to brief, live modeling which involves no more than a few sentences to complete the whole modeling sequence. One common place in which such modeling can be used is when the group participants report on their homework and sundry experiences with assertion during the week. Instead of just having the members generally report their assertive experience, encouraging the members to demonstrate exactly what they said and how they said it provides modeling for the other group members. Failures in carrying out assertion homework often provide good opportunities for inviting other group members to quickly model several alternative assertions for the group member who reported nonassertive or aggressive behavior and who simply lacked information on how the situation could have been approached differently. Trainers can also use mini-modeling during the initial group sessions when the basic concepts of assertion are being presented. A discrimination tape (see Chapter 4, p. 82) can be used to directly model assertive responses as well as provide a stimulus for the group members to devise assertive alternatives to the aggressive and nonassertive statements presented on the discrimination tape.

Assertion Exercises

Needless to say, many of the group exercises described in Chapter 4 involve member-to-member modeling of assertive behaviors. In addition to these exercises, the Assertion Game, developed by Dr. Larry Kiel (personal communication, 1973), incorporates both modeling and behavior rehearsal features.

In this exercise, assertion situations which the group participants find difficult are briefly described on index cards. A member of the group is given a stack of these cards, takes the top card and role plays the situation with the person sitting on the immediate right. Afterwards, the group rates (Yes or No) whether the member played the scene realistically, whether the member's assertion was appropriate for the situation, consistent with the specified goals, and whether verbal and nonverbal behaviors were natural, yet congruent and assertive. Members who vote negatively are asked to demonstrate (model) more assertive ways of handling the situation. Additional voting points are awarded for both the group member who served as the model and for the member who afterwards practiced the modeled assertion. For added interest, the voting points may be tallied on a scoreboard on which members advance so many squares for their points. Trainers who decide to use this modeling behavior rehearsal game must consider whether the group members are likely to feel comfortable in such a game format and have ability to model for each other.

Modeling within Behavior Rehearsal

In assertion training groups, informal modeling is most commonly used in conjunction with behavior rehearsal procedures. As Chapter 6 illustrated, behavior rehearsal can be done without the modeling component. The decision to use modeling rests upon the answers to two major questions: Will the modeling impose the trainer's values upon the group member? Would the person benefit more from modeling or from the sole use of self-evaluation and trainer/group feedback?

Since Chapter 6 has described the behavior rehearsal sequence in some detail, at this point we shall just briefly describe at what point(s) the modeling sequence would be used. After the group member has identified the problem situation and his assertive goals, and provided background information on the context of the situation, the first role play is started with the member playing himself and the trainers taking the role of the other person in the interaction. After a few minutes, the role play is stopped and briefly analyzed in terms of its strengths and areas for improvement. The trainer then takes the role of the group member and models an alternative way of assertively handling the situation. After the modeling is completed, the trainer and member assess the role play and the member then goes on to practice the modeled assertion in his own words. The sequence of practice-modeling-practice is illustrated in the following situation in which the group member has previously antagonized a housemate, Jerry, about his failure to take phone messages for the group member.

Member: Hi Jerry, what's happening?

Trainer: (As Jerry) Not much. What are you in to?

Member: Well something's been on my mind. It's about the phone. Jerry, when I get a phone call, why can't you just call me or walk over to my room to see if I'm in.

Trainer: (As Jerry) Hell, are you going to crab about that again!

Member: (Laughing) And that's just about the way it would go too!

Trainer: OK, let's stop here. What did you like and dislike about what you did?

Member: I liked my coming straight to the point and my eye contact, but I felt I was becoming defensive.

Trainer: Both are good observations. Let me try another approach and see how that goes.

Trainer: (As Member) Hi Jerry. That music really sounds good. Jerry, do you mind if we have a talk about something?

Member: (As Jerry) What's bugging you?

Trainer: (As Member) Yeah, I did want to talk to you about something. But first I want to make sure that this is an OK time for you to talk.

Member: (As Jerry) Well, I guess so.

Trainer: (As Member) Thanks, Jerry, I appreciate that. I'm kind of hesitant to bring it up because it's a sore spot, the phone, I mean, but I'd really like to talk to you and hear your side of it too.

Member: (As Jerry) Are you going to crab about that again?

Trainer: (As Member) No, I'm not going to crab. I did that the last time with you. *This time* I'd like to problem solve and hear you out too.

Member: Hey that really got to me. I felt good when you said that.

Trainer: OK, let's stop here. What did *you* see that was different about the way I approached Jerry?

Member: Well to start off with, somehow the whole atmosphere was different right off the bat. I don't remember exactly what you said. And then that last thing you said was really good. I liked that.

Trainer: You pinpointed two important things. Now the exact words I used aren't too important since you'll want to use your own words anyway. Here's the principle I was following: *First* of all, Jerry's apt to be touchy from what you said before. So it's important to show him right away some consideration,

187

that you have some awareness of his feelings. That's what I did when I checked with him about whether this was a good time for him to talk and I hung in there until he said it was OK. Then I let him know that I appreciated it by thanking him. *Second,* I let him know that I was prepared to hear his side *too* which implied that I wanted him to also hear my side. This is important in light of that previous negative encounter the two of you had. I kept thinking to myself—be *firm but friendly.* That's different from being diffident or apologetic.

Member: That makes sense to me. It's like remembering: One, let Jerry know that you're being considerate about the timing for the talk. Two, show appreciation. Three, when I broach the phone subject, let him know I'm also interested in his side so I can *solve* the problem.

Trainer: Good, let's have you play yourself and I'll play Jerry.

While the above example illustrated a trainer's modeling for the group member, trainers have several other modeling options that could be used. One option is to have other group members be the models instead of the trainer. This format has the advantage of providing several members with assertive experience and possibly reinforcing their existing assertive skills. It also helps pull the group together and reduces the danger of the trainer devoting too much time to just one member while the rest of the group withers away. It does have the disadvantage, however, of the trainer having less control over the behavior rehearsal process.

Another option is to work with one group member, as illustrated in the previous example, while instructing the rest of the group on the behavior rehearsal process itself. Afterwards the group members can form triads. One person, the "client," presents a problem for rehearsal, another person, the "helper," takes the trainer's role, and the third person takes the role of the "coach," who, together with the helper provides both positive feedback and discusses areas for improvement with the "client." The assertion coach also stops the role play when it looks like it is going nowhere or that the client is having trouble carrying out the assertion practice, or when the helper has misunderstood the client, has imposed personal values, or is becoming too critical. The helper and coach can exchange roles when the helper cannot model assertive behavior or the coach has some modeling ideas to share with the client. In this format, after one person has been helped, the roles are exchanged, and either the helper or coach present their own assertion problem. Trainers who use this format can provide all members with guidelines for giving feedback (see Figure 3, p. 195).

SUMMARY

Modeling is another important instructional component in the assertion training process. Modeling involves presenting either a live or taped model who demonstrates alternative assertive behaviors or parts of one specific assertive behavior. The general modeling research has established the efficacy of such procedures. The available research suggests that modeling has a place in assertion training, although additional research is needed which clearly establishes the precise contribution which modeling makes to assertion training.

Trainers may either use formal or informal modeling procedures. Formal modeling involves presenting highly structured video or audio modeling tapes for the group to observe and afterwards discuss and practice the modeled assertion. Various considerations which are important in developing such formal modeling procedures were discussed. Informal modeling involves the trainer and/or group participants serving as live models for another group member.

REVIEW QUESTIONS AND EXERCISES

1. Evaluate this statement: The potential advantages of modeling in assertion training groups outweigh the potential disadvantages.

2. In your own words, summarize the major results of the modeling research.

3. Name three areas in which additional research is needed regarding the role of modeling in assertion training.

4. If you, as a trainer, decided to use formal modeling procedures in assertion training, would you choose video or audio modeling? Why?

5. Describe Bandura's four subsystems and explain the practical relevance of each system.

6. What do the terms "coaching" and "coding" mean? Why are these considered to be important variables in assertion training?

7. Explain several cautions a trainer should keep in mind when using modeling in assertion training.

8. Obtain one of the paper-and-pencil measures of assertion, i.e., Galassi et al. (1974) or Rathus (1973a) and where appropriate, read the situation and tape record your own assertive response. Evaluate your own modeling for clarity and appropriateness. Then modify the situations to reflect different assertive goals and again provide a verbal modeling assertive statement. Listen carefully to your modeled assertive statements and check whether they do reflect a change in goals.

Figure 1
Modeling Sequence for Making Requests

You are receiving financial aid from the school for tuition and living expenses (e.g., room and board). Your parents have usually paid for your books and other supplies. However, because of a recent emergency, your family will not be able to help you. So you have come to the financial aid office to ask for the money you need.

Notice how the student quickly comes to the point. When the financial aid officer says there is nothing that can be done, notice how the student briefly expresses her understanding, but points out how the situation has changed and asks for new consideration.

Student: I came in because I need to buy books and supplies. My parents are having a financial emergency and won't be able to give me the hundred dollars to buy them for this semester.

Officer: I can understand your need. But we have given you all the money we could according to your parents' financial statement. We are not in a position to increase scholarship money.

Student: I understand that, but now my parents' financial situation has changed, so I was wondering if it could be adjusted.

When the officer makes a suggestion, notice how the student doesn't accept it but offers her own.

Officer: I know what you are asking for, but it is impossible for this semester. We can do something about that for next semester. I don't see but one option really, and that's a loan. You or your family could take a personal loan at a bank.

Student: I really feel I can't ask my parents to take out a loan because of what's going on with them right now, financially.

Officer: I see.

Student: And as a student, I don't think I'd qualify for a loan. However, I am more than willing to work for the hundred dollars.

Watch how the student repeats her suggestion when it was overlooked. She accepts a compromise of both their suggestions.

Officer: There is a possibility that you could take a loan through the university. We have money available for small loans. I'll give you a form to fill out. You can get an answer within two to three days. Is that OK?

Student: That sounds good, except for one part.

Officer: What's the problem?

Student: The problem is I really would like to find a way of paying it back right away instead of having it added onto what I already owe the school.

Officer: That's possible. There are a few job openings for students on campus which would allow you to earn a small amount of money. I could give you the information and you can look into them.

Notice how the student ends the interview on a positive note.

Student: I'd appreciate it. That sounds really good to me. Thank you.

Officer: You're welcome.

Reprinted with permission from Leon Ashford and Janice Van Buren.

Figure 2
Modeling Sequence for Expressing Disagreement

During a lecture on measurement and intelligence tests, your instructor made the following statements: "The literature indicates that blacks are somewhat less intelligent than whites and this is evident by their scores on intelligence tests." You think his statement is too general and inaccurate. You have read recent publications that give a different interpretation of these test scores. You have decided to approach him in his office after class to express your disagreement.

Notice that the student describes his feelings and then goes right to the point of his visit.

Student: Can I come in and speak to you a minute?

Instructor: Sure.

Student: I have something that has been bothering me and I want to speak to you about it.

Instructor: What is it?

Student: You mentioned in class today that there is evidence that blacks score lower on the intelligence test than most whites.

When the instructor explains his position, notice how the student briefly explains where he disagrees.

Instructor: Yes, I said in class, the research indicates that blacks score one standard deviation below the mean on all the standardized intelligence tests.

Student: I was disagreeing with what you were saying because I think more recent evidence indicates that's not an accurate picture.

Instructor: How do you mean that's not accurate?

Student: There are some other factors involved which make that statement too general.

When the instructor becomes defensive on two points, notice how the student maintains his ground without backing off and calmly repeats what he wants.

Instructor: Are you questioning the validity of my statement?

Student: Well, yes. I'm asking you to consider other possibilities or alternatives. There are other things that need to be taken into consideration when talking about the low performance of blacks on IQ tests.

Instructor: Are you saying I didn't prepare very well for this lecture?

Student: No, I can't say that because I don't know what you looked at in preparation. But I want to bring some materials to your attention to see if you would consider them.

Instructor: OK, what material?

Student: Well, I don't have them with me now and I'd like to come back and drop them off. If it's OK.

Instructor: OK. Can you give me an idea of what they are about?

Notice how the student briefly presents specific information. Listen to how the student emphasizes key words which show how important these alternatives are to him.

Student: Yes. For example, the difference in language style between blacks and whites is one factor. Another is that these tests are culturally biased in favor of the white middle class.

Instructor: All right. You know, I haven't really looked at some of that. I've been thinking about it, and if you noticed what I said today, I didn't really get into those details.

Student: Yes.

Instructor: It's something I've been putting off and, for the most part, people haven't raised that kind of issue. But since you raised the question, I'll take a look at those materials.

Notice how the student ends the interview on a positive note by expressing his sincere appreciation.

Student: I would really appreciate that and I appreciate your listening to me. I feel much better about it now.

Instructor: OK, good, I'm glad you came in.

Student: Thank you very much.

Reprinted with permission from Janice Van Buren and Leon Ashford.

Figure 3
Guidelines for Giving Feedback

1. Start off with the strengths of the performance. Specify exactly which behaviors were positive.

   Verbal Behaviors
   Was the statement direct and to the point?
   Was the statement firm but not hostile?
   Did the statement show some consideration, respect, or recognition of the other person?
   Did the statement accurately reflect the speaker's goals?
   Did the statement leave room for escalation?
   If the statement included an explanation, was it short rather than a series of excuses?
   Did the statement include sarcasm, pleading, or whining?
   Did the statement blame the other person for the speaker's feelings?

   Nonverbal Behaviors
   Was eye contact present?
   Was the speaker's voice level appropriately loud?
   Was the statement filled with pauses?
   Did the speaker look confident or were nervous gestures or inappropriate laughter present?
   Was the statement flat or expressive?

2. After all positive feedback has been given, offer feedback suggestions.

   Describe the behavior, rather than give a label. Be objective rather than judgmental.
   Offer a possible way of improvement. This should be expressed in a tentative rather than absolute manner. Do not impose a suggestion.
   Ask the group member for a reaction to the suggestions, allowing the member to accept, refuse, or modify the suggestion.

Note: Stick to the basic assertive problem and do not get involved with long and complex descriptions of the history of the problem or the anticipated negative reactions of the other person.

8
Planning and Conducting Stages in the Life of an Assertion Group

This chapter contains recommendations for the development and conduct of assertion training groups from the initial decision to conduct a group to the last contact with the participants. In planning the functional aspects of an assertion group, we recommend that the groups consist of seven to ten participants. With too large a group it is difficult to maintain member involvement, particularly during the cognitive restructuring and behavior rehearsal stages. The group might be same sex or male and female depending upon the goals and issues to be raised in the group (which might be determined in advance by the trainers or evolve from conversations with those interested in the group).

If possible, two trainers should conduct a group since (1) it is particularly valuable to have two different ongoing models of assertive behavior; (2) the trainers can support and reinforce each other's points; (3) each trainer does not have to maintain such a high energy level or hold the group focus as long; (4) one trainer can lead an exercise or procedure while the other observes what is happening more fully; and (5) evaluation of each session is facilitated. With a male-female group, it is particularly preferable to have a male and a female trainer. With same-sex groups, probably both trainers, or at least one, should be of that sex (although we have had success working with groups of the opposite sex).

The group might continue for six to nine sessions (possibly longer if people actively want to continue working, although by that time participants seem to be able to work on their own) with each session being about two hours. Beyond two hours, participants tend to be less energized and less involved. When planning a group, variations on these basic recommendations are quite appropriate to meet the particular characteristics and needs of the participants.

Once the initial planning is done, the trainers may want to advertise the group. Advertising will vary with the population sought (personnel in a business or university; high school or university students; the general public; referrals from counselors or psychotherapists) and with the vehicle for advertising (professional newsletter, personnel memo, student newspaper, or a women's center newsletter). The ethical standards of the American Psychological Association state that announcements of services should adhere to professional, rather than commercial, standards in making known the availability of professional services. Particularly if the assertion group is organized on a fee basis, the trainers should be careful to avoid advertising which is solicitous or competitive. Brief descriptions of the process, focus, and population sought seem appropriate as an announcement of services, particularly at a service agency such as a university counseling center, a women's center, or a mental health center. A statement of the superiority of services is inappropriate and the information should be presented in an informational manner. For example, the following is a possible flier or brief note in a newsletter or campus paper.

> An assertion training group will be conducted at the University Counseling Center by Arthur Lange, Ed.D. and Patricia Jakubowski, Ed.D., counseling psychologists at the center. The group will focus on (1) discrimination between nonassertive, assertive, and aggressive responses to specific situations, (2) identifying and developing a belief system which has a high regard for personal rights and the rights of others, (3) identifying the irrational thinking which often precedes unassertive behavior, and (4) practicing alternative assertive responses to specific situations. The group will consist of men and women and is open to anyone affiliated with the university. Contact the trainers for further information regarding the group at (phone number).

SCREENING

Not all persons expressing interest in assertion training have concerns applicable to such a group. Consequently, a screening procedure is important to assess the appropriateness of concerns for assertion training. The trainers should have a brief interview with all of the candidates, preferably in person, to explain clearly what the goals and format for the group are and to identify their needs for assertion training. The trainers may wish to simply question the candidates about their expectations and needs or they may administer an assessment questionnaire (such as those cited in Chapter 13), either to determine their appropriateness for assertion training or as a pre-measure to assess the impact of training.

During a brief discussion with a candidate, one can determine if assertion training seems appropriate. The trainer might briefly describe the outcome goals and process of the group and elicit reactions from the prospective member. Trainers should also explore the expectations and needs of the candidate. For example, a person might be looking for more of an encounter group experience where the members would generate and share reactions to each other in the "here and now" of the group. Others might wish to discuss and get advice regarding important life decisions, and although some aspects of assertion training might ultimately be helpful, the person's immediate need is to consider various alternative decisions. It is as important that the prospective group member be seeking the *process* of assertion training as well as the outcomes since other groups and other procedures might be preferred and lead to similar outcomes.

We have also found some unassertive persons to have very low energy levels, that is, they seem to think, feel, and behave minimally. This may be manipulative behavior seeking rescuers or safety in inactivity and uninvolvement. Regardless of their motives, involvement in the group is more demanding for them and the likelihood of their having a successful experience is low. Hopefully such persons would be identified during the screening process and not admitted to the group, but rather to individual counseling at that time. If, however, a person is already in a group, the trainer can talk with the person outside the group, noting lack of energy and involvement. If the person seems to be manipulating for attention, the trainer might share that observation and suggest that the person work on getting his needs met more directly in the group. In other cases, the trainer might suggest that the person make a contract to systematically identify his thoughts, feelings, and behaviors in the group and possibly utilize the cognitive restructuring and behavior rehearsal procedures. The trainer, however, should clearly realize that participants do not *have* to be involved fully and at all times.

Another serious and much less easily determined factor is the prospective member's readiness to profit from the action-oriented focus of the group. Some persons have deeper investments in holding onto their irrational assumptions and dysfunctional or ineffective behaviors. In the transactional analysis sense, they have been seeking and getting a "payoff" for their dysfunctional behaviors (such as collecting enough abuses to warrant a blow up or being helpless so that others will "rescue"). They are reticent, or at least ambivalent, about giving up those behavior patterns and their subsequent "payoffs" in favor of more assertive interactions. Moreover, "gamey" behavior patterns and their "payoffs" are not fully apparent to the behaver. Consequently, some persons would profit from a period of exploration and clarification of the psychological investments they have in maintaining their dysfunctional thinking, feeling, and behaving. This might be done in individual or traditional group therapy from any of a variety of theoretical orientations. The typical assertion group does not provide for in-depth, lengthy exploration of these deeper investments. The cognitive restructuring and rehearsal procedures provide for substantial exploration, but not to the extent needed for some persons. Experienced diagnostic and clinical assessment skills utilized during the screening session are the best tools for judging readiness.

If, however, a person is already in an assertion group and appears to be resistant to giving up dysfunctional behavior, the trainers might choose from several courses of action. If a person behaves in a manner which is clearly an attempt to disrupt or immobilize the group, the trainers might confront that person outside the group with the specific dysfunctional behaviors and make a contract to halt those behaviors in the group. If the participant wishes to work further on changing that behavior, the trainer might do so within the group or refer the person to a more appropriate mode of counseling or therapy. If a person does not make changes in disruptive behavior, as agreed upon, the trainers can (outside the group) legitimately ask the person to leave the group. It is worth noting that although it is important to have this last resort available, we have never exercised it. By being assertive themselves, the trainers can minimize the effects of dysfunctional behaviors by the way they deal with participants inside the group, particularly by effectively keeping the group focus on the situation, issue, or person working, and not supporting distractions or digressions of a disruptive nature.

If a participant is not disruptive but is more resistive or ambivalent about letting go of old patterns, the cognitive and behavioral interventions described in the next three chapters might be utilized. The trainers should avoid attempting to convince or push a participant into changing. The choices to work and what to work on rest with the participant. The trainers can "invite" participants to work and to explore what might be blocking them from changing, but it would be a violation of the participants' personal rights to attempt to make them change. Particularly with nonassertive participants, it is quite a temptation as a trainer to step in and exhort a participant to make changes which will clearly be good for him.

Some participants may not be ready to change or to practice alternative behaviors. These persons can still learn and understand much from what is said and done in the group, and often will utilize this learning at a later time when they are ready to add some new behaviors or change some thinking.

Assertiveness is often an underlying issue for many psychological problems including depression, lack of decision-making, low self-esteem, and sexual dysfunction (see Chapter 13). Assertion training is not, however, a panacea for all psychological dysfunctions. For example, one person seen in individual counseling cited a problem situation where he was in a bar when a close friend recognized him and said she would join him shortly. In a few moments, however, he saw her leave without ever having come back. He became disconsolate and, feeling rejected, quickly escalated the importance of the incident out of proportion. After leaving the bar, he made a suicidal gesture which was not serious. Clearly, his cognitive, emotional, and behavioral responses were inappropriate, yet assertion training would not be enough to resolve the complex dynamics operating here. As individual therapy progressed, however, this client did become a participant in an assertion group and worked on expressing his needs in a direct and reasonable manner in a number of situations.

We recommend that trainers who are working with generally well-functioning participants avoid including members who would be diagnosed as seriously depressed, alcoholic, drug addicted, suicidal, schizophrenic, or hysterical. Such persons are likely to require more attention and have a disruptive influence on the group process. During the screening interview, the trainers should be assessing the prospective participant's level of dysfunction.

Another primary consideration in determining who should be in a group is the trainer's assessment of her own clinical capabilities and experiences. Assertion trainers with relatively little counseling or therapy training can be very effective with persons who are functioning well and are seeking personal growth. Clinically trained leaders usually can work with more dysfunctional participants in the group. If handled correctly, there is little potential for psychological casualties in assertion training groups. However, with any experience focusing closely on human behavior, that potential is always present. There is no ironclad formula for determining who is an effective trainer. Academic credentials do not guarantee competence. We believe, however, that trainers should have basic knowledge of the relevant cognitive and behavioral principles, be experienced in group work, be prepared to handle unexpected psychological dynamics, and have adequate supervisory backup personnel available. In regard to specific preparation to do assertion training, we recommend that prospective trainers go through a three-stage sequence before conducting their own groups: (1) be a participant in a group with an experienced leader, (2) co-lead a group with an experienced trainer with supervision by that person outside the group, and (3) lead a group alone or with another "trainer in training" with supervision by an experienced trainer.*

SUGGESTIONS FOR PLANNING EXERCISE-ORIENTED SESSIONS

In this section, we will describe a specific format for individual sessions which we have employed. The unique nature of the group and the needs of its members should be the prime consideration when trainers plan the content and number of sessions for their own groups.

The following is a recommended sequence for a nine-week group, where the participants are generally unassertive but are functioning reasonably well. This group would be more likely characterized as a personal growth-learning experience than a therapy group.

SESSION 1

Introductory Mini-lecture

This introductory lecture should provide (1) a brief overview of the nine sessions describing the focus of exercises and the general nature of cognitive restructuring and behavior rehearsal, (2) a clear definition of

---

* For example, the University of California at Irvine extension program offers a 15-unit certificate program in assertion training to prepare trainers to conduct groups.

assertive behavior as contrasted with nonassertive and aggressive behavior, and (3) some generalizations about reasonable expectations as a result of being in the group. For example, after the trainer introduces himself, he could continue with:

I want to start this session by giving you a brief overview of what we'll be doing over the next nine weeks. For the first five sessions I will bring in some structured exercises which will focus on different situations or types of assertive behavior. For example, we'll practice giving and receiving compliments, dealing with conflict situations especially with people close to you, responding in difficult situations, and role playing specific situations where you can identify the personal rights you have and how you might act on them assertively as opposed to nonassertively and aggressively. You will also have a chance to discover how your thoughts affect your feelings and behaviors. The last four sessions will also be structured; we will focus on specific situations, but you will bring in the situations which are real for you and one person will work at a time.

We expect that after you've completed the group, you will be better able to handle a number of situations more assertively. You will be less anxious in those situations, you will have a wider repertoire of responses available to you, you will be able to identify your personal rights and be more inclined to act on them. And you will have learned some ways to work by yourself on new situations which initially you might avoid or not handle as well as you'd like. Those are pretty ambitious goals and we need to be realistic about what can be done in roughly sixteen hours together, but if during the week, we actively make use of what we do in the group, some really fine changes can occur.

Before we begin the exercises, I'd like to define assertiveness so that we can all have a more accurate sense of what we are working toward. Assertiveness is being able to communicate my opinions, thoughts, needs, and feelings in a direct, honest, and appropriate manner. When I am nonassertive, I am communicating less than I'd like to express and I am denying my own interpersonal rights. Aggressiveness is standing up for my own rights but in such a way that the rights of others are violated. We'll do a lot more with defining and discriminating between these three behaviors in the exercises coming up.

This lecture also provides the opportunity to raise issues such as group confidentiality and how the participants should notify the group about planned absences.

This brief introduction allows the participants to get involved in the group as listeners and gives them some sense of what to expect. It also stimulates some thinking about what assertiveness is and what the group and the trainers are all about. It should be as brief as possible (no more than ten minutes) since the participants will lose attention and not retain much if it becomes a lecture (even a stimulating one). The content issues are more appropriately discussed later within the context of specific exercises and the rehearsals.

Exercises

Introductions	10 minutes
Inane Topics	20 minutes
Yes-No Exercise	10 minutes
Giving and Receiving Compliments	20 minutes
Social Conversations	25 minutes
Homework and Whip	15 minutes

These exercises (described in Chapter 4) are used for the first session because (1) they deal with positive assertions which are important and often neglected in assertion training, (2) they are brief and positive which increases the likelihood of a successful experience in the group, and (3) they are excellent preparations for the more complex behavior rehearsals to come later. With the focus on positive assertions and processing the effective behaviors of the participants, a highly supportive atmosphere develops which helps participants to feel comfortable about working on their interpersonal concerns.

The amount of time recommended for each exercise is only a rough estimate. It is unlikely that more exercises could be completed, but the trainers may wish to go slower or direct more attention to a particular exercise.

SESSION 2

Begin with a discussion of the participants' homework   15 minutes
and any incidents (not necessarily major events) which

204

they believed they handled assertively or did not deal with as effectively as they would have liked.

Discrimination tape exercise (including mini-lecture on types of assertive responses)	30 minutes
Identifying Personal Rights exercise	60 minutes
Homework and Whip	15 minutes

This session shifts the focus from positive assertions to the more complex process of recognizing and acting on personal rights. It is very important to give participants an opportunity to discriminate among assertive, nonassertive, and aggressive responses and to recognize how their belief system regarding personal rights directly effects which responses they choose. As with the first session's exercises, these too deal with important issues of assertiveness and focus on an important cognitive component of the rehearsals to come later. Assertion training must include such cognitive assessment procedures.

SESSION 3

Discussion of week's homework and situations	15 minutes
Brief Introduction to Rational-Emotive Principles exercise and Rational Self-Analysis exercise	30 minutes
Rational-Emotive Imagery or Emotive Imagery exercise	30 minutes
Discussion of cognitive restructuring (as described in Chapter 5), where participants discover their negative self-statements, recognize their relationship to their behavior, and make plans to alter them with the help of the trainer's cognitive intervention techniques.	30 minutes

This session is designed to lay the conceptual groundwork for utilizing cognitive restructuring procedures in conjunction with the behavior rehearsal procedures.

SESSION 4

Discussion of week's homework and situations	15 minutes
Making and Refusing Requests exercise	30 minutes
Making Statements Without Explanation exercise	30 minutes
Dealing with Persistent Persons exercise	30 minutes

205

Homework and Whip	15 minutes

SESSION 5

Discussion of week's homework and situations	15 minutes
Small Group Behavior Rehearsal Line exercise	60 minutes
Defining One's Own Behavior exercise	30 minutes
Homework and Whip	15 minutes

These exercises in Sessions 4 and 5 attend to situations that are more complex than in the first session and deal more with acting on personal rights. It is extremely important for participants to act out these exercises, as opposed to talking about them. None of the principles or skills is difficult to understand, but they are difficult to do; hence, practice is the more effective means for learning.

SESSIONS 6 THROUGH 9

Continue to begin and end the group as in earlier sessions.	15 minutes at beginning
	10 minutes at end
Employ the cognitive restructuring and behavior rehearsal procedures with participants who volunteer to work on situations of their own concern. The amount of time varies greatly for each situation. The participant may need to do a good bit of cognitive work or may want to practice several different escalations of the situation. If one series of rehearsals goes beyond a half hour, the trainers may want to seek closure depending on the degree of involvement and attention. The person may then work on other escalations at a later time. Usually three separate sets of rehearsals is reasonable to complete in this time.	95 minutes

For the last session, Alberti & Emmons (1974) recommend ending groups in a positive manner in two interesting ways. Part of the session is devoted to identifying potential reinforcers and sources of support for assertive behavior outside the group that each member might utilize when the group ends. Secondly, during part of the session, individuals

206

make positive self-statements for one minute and hear specific positive statements about themselves from others for two minutes.

In summary, beginning with Session 1, the flow is from brief, positive interactions through the more cognitive discrimination exercises of Sessions 2 and 3, to the more complex and conflict-laden situations of Sessions 4 and 5. The more personal and more complex situations are raised by the participants in Sessions 6 through 9.

USE OF VIDEO TAPE

If the trainers have access to the equipment, video taping can be used in a variety of ways in assertion training. We have used video taping to record behavior rehearsals as a means for the participants to observe and assess both the content and the behavioral components of their communication. Playing back only the video portion (no sound) can sometimes be a valuable source of feedback on nonverbal behaviors. In addition, trainers may adapt the technique of Interpersonal Process Recall (Kagan, 1975) to enable the person working to focus during playback on what her thoughts and feelings were during the rehearsal, and thus discover her faulty internal dialogs.

The trainers might play back initial rehearsals for analysis and contrast them with successive, more assertive rehearsals. The trainers might also have some particularly nonassertive participants "exaggerate" their behaviors, since what the person worried would be aggressive, upon observation, might not be as catastrophic as he imagines. It is not suggested that the participants behave in an aggressive manner, but rather that they assess how restricted their range of behaviors might have been.

FOLLOW-UPS

After the sessions have ended, the trainers might have a follow-up group session, administer a measure of assertiveness, or arrange a behavioral assessment procedure to determine any significant changes in the participants (see Chapter 13 for assessment and measurement procedures). As a practitioner or researcher, it would be valuable to have information on the stability of changes over time and the degree of generalization of assertiveness to other situations, as well as the long-term effects of the group experience on the participants.

SUMMARY

In setting up assertion training groups, trainers need to follow ethical standards in advertising. The process of selecting members for the group is also important. We recommend that screening interviews be conducted with all interested persons. In these interviews, the trainer would determine if assertion training is appropriate for the candidate, describe the outcome goals and process of the group, and explore the expectations and needs of the candidate.

A nine-week exercise-oriented group was described. In this type of group, we have found that approximately nine sessions are needed to teach the participants the basic skills of assertiveness. After such a basic group, some participants ask for an "advanced" training group in which more time can be devoted to individual behavior rehearsal. Trainers who do exercise-oriented groups would, of course, determine what sequence of exercises would best fit the needs of their particular group.

It is recommended that inexperienced assertion trainers go through a three-stage sequence before conducting their own groups.

REVIEW QUESTIONS

1a. What is the recommended training sequence for inexperienced assertion trainers?

b. What other knowledge or experience should trainers have?

c. What other professional action and precautions should be taken for any relatively inexperienced assertion trainer?

2. Identify and describe the goals held for the screening interview.

3. What are the advantages of having co-trainers?

4. What are the ethical and professional issues regarding advertising an assertion group?

5. What alternatives are available to trainers for dealing with disruptive or withdrawn participants?

6. Identify two uses of video tape in assertion training.

9
Theme-Oriented Assertion Groups

In theme-oriented groups, the individual sessions are devoted to one theme or topic around which the lecture, discussion, cognitive restructuring procedures, behavior rehearsals, and homework assignments are centered. These themes are based on the members' common problems which have been assessed prior to training. Although theme-oriented and exercise-oriented assertion training groups overlap to some extent, they differ in that the themes generally encompass a wider variety of assertion problems and the behavior rehearsals are usually not in the form of specifically designed exercises. In addition, a single theme may be carried over several sessions. Thematic groups have the advantages of providing a topic which is of general concern and interest for all the members (thus increasing group cohesiveness), providing a conceptual structure which ties together several separate sessions, and maximizing the members' opportunity to discuss a variety of personal situations which relate to the general theme.

SESSION FORMAT
The general format for each theme-oriented session is (1) identification of the theme; (2) a lecture which deals with self-defeating internal messages, personal rights, and where possible, provides specific guidelines for assertion; (3) rehearsal of assertive behavior; and (4) assignment of homework.

    In the following example, the theme "assertively giving criticism in a work situation" has been identified as a major concern by a training group consisting of supervisors and managers.

Lecture

This particular lecture focuses on guidelines for acting assertively, rather than on personal rights.

As you well know, one of your hardest jobs is to give criticism which is honest and not derogatory, and which causes the receiver to take the criticism seriously and yet not become discouraged or antagonistic.

The first guideline for acting assertively in this situation is *Get your own head together before you see the person.* Your internal self-messages play an important role here. If you tell yourself that it's a catastrophy that the person didn't do all the work correctly, chances are you'll aggressively overreact in the talk. If you tell yourself that the person is too weak to handle criticism, you'll be apt to water down your criticism with inappropriate smiling and the like.

Take a minute now to picture yourself in a situation where you gave criticism and were dissatisfied with the way you handled the situation. What were some things you were telling yourself that messed you up? (In the group discussion, the trainer lists the self-defeating internal messages identified by the group.) How could you change these messages to make them work for you instead of against you? Now picture yourself in a situation where you were pleased with how you criticized. What were you saying to yourself then? (Group discussion follows during which the trainer identifies and reinforces the productive self-messages and contrasts these to the list of self-defeating messages.)

After psyching yourself up and clarifying for yourself the specific good and bad points about the person's work, you're ready to see him. Now for the second guideline, *Get immediately to the point.* Don't beat around the bush; that will make the employee suspicious of your ulterior motives and will arouse defensiveness. Don't use the socratic-lawyer approach of asking a stream of incriminating questions. The employee quickly senses that your questions are intended to bring out a confession. This approach causes him to feel under personal attack, and he is likely to counterattack or grow increasingly rigid in his denial of blame. Do come quickly to the point and let the person know the behavior that is incorrect or less effective. Don't overwhelm the person with a flow of criticism.

The third guideline, *Be specific*. Don't use labels in describing the person's failings. Saying, "You're a sloppy, careless, lazy, or irresponsible person" is labeling the worker. Clearly describe the incorrect behavior and show how it has a concrete effect on you or others. Use the I-message we've discussed earlier. For example, "I've noticed that you've been late to work three days this week. When you're late, other people have to take over your duties, and I have to rearrange the work load, which takes me away from my other work."

The fourth guideline, *Create a positive atmosphere* in which the person will know that you're providing corrective feedback rather than personal attack. If possible, give a brief rationale so that the individuals can see that it's to their advantage to change their behavior. Needless to say, such rationales should be sincere. For example, "I wanted to tell you this because I know you're interested in getting ahead in the company and would want to know when you're doing something that may get in the way of a promotion"; "Because I know you're trying very hard to do a good job and would want to know when you've unintentionally done something wrong"; "Because I thought you'd want to know so you could improve your work"; or "Because I didn't want to ignore it and blow up later."

The fifth guideline is *Get her reaction to your criticism*. Then the person is less likely to feel that she's been dumped on and that you're being judgmental. You could say, "What's your reaction to what I've said?" or "What do you think?" or "Do you see it a lot differently than I do?" If you disagree with the reaction, e.g., denial of coming late to work, you may restate your position and give a brief explanation; or you may suggest that you both keep a record of the behavior in question and later compare notes. Be open to the possibility of countercriticism, e.g., "All you ever do is criticize." Often there is some truth to countercriticism, and it's important to recognize valid criticism so that you can improve your own work.

The sixth guideline, *Ask for his suggestions and determine if there's an obstacle to the person's changing his behavior*. Asking for suggestions opens up the possibility of mutual problem-solving. The obstacles will need to be dealt with. For example, if individuals come late to work because they manage their time poorly, you may ask if they want your suggestions on organizing their time. If they are late because they can't assert themselves with their car-pool driver, you might ask if they'd like to learn how to be more assertive with their driver. If the person has struck a hidden bargain of doing extra work in exchange for the right to come to work late, you might say that you'll try to get him monetary compensation instead of the privilege of coming late to work.

The last guideline, *Get a commitment to change* and ask for suggestions on what you should do if he fails to change.

After the lecture the trainer can ask the following discussion questions: How can you maintain your assertion with people who get antagonistic, who react with hurt or tears, who are resentful but "clam up," who discount your criticism, or who become evasive and try to change the topic? What messages can you give yourself when you find yourself starting to back down under pressure, when you get personal in your criticism, or when the employee counterattacks?

Behavior Rehearsal

There are several ways in which the members can practice being assertive and giving criticism: (1) the members can watch a video modeling tape, after which they form pairs or triads and practice assertive criticisms which are relevant to their own individual situation; (2) the trainer can provide live modeling with a co-trainer or another member of the group, and then the group forms pairs or triads; or (3) the members can form two groups of five in the line exercise and practice their own self-identified situations (see Chapter 4).

Homework Assignments

Each group member makes a contract to give supervisory criticism during the following week. If this is not realistic, the member agrees to carry out the homework assignment in the next two weeks.

FILM THEMES

Trainers who wish to use the theme-oriented format can use the stimulus films, *Assertive Training for Women* (Jakubowski-Spector, Pearlman & Coburn, 1973) to set the theme for each session in a way that maximizes the emotional involvement of the members. Although the films were designed for women, they have been successfully used with men. The films are on two reels with ten and eleven vignettes respectively; Part One is appropriate for younger college students while Part Two is designed for older college and noncollege adult populations. Each vignette shows a person who talks directly to the viewers in such a way that the viewers' rights will be violated unless the viewers assert themselves. The vignettes stimulate the group members to recall other similar situations in which they've failed to act assertively. Each of the vignettes serves to set the general theme for the session. Some of the themes dealt with are: relationships where you always do favors for other people, not wanting to be with someone and hesitating to hurt their feelings, requesting a service in a store or restaurant only to have the request ignored, being pressured by someone to relinquish time you wanted for yourself, being intimidated by a busy professional from whom you wanted to get more information, having someone assume responsibility for things you were capable of doing, being asked to do something for a worthy cause that you'd rather not do, having your opinions or feelings ridiculed, being pressured for more time when you are busy, having a passive person shift all the responsibility to you, and being overwhelmed by someone's strong and rigid stand.

GENERAL THEMES

Those trainers who wish to create their own themes for a particular assertion training group may wish to consider using the following general themes which are sufficiently broad to meet the needs of virtually any kind of group.

1. Being assertive with people who demand personal favors. Examples: requests to borrow personal belongings such as cars, class notes, books, sports or hunting equipment; requests to co-sign loans or borrow money, to take care of someone's pet, or to exchange vacation times at work.
2. Being assertive with people who request that you spend more time with them and whose requests are excessive or whose company is unpleasant. Examples: people who ask for dates or more friendship than you wish to provide; clients who demand too many counseling sessions from the therapist; relatives who want you to visit more frequently; neighbors who want to coffee clatch, or friends who visit late at night.
3. Being assertive with people who request that you participate in a worthy cause. Examples: requests to solicit for charity, to

organize drives, to sponsor showers or foreign students, to be a student representative on a committee, to give free lectures.

4. Being assertive with people who ask for your help or assistance. Examples: people who want help in writing papers, taking class notes for another student, learning how to drive, needlepoint, change car oil, write research grants; people who want you to take part of their work load.

5. Giving ourselves permission to need help and to make requests of others. Examples: same as in the above refusal of requests.

6. Being assertive with high status professionals who are very busy or condescending. Examples: doctors, tax accountants, dentists, lawyers, professors.

7. Going beyond assertion and negotiating a behavior-change contract with others. Examples: children, mates, friends, office employees, students, teachers, parents, roommates.

8. Maintaining our assertion in the face of someone's aggression and personal attack. Examples: any persons who are aggressive. This theme cuts across a variety of situations.

9. Being assertive with people who force their views and values on you. Examples: religious, sexist, racist, political, or business views as well as views on how you should run your house, personal life, or raise your children.

HOME THEMES

In addition to these general themes, the following themes would be appropriate for groups whose members are concerned with being assertive in home-related situations.

1. Being assertive with repair people who overcharge, do not do the work properly, or do not show up for appointments. Examples: garage mechanics, plumbers, painters, TV repairmen.

2. Negotiating money and work expectations with people who work for you at home. Examples: grass-cutters, maids, general handymen, babysitters.

3 Being assertive with high pressure salespeople. Examples: people who sell cosmetics, religious items, vacuum cleaners, land deals, magazine subscriptions, and insurance policies.

4. Getting the commercial service you deserve. Examples: getting seated at the table you'd like, getting service from a busy clerk, getting correct change, dealing with taxi drivers.

WORK THEMES
The following themes would be appropriate for groups whose members are concerned with being assertive in work situations.

1. Being assertive when giving supervisory criticism.
2. Presenting yourself at a task meeting where others ignore, discount, or put down your ideas.
3. Negotiating salary increases, changes in job title or job function.
4. Being assertive in job interviews.
5. Presenting discrimination complaints to a business or educational employer.
6. Being assertive with colleagues who make sexist, racist, or condescending remarks.

INTIMATE RELATIONSHIPS THEMES
Lastly, the following themes would be appropriate for groups whose members are concerned about being assertive with people who are emotionally close to them.

1. Being assertive with intimates who are passive and shift all the responsibility to you.
2. Expressing feelings of hurt, anger, and disappointment.
3. Expressing feelings of love, affection, and tenderness.
4. Asking for a personal commitment in a relationship.
5. Renegotiating the marriage contract or intimate relationship.
6. Being assertive and tender in sexual relationships.
7. Being assertive with people who ask for greater sexual intimacy than you'd like or whose requests come too early in the development of the relationship.
8. Being assertive in asking for greater sexual intimacy.
9. Responding to people who impose expectations on you (e.g., men suggesting Dutch treats on dates; women calling men for dates; people who don't want to have children; men who wash the dishes and take care of the children).

In developing a theme-oriented assertion training group, a trainer may choose themes from any of the above lists, and have the prospective group participants indicate which of these topics they would like to cover in their assertion training group (Table 6 on page 218 presents a check list of possible topics). In addition, a trainer may create new themes which would be uniquely appropriate for the group.

SUMMARY

In theme-oriented training groups, each session is devoted to a particular theme or topic around which the lecture, discussion, cognitive restructuring procedures, behavior rehearsals, and homework assignments are centered. Theme-oriented groups differ from exercise-oriented groups in that the themes generally encompass a wider variety of assertion problems and the behavior rehearsals are usually not specifically designed exercises. In addition, a single theme may be carried over several sessions. This chapter illustrated how the theme of "assertively giving criticism in work situations" could be implemented in a theme-oriented assertion training group.

Examples of various themes were given which were appropriate for group participants who had issues involving home-related situations, work-related situations, issues in being assertive with people who are intimates rather than strangers, as well as issues which would be generally appropriate for any group. A check list was also provided for trainers to use in organizing a particular theme-oriented assertion training group.

REVIEW QUESTIONS AND EXERCISES

1. What is a theme-oriented assertion training group?

2. How does a theme-oriented group differ from an exercise-oriented group?

3. What is the sequence of activities in a thematic session?

4. Give the check list of topics to three friends or members of the target population you're likely to work with, and determine the themes which would be common issues for the three people. Or interview three friends, determine the problems they have in common, and create appropriate themes. Or decide on a target group you're likely to work with and select from the check list in this chapter those themes which would likely be appropriate for that group. Add any additional themes which are missing.

5. Develop lectures for each theme. Present the lectures to sample members of the target population or friends to determine if the lecture provides helpful information on rights, self-defeating internal messages, and guidelines for acting assertively.

6. Develop homework assignments which would be appropriate for each theme. Carry out the homework assignments yourself during the next two weeks to determine how reasonable the assignments are.

Table 6
Check List of Possible Topics
for Your Assertion Training Group

Name_____ Home phone _____

Address _____ Work phone _____

Age_____ Occupation _____

Please rate the following topics as to how much you'd like to see them covered in your assertion training group. Then indicate the top 10 in rank order of importance, since not all of the topics can be covered in this group. All the members will be polled and a common list of topics will become the focus for the assertion practice sessions. Please add any topics that you're interested in.

1	2	3	4	5
No interest		Average		Tremendous interest

Topics	Interest Rating 1-5	Rank Order of Top 10 Topics
1. Being assertive with people who demand personal favors	_____	_____
2. Being assertive with people who request that you spend more time with them and whose requests are excessive or whose company is unpleasant	_____	_____
3. Being assertive with people who request that you participate in a worthy cause	_____	_____
4. Being assertive with people who ask for your help or assistance	_____	_____
5. Giving yourself permission to need help and to make requests of others	_____	_____
6. Being assertive with high status professionals who are very busy and/or condescending	_____	_____

Topics	Interest Rating 1-5	Rank Order of Top 10 Topics
7. Going beyond assertion and negotiating a behavior-change contract with others	_____	_____
8. Maintaining assertion in the face of someone's aggression and personal attack	_____	_____
9. Being assertive with people who force their views and values on you	_____	_____
10. Being assertive with repair people who overcharge, do not properly do the work, or do not show up for the appointment	_____	_____
11. Negotiating money and work expectations with people who work for you at home	_____	_____
12. Being assertive with high pressure sales personnel	_____	_____
13. Getting the service you deserve in stores and restaurants	_____	_____
14. Giving supervisory criticism	_____	_____
15. Presenting yourself at a task meeting where others ignore, discount, or put down your ideas	_____	_____
16. Negotiating salary increases, changes in job title or job function	_____	_____
17. Being assertive in job interviews	_____	_____
18. Presenting discrimination complaints to a business or educational employer	_____	_____
19. Being assertive with colleagues who make sexist, racist, or condescending remarks	_____	_____
20. Being assertive with intimates who are passive and shift all the responsibility to you	_____	_____
21. Expressing feelings of hurt, anger, and disappointment with people who are close to you	_____	_____

	Interest Rating 1-5	Rank Order of Top 10 Topics
Topics		

22. Expressing feelings of love, affection, and tenderness _____ _____

23. Asking for a personal commitment in a relationship _____ _____

24. Renegotiating the marriage contract or intimate relationship _____ _____

25. Being assertive and tender in sexual relationships _____ _____

26. Being assertive with people who ask for greater sexual intimacy than you'd like _____ _____

27. Responding to people who impose sex-role expectations on you _____ _____

28. Being assertive and asking for greater sexual intimacy _____ _____

29. Talking positively about your accomplishments _____ _____

30. Accepting compliments _____ _____

31. Giving compliments and expressing positive feelings _____ _____

32. Handling social conversations _____ _____

10
Assertion Training +
Consciousness-Raising Groups

A third basic type of assertion training is the semi-structured group which uses some behavior rehearsal exercises in combination with other procedures, such as values clarification, conflict resolution, and decision-making. This chapter discusses a combination of assertion training with consciousness-raising discussion and exercises.

Women's consciousness-raising groups emerged in the Sixties to achieve five basic goals: (1) to increase awareness of how women's behavior is controlled by cultural stereotypes of femininity; (2) to increase awareness of women's individuality; (3) to experience and nurture women's potency; (4) to develop feelings of acceptance for self and other women; and (5) to support women in whatever changes they make in their lives (Whiteley et al., 1973). In the Seventies, men's consciousness-raising groups are forming with similar goals: (1) to increase awareness of how men's behavior is restricted by stereotypes of masculinity and how men's expectations of women are conditioned by their stereotypes of femininity; (2) to increase men's openness and ability to admit weakness and display softness; (3) to reduce feelings of competition with other men; and (4) to challenge men to re-examine their attitudes towards themselves, women, and other men (Farrell, 1975). At this time the women's groups—more so than the men's groups—are starting to include skill-building so that the members have the skills to act on their newly acquired self-awareness. Assertion training is emerging as one of the most important skill-building strategies.

Combining assertion exercises and consciousness-raising experiences has two important benefits. *First,* consciousness-raising increases the participants' awareness that their problems are not solely individual

221

failures, but rather are a common problem due to cultural stereotypes of femininity and masculinity. This tends to reduce the participants' feelings of personal inadequacy about their failure to act assertively; when inadequacy feelings are diminished, it is often easier to act assertively. *Second,* consciousness-raising may result in major changes in how the participants view themselves, other people, and their interpersonal relationships. It is reasonable to believe that such cognitive changes would facilitate the generalization of assertion skills to new situations. For example, when a woman realizes that she acts dumb so as not to threaten men, she may more easily recognize and possibly change her nonassertive behavior in such diverse situations as failing to defend her opinions in meetings which are dominated by men to failing to express her views on a controversial movie to a male friend.

However, trainers should be aware that such consciousness-raising may result in a temporary general anger towards the opposite sex. For women, this anger is one stage of feminism (Carter, 1974). As women become aware of being treated less fairly and of not being allowed to be fully competent and powerful simply because they are women, great anger results—especially at men, who are seen as perpetuating the unfairness. Men often go through a similar anger towards women, as they recognize how women treat them as "security objects, in which they are always expected to be strong and secure—economically, emotionally, and physically" (Farrell, 1975). An additional source of resentment may be women's complaints about their own unfair treatment; these men often feel that their own problems about the masculinity myth are neglected by women.

If group members go through the anger stage of consciousness-raising, it is important that they learn how to express their anger assertively—rather than aggressively. Since assertion exercises provide some skills for dealing with discriminatory situations, the participants' sense of powerlessness, hopelessness, and resulting anger may be reduced. Thus assertion training may possibly shorten this anger stage.

STRUCTURE OF ASSERTION TRAINING + CONSCIOUSNESS-RAISING GROUPS

These groups range in size from six to ten members of the same sex. The same-sex composition of the groups facilitates self-disclosure of problems and feelings which would not ordinarily be revealed in the presence of the opposite sex. For example, in front of men, women do not as readily talk about competition, jealousy, sex, or ways they manipulate men. Likewise with women, men do not as easily talk about their resentments towards women, their sexual insecurity, competency fears, inadequacy feelings, or ways they manipulate women. In same-sex groups, self-disclosure, cohesiveness, and intimacy usually develop more quickly than in mixed-sex groups (Brumage & Willis, 1974).

When the original purpose of a group is consciousness-raising and the group goals eventually shift to assertion training, the group lasts a longer period of time. Usually eight or more months of consciousness-raising are then followed by six to eight assertion training sessions. In contrast, when assertion training is the main goal with consciousness-raising an important subcomponent, the total group sessions are fewer, usually ten to twelve in number, with consciousness-raising exercises used in conjunction with preplanned assertion topics. These consciousness-raising exercises lead to increased insight and motivation to change, after which the assertion exercises are used to promote actual behavior change.

This chapter will focus on assertion training groups which use some consciousness-raising procedures. Since the various assertion training procedures have already been described in previous chapters, this chapter will simply describe the general kinds of consciousness-raising topics and some related exercises which can be used in this type of group.

CONSCIOUSNESS-RAISING TOPICS IN WOMEN'S GROUPS

Self-Acceptance and Acceptance of Other Women
In these groups a central topic concerns the extent to which women accept other women. Many women are alienated from other women. The culture has taught them to expect women to be less intelligent than men, to be overly emotional, petty, manipulative, and weak, and to be potential competitors for men. In sum, women initially value men more highly than other women. In the process of various group discussions in which the participants *help each other* to resolve problems and share heretofore unexpressed fears and self-doubts, women come to experience each other as strong, intelligent, and supportive. This generally results in the women gradually coming to accept—not tolerate—other women and to start valuing themselves, as well as each other, as individuals and as women (Whiteley et al., 1973). As their self-acceptance

grows, the women feel more self-worth, which then makes it easier for them to refuse others' discounts, interruptions, put-downs, and to stop using manipulative games to achieve their goals.

An additional side benefit is that a sense of new-found freedom often emerges. The group members feel freed of the need to seek intellectual discussions only with men, free from feeling that the only way they can feel OK is through getting a man, and free from having to be weak and helpless as a way to get approval from other people.

Achieving Personal Power

Achieving personal power is a second important topic in these groups. The development of competence and personal power allows women to accept compliments instead of rejecting them or attributing their positive accomplishments to luck, accident, or to other people; stop automatically assuming that they are wrong when their opinions differ from other people's; ask for pay increases or job promotions instead of simply accepting the status quo; and in conversations, decrease reflecting other people's ideas and instead, increase expressing their own ideas. In short, the development of competence and personal power means ceasing to be inappropriately apologetic about their thoughts, feelings, and opinions.

Traditionally, women are supposed to act in ways which are non-threatening to other people—especially men. When women have power, it is usually more socially acceptable if it is used "behind the scenes," that is, indirectly through someone else. Many women find that showing their competence and personal power is frightening. Their biggest fear is that other people—especially men—will withdraw. The dreaded price of being a competent woman is being alone and rejected. In addition, many women fear that their competence might somehow de-masculinize men. While being unthreatening and weak holds a certain attraction by eliciting rescuing and support from other people, the price of such behavior is lowered feelings of self-respect and an increased sense of powerlessness. In the assertion training + consciousness-raising groups, women are helped to accept their competence and strength by having their basic assumptions and fears challenged. For example: Is it true that *no* man is capable of desiring and appreciating a strong woman? Is it true that *all* men must be as competent as women or even more so? Or is this belief merely part of a cultural myth? Is it true that you *cannot* live without a man? Is it true that *only* men can provide the sense of belonging that you desire? Is it true that *only* men can fulfill all of your important needs?

Women frequently dilute their personal power by using self-effacing body language in an attempt to conform to the stereotype of always being sweet and unthreatening, e.g., speaking softly and hesitantly or covering their mouth with their hands when speaking. Smiling when expressing anger is particularly common among women. Furthermore, women often engage in random smiling since they have been frequently encouraged to smile even when they have nothing to smile about ("How about a smile; life's not all that serious!" "I haven't seen you smile all evening").

Giving women permission to be strong, giving them opportunities in the group to practice using their bodies in a confident manner, examining the femininity myth are all methods which can be used to help women deal with the issue of personal power. Various consciousness-raising exercises can be used to increase women's awareness of personal power. The following exercises, which are partially modified from John Stevens' *Awareness* (1971), can be used to pave the way for the assertion exercises which are later used in the group.

Parent-Child Dialog / In this exercise, women work in pairs, one of whom plays the parent who tries to get the child to do something, e.g., go to bed, wash up, etc. The other person plays the child who tries to resist the parent. After five minutes the partners reverse roles. Afterwards the partners discuss the following questions: As the parent, what methods did you use to try to manage the child? As the child, what methods did you use to try to evade this control? Was your control open or indirect? After the pairs discuss these questions, the trainer can encourage a group discussion on how they control others through manipulation instead of assertively setting limits and expressing their feelings, how they adapt to a child role when they face another person's power, how the members can change their ineffective patterns of exerting power and responding to other people's power.

I Am—I Play / This exercise also involves partners. For three minutes, one woman describes her most salient characteristics, beginning each statement with "I am...," while the partner listens silently. The partners then reverse roles, after which the original speaker for three minutes again repeats the statement "I am..." and adds "I play...." She pauses after each statement to briefly consider the extent to which she does actually play a game and misrepresents herself. The "I am—I play" statement is then repeated a third time, and the woman adds anything that comes to her mind. For example, "I am capable. I play dumb and I don't like myself when I do that. I don't really think I fool anybody with my dumb act." Following this series of statements, the second partner follows the same pattern, repeating her own "I am—I play" statements.

Indirect No / Once again in pairs, one woman asks the other for something which she knows that the partner does not want to give her. The partner is instructed to indirectly refuse, without actually saying no. The roles are then reversed after four minutes. Both partners are asked to be aware of how they evade the other person without actually saying no. This exercise can help women become more aware of the various methods they use in avoiding directly refusing others' requests. Talking about the body tension the members experienced in this double-bind communication often helps to increase their motivation to change their nonassertive behavior. Trainers may question those women who enjoyed thwarting the other person in this exercise about what they gain by continuing the power-thwarting game and whether they really want to give it up at this time.

When women can more easily accept their strength and have a greater awareness of the ways they dilute their power and use manipulation, various assertion exercises can then be profitably used. These exercises include accepting compliments, talking positively about personal achievements, disagreeing with others' opinions, assertively stating opinions, and refusing others' requests.

Valuing One's Own Needs

A third basic issue concerns women's discounting their own needs and instead taking care of other people's needs. This is not to say that it would be desirable for women (or men) to solely attend to their own needs and to neglect other people. It is satisfying to have personal relationships where people care about each other's development and are willing to put aside some of their own needs in order to further another's growth. But for many women, there is an overemphasis on self-sacrifice and building a man's ego at the expense of the woman. Many women really believe that their needs are not as important as the needs of other people and that it is selfish for them to even want their

226

needs to be as important—and on occasion, even more important—than the needs of other people. Sometimes women even believe that their main purpose in living is to take care of other people.

In terms of assertion issues, many women have great difficulty refusing requests to solicit for charity because they perceive their own needs for rest or time for themselves to be less important than the needs of the charity solicitor—even if they are already overcommitted in their volunteer work. Moreover, some women automatically volunteer their services—even when they are not asked—upon perceiving another person's need. Women often hesitate to ask for help for fear of inconveniencing other people (e.g., asking a gasoline attendant to check the tires and water). One woman found that she did not express her anger towards her male friend because he was uncomfortable with such "emotional displays." Suppressing her anger was an attempt to protect him and to make life easier for him even though denying her feelings resulted in tension headaches for her.

Women can be helped to respect their own needs when the trainers supportively challenge their basic assumption that their needs are not important and when the trainer provides more accurate information about personal rights.

A method which can be used to help the participants become more aware of their own needs is to have the participants construct an "I want list"; for example, I want to be held when I feel sad; I want twenty minutes a day just for myself; I want to eat dinner out twice a month. The group can then discuss how realistic these wants are, how they could be achieved, etc. In some cases the participants could have close friends or mates construct their own want lists, and then discuss how each of their individual wants could be met in the relationship.

Expressing Anger

A fourth issue involves expressing anger and irritation. Generally women express hurt more easily than anger. Women often fear that expressing their anger will cause other people to withdraw or to dislike them. Some women have found that when they have been openly angry, they were criticized for being unattractive or overly emotional. While a male's rage is often considered manly, a woman's rage is more likely to be viewed as hysterical or shrewish. In other cases women have simply not learned how to constructively express their anger with other people. Instead, they have directed it inwards on themselves and have

227

become depressed, or they have indirectly expressed anger through snide comments or in passive-aggressive ways. Sometimes women cry when they are extremely angry. These tears are the result of simultaneous feelings of great anger and helplessness in being unable to make an impact on the other person.

In assertion training + consciousness-raising groups, a trainer needs to help members realize that all people—females and males—have the right to have angry feelings. However, having the right to experience anger does not also entail automatically expressing these feelings. Sometimes anger is illegitimate in the sense that it is not caused by others violating personal rights, but instead occurs when other people simply do not conform to one's expectations. For example: "My son *should* keep his room neat—I get very angry when he doesn't"; "When I ask my secretary for some information, he *should* have the information immediately at his fingertips"; "Students *should* want to do a good job in school and study hard." In such cases, expressing immediate anger would be inappropriate. The rational self-analysis method (see Chapter 4) could be used to help women reduce their excessive anger in these situations. At other times, a woman may discover that she is using anger to cover up other feelings, such as anxiety, hurt, and disappointment—feelings which she believes she has no right to experience. Here it is important that a trainer help the participants become aware of their hurt and disappointment and learn to express these feelings instead of, or in addition to, expressing their anger.

Besides helping the group members to discriminate when it is appropriate to express anger, a trainer can use exercises which give the participants permission to express anger. One such exercise involves one member facing each of the other group members in turn. As she faces them, she completes the sentence stem "I can get angry when. . . ." After each statement, a group member gives "permission" for the woman to experience and express her anger; for example, "I can accept your anger"; "I prefer it when you tell me directly when you're mad"; "I get angry too and I can live with your anger." Trainers can also use cognitive restructuring procedures to help the participants deal with their anger, for example, having them concentrate on some of the following thoughts when they become aware of the fact that they are suppressing legitimate irritation: "My anger won't destroy people," or "I have a right to be angry in this situation."

These exercises are not intended to produce anger, but instead are designed to give women permission to directly express their legitimate grievances.

In addition to the exercises for women's groups described in this section, other procedures may be found in Osborn & Harris (1975), Phelps & Austin (1975), and Bloom, Coburn & Pearlman (1975).

CONSCIOUSNESS-RAISING TOPICS IN MEN'S GROUPS
Since men and women who join assertion training groups are more likely to have problems with nonassertion than with aggression (although the two problems interrelate as discussed in Chapter 2), many of the topics raised in the men's groups will be the same as those raised in the women's groups. Nonetheless, some issues are more characteristic of men's groups.

Listening to Other People
According to Warren Farrell, author of *The Liberated Man* (1975), a major issue in men's groups involves helping them to learn how to listen to other men rather than doing "self-listening." This self-listening process involves (1) listening to the first statement or two that the other person makes, (2) assuming that he knows what will be said next, and (3) starting to form his own story, which is related to his own ego or accomplishments, *while the other person is still talking.* This self-listening process is subtly different from listening to the other person talk and then trying to relate to oneself what that person is saying so that one can make a self-disclosing statement as an entrance *into* the conversation. When an individual is only trying to get *into* a conversation—instead of trying to get the conversation *away* from another person—the individual usually ends his self-disclosing remarks with a question or comment directed back to the other person, which results in the other person coming back into the conversation. In contrast, self-listening is used as an attempt to dominate the discussion and as a way of cutting off other people. In terms of assertion, being able to accurately listen to other people is important so that one does not discount or cut off another person's legitimate points, and thus inadvertently engage in aggressive behavior.

In his consciousness-raising groups, Farrell uses several exercises to promote men's genuine listening to each other. One such exercise involves starting off each group session with the question, "What's been happening with you this week?" which each man is asked in turn.

During this time, no interruptions are permitted. Sometimes the group is instructed to have a minute of silence after each man's contribution, during which time the members silently reflect upon what the speaker has said.

Self-Disclosing of Vulnerability

A second major issue concerns the participants' becoming self-revealing and expressing their personal feelings, rather than intellectualizing or pontificating. Since the masculinity myth calls for men to always be strong, confident, knowledgeable, and striving, it is often threatening for men to reveal weakness, sadness, anxiety, and fear, which are often initially viewed as feminine behavior. However, when a trainer shows no embarrassment in his own self-disclosures and encourages the participants to support and share their feelings, the men gradually start to feel freed of the burden of having to always be strong. In addition, a trainer can use cognitive restructuring procedures to replace the unrealistic socialization messages with more healthy ones (see Table 7, p. 235).

Many of the participants find revealing their vulnerability in front of women particularly difficult. Their main fear is that women may think they are less of a man. Unfortunately, this sometimes does happen, especially with those women who discount their own competence and personal power and rely on men to take care of them. However, many other women welcome such displays of male vulnerability and are supportive when men express these feelings. A trainer can help men to express their vulnerabilities by pointing out that it is human to feel scared and vulnerable at times. Furthermore, men who cover up these feelings pay the price of using their energy to conceal their feelings from other people, and consequently have less energy to be genuine in relationships. Increased sharing of vulnerability also leads to relationships which are emotionally close and more satisfying.

When men try to conceal their vulnerability, aggressive behavior may result. For example, instead of admitting that he had made an error in balancing the family checkbook, one man blamed his mate for not double checking the check stubs. Another man, while carrying his young child, accidentally bumped the child's head against the wall. Instead of admitting his carelessness and fear that he had hurt the child, he attacked his wife for her failure to offer to help him with their child.

Trainers can use discussion topics such as "Times I have felt rejected" or "What do I presently feel most vulnerable about this group

230

discovering about me?" to help the group members to become more self-revealing. Farrell also suggests having the members anonymously write their response to the question, "What would a woman have to do to make me vulnerable?" after which the papers are shuffled and each member reads another's response to the group.

Reducing Competitive Feelings
A third issue concerns the men's feelings of competition with other men and women. This competition frequently involves proving that the man is as potent and as intelligent as other men. It is generally more difficult for the group members to discuss their feelings of competition with women. Since many men have accepted the masculinity myth that they should always be competent and the femininity myth that women are weak, when a woman proves to be more competent than a man, the man often feels very threatened and highly competitive. Strong feelings of competition usually result in attempts to make the other person feel less adequate and not-OK. Thus, aggressive behavior is often associated with strong competitive feelings. Trainers can help the participants to deal with their strong competitive feelings by pointing out that such strong feelings are enslaving, result in constant pressure, and often in increased vulnerability because energies are used to worry about other people's greater or equal competence, instead of being used to learn from other people.

In the group, a trainer can use the general discussion topic of "How do I feel competitive at work, in the group, and with my women friends?" to stimulate insight and to promote change. Farrell also uses an exercise in which the group members, in pairs, draw a picture together. Afterwards, the group analyzes how the picture was developed, who created the basic design, how decisions were made as the picture was created, who dominated, and what feelings of jealousy and competition were evoked.

Expressing Affection
A fourth common issue concerns difficulty in directly expressing affection and liking for other people, especially other men. Rather than openly expressing their joy at seeing a male friend, many men cover up their feelings with aggressive sarcastic comments, such as one man who said to a male friend, "Where have you been—hiding under a rock? I wouldn't blame you if you were, with that Buster Brown haircut," to

231

which the friend retorted, "Sure. You think I'd want to waste my time talking with you?" Personal relationships are kept at a distance when men have great difficulty expressing tender feelings. For example, it is not uncommon for two men to separately confide in a mutual woman friend that they like each other. But when the two men are together, they may be frequently sarcastic to each other and give every indication of mutual dislike. Some unmarried older men may have trouble forming close male relationships if they fear that overtures of friendship or affection will be perceived as sexual advances. Finally, many group members often have difficulty displaying affection through touching each other. As one man said, "When I see another man that I feel close to, the first thing that happens is my hand leaps out—like an automatic jerk—when I'd really prefer to hug him. But I'd feel awkward doing that!" Although men are usually more comfortable with touching women, for many men, their touching is more of an attempt at domination or sexuality, than it is an expression of affection and tenderness.

Farrell suggests that one way in which a trainer can help group members deal with these affection issues is to have the participants form a circle and hold hands while talking in the group. Another procedure involves having the members read their own poems to one man and then the whole group. These procedures are intended to help men get in touch with their own tenderness and to feel at ease when expressing these feelings. The Giving and Receiving Compliments exercise described in Chapter 4 may follow naturally as a skill-building exercise in asserting positive feelings toward other people.

SUMMARY
The third basic type of group is a semi-structured assertion training group which uses behavioral rehearsal exercises in combination with other therapeutic procedures—in this case, consciousness-raising discussion and exercises. In the women's assertion training + consciousness-raising groups, common topics include accepting other women, achieving personal power, valuing personal needs, and expressing anger. For the men's groups, common consciousness-raising topics include listening to other people instead of self-listening, disclosing vulnerability, reducing strong feelings of personal competition, and expressing affection for other people, especially other men.

REVIEW QUESTIONS AND EXERCISES

1. What are some advantages of using consciousness-raising experiences in an assertion training group?

2. Why are women's groups concerned with issues of personal power while men's groups are more likely to be dealing with expressing affection?

3. What are some methods a trainer can use to help the group members deal with personal power issues?

4. Evaluate this statement: Trainers should be primarily concerned with helping their group members to take care of their own needs and to cease worrying about the needs of other people.

5. Evaluate this statement: Trainers should help the group participants to get in touch with their angry feelings and learn how to immediately express them.

6. What is self-listening?

7. How is aggression related to attempts to cover up a sense of personal vulnerability?

8. How is aggression related to strong feelings of personal competition?

9. How is helping group members feel comfortable expressing affection related to assertion?

10. Read the following materials which were cited in this chapter: Whiteley et al. (1973), Stevens (1971), Osborn & Harris (1975), Farrell (1975), Bloom, Coburn & Pearlman (1975), Phelps & Austin (1975).

11. Conduct the following exercises with a group of friends: Parent-Child Dialog, I Am—I Play, and Indirect No. Tape record your session and assess the degree to which your directions were clear, your discussion questions helpful and supportive, and the extent to which you facilitated the group members' self-understanding.

12. Observe your own behavior while carrying on social conversations. Check the degree to which you engage in self-listening.

13. Observe yourself during the week and notice the degree to which you express vulnerability instead of covering it up.

14. Observe yourself during the week and notice how you express affection to other people and how you respond to other people's affectionate overtures.

Table 7
Men's Common Socialization Messages

Socialization Message	Healthy Message
Keep your feelings to yourself. Don't bother other people with your feelings.	It is undesirable to incessantly complain about personal problems. However, it is rigidity and not true strength to cover up vulnerability. Sharing your own scared and sad feelings is not the same as being a weakling. Such sharing brings you closer to other people. It takes courage and true strength to risk revealing your feelings to other people.
Be thoroughly competent. Don't be lazy, strive to be the best.	It is undesirable to give up at the first sign of difficulty. However, always trying to be the best is not only impossible, it is undesirable. All human beings have limitations and so it is impossible to be more competent than other people in all areas of life. Moreover, constant striving results in your neglecting other important needs.
Take care of yourself. Don't depend on other people. Don't be a weakling.	It is undesirable to always rely on others for help, especially when you don't need it. However, you are not a weakling just because you need some help occasionally. Instead, it's weak *not to ask* for help when you need it. No man is an island unto himself. All human beings have some desires for support, help, and encouragement. Other people are more likely to give this to you if you ask for it directly and let other people know what your problems are and what you want.

Socialization Message

Be logical. Use your head. Don't give in to irrational feelings.

Healthy Message

It is undesirable to respond to every life situation solely on a feeling basis. A full human being is one who can think *and* also feel. Feelings don't have to be irrational. By keeping in contact with your feelings, you can make better judgments about your life. If you take the time and patience to understand your feelings and to allow yourself to experience them, they will not be alien and scary. When your feelings seem like an overreaction, you can analyze them and change the thoughts that produce these feelings. This is more healthy and productive than simply trying to ignore or suppress your feelings. Feelings do not go away by simply trying to ignore their existence. Instead, they merely go underground and cause worse problems in the long run.

Be cool. Don't be a softy and express affectionate and tender feelings, especially towards men.

It is undesirable to constantly display tender feelings. However, it's healthy and normal to be able to express truly felt affectionate feelings towards others when one wishes. Being able to express such feelings results in closer relationships. Expressing tenderness, joy, and affection is not the same thing as sex. Touching another person in an affectionate manner does not necessarily have to arouse sexual feelings in the other person.

11
General Applications of Training Groups

When considering the possible contexts for employing assertion training, we are struck by the great potential for its application. When viewed as a means to facilitate more direct and honest communication, assertion training procedures can be a valuable contribution to almost any interactive context. The limitations on its effect are more a function of the present level of assertiveness and a person's readiness to be involved. In this chapter, we will identify and briefly describe some of the specific contexts and special populations who can utilize assertion training. It is important to note that although we are citing specific populations, assertion training groups can also be offered to a general population which has no particular commonality among the participants.

HIGHER EDUCATION
Assertion training is widely offered on college campuses to students, faculty, and staff, usually through the university counseling center or continuing education.

The university setting can be a highly interactive experience. Assertion training is offered to help participants maximize their university experience. The training focus is primarily on how the participants can be more effective in their social and educational interactions. More specifically, participants might work on improving their social skills, speaking up in classes, initiating interactions with professors, dealing assertively with university staff and administrators, giving presentations, relating to their parents, dealing with living companions. The situations are unlimited.

The outcome goal is to enable the participants to give and get what they want in what can be a highly stimulating environment. This goal applies to other members of the university community as well as to students. Assertion training groups have been conducted with civil service staff, professors, professional academic staff (academic advisors, librarians, administrators), coaches, campus police, and student affairs staff (housing, financial aids, admissions, career planning, student activities) to enable them to function more assertively in their positions. Assertion training procedures also have been utilized in student leadership training programs. Peer counselors have used assertion training procedures with ethnic minority students to enable them to get their needs met in the university. Residence hall staff have particularly profited from assertion training in conjunction with basic counseling skills training as they function on the front line with students. Assertion groups have been conducted with married couples (usually graduate students) who are often at a highly stressful period in their lives when great financial, time, and energy demands are made upon them. Particularly when both partners participate, the assertion group experience greatly facilitates straighter communication and diminishes the potential for tension buildups. In addition, assertion training procedures have been employed in a number of undergraduate credit courses (usually in psychology or education) on communication skills, applied behavioral principles, personal growth, classroom or group process, the psychology of women, and psychological self-help. Naturally, graduate courses on how to do assertion training and behavioral counseling and therapy are also being offered in psychology, education, and other helping professions including rehabilitation counseling, pastoral counseling, corrections, and business management.

Several counseling skills trainers (e.g., counselor educators) have begun a highly promising integration of assertion training with their regular counseling skills training programs. These trainers have recognized that the more active skills like confrontation, interpretation, and self-disclosure require considerable personal assertiveness. Trainees, then, not only learn the specific counseling skills but also, through assertion procedures, work on any cognitive, emotional, or behavioral blocks, thus helping them to utilize the skills effectively. The addition of assertion training is crucial to counselor skills training, which often has not attended adequately to personal trainee dynamics which might mitigate against effective use of the new counseling skills.

238

Career development services have utilized assertion training in their programs (see Chapter 12). Much attention has been given to the question of the effect of personal qualities on the academic success of students admitted without meeting the regular admissions criteria. On many campuses assertion training has been integrated into a larger training program to help these students function more effectively in the educational community.

We believe that the atmosphere of an institution can be effectively altered toward greater mutual respect and appreciation as people become more assertive with each other. The goal is not a new one; assertion training procedures, however, provide an effective, relevant approach to meeting individual needs for interpersonal growth.

The following is a more detailed account of one creative application of assertion training procedures to a specific population within the university setting. One author conducted an assertion training workshop with the faculty, staff, and students who would be running a ten-week pre-entrance academic skill-building program primarily with black and native American students. The workshop participants decided to conduct assertion training groups as part of this summer program for several reasons. *First*, previous students experienced a typical lack of assertiveness including situational anxiety, irrational thinking and catastrophizing, low self-image, and situational behavior deficits. The workshop participants learned the rationale and procedures for conducting assertion groups (each group included at least one experienced counselor). They also devised a number of exercises and scenes for stimulus video tapes which were appropriate to the students in the program and the situations they were likely to encounter. Much of the focus was on interaction between students and faculty or administrators: getting information and clarification from professors in class, expressing opinions in class, discussing an issue in class, talking with a professor after class (either seeking information, expressing opinions, or asking for help). The groups focused on social interactions (e.g., dating, handling roommate conflicts, dealing with subtle racial conflict) and college-related interactions with administrators and counselors.

Second, the assertion training model was utilized to build a support system within the groups. Utilizing the positive assertion exercises and genuine positive reinforcement, the groups began to serve as a locus of support for each member.

Third, the assertion procedures dealt with several intrapsychic dynamics which have occurred with some students in previous years. The students in this program had demonstrated their ability to do college work (through high school grades and admissions tests), although they fell in the low percentiles of the entering class. Many students in this program preferred to take care of their own needs; they were often fearful of looking stupid in class, feared rejection or condescension, and felt stigmatized even by being invited to such a pre-entrance program. In some cases, when the student did get behind or did not understand some important academic material, he did not seek assistance and tended to deny that anything was going wrong. Getting some students to "face the facts" realistically required more than straight confrontation. The group leaders utilized the cognitive restructuring procedures and, at times, the rehearsal procedures to discuss and challenge the basic underlying irrational assumptions, catastrophizing, and abdication of personal rights. The leaders identified these dysfunctional patterns of thinking and behaving, and discussed how the underlying values and assumptions could work against the students when they denied or avoided. For example, if a student acted as if nothing was wrong when he was clearly getting behind in his academic work, the issue could be openly discussed in the group.

The ultimate goals for the summer program were to help students to utilize their own cognitive capabilities and to help them to utilize maximally the university's resources. The assertion training segment of the program focused on the often neglected cognitive and behavioral dynamics which can interfere with personal effectiveness. Specifically, the outcome goals for the assertion groups were: (1) to increase the students' repertoire of assertive responses in academic and other college-related interactions, (2) to reduce anxiety in those situations, (3) to increase self-confidence, (4) to increase student utilization of college resources (faculty, counselors, tutors, study skills specialists, advisors) *when appropriate*, (5) to change the irrational thinking regarding fear of appearing dumb and fear of stigmatization, (6) to learn to discriminate between those professors and staff who will be responsive and those who will not, and (7) to build a positive support system among the members of the group where they directly express support and concern for each other.

SECONDARY AND ELEMENTARY EDUCATION

Assertion training has been utilized with teachers, counselors, administrators, and students. Psychological education instructors have incorporated assertion training procedures into their courses. For students, this training is a useful procedure to help them deal with the typical developmental concerns of their age (see Steel & Hochmann, in press, a, b, c; Rausbaum-Selig, in press). Interestingly, in conducting assertion training with teachers, the focus of rehearsals was as much on interactions with peers, supervisors, principals, parents, and central administration specialists as with students.

OTHER PROFESSIONAL PSYCHOLOGY SETTINGS

Therapists have utilized assertion training with in-patients to reduce anxiety and to help them respond effectively to hospital personnel. Essentially, training has often led to a greater sense of control and direction. Assertion training has also been utilized in conjunction with other treatment modes with both in-patients and out-patients. Many community mental health centers are also offering assertion groups as a personal growth and preventive mental health program, with mental health staff also joining the training group.

A number of counselors and psychologists in correctional settings conduct assertion groups to help inmates function more effectively while in the highly restrictive prison setting and, even more importantly, to handle assertively those situations likely to be encountered upon release. Some corrections counselors report using a more practical approach to justifying learning assertive behaviors, particularly with aggressive inmates, i.e., "You're likely to wind up in the slammer again if you don't start functioning more effectively, so why not try it and see if it pays off?"

Psychologists in private practice and at private institutes (such as the Institute for Rational Living in New York) are regularly offering assertion training groups to the general population as well as specific subgroups.

Pastoral counselors, social workers, youth group counselors, and crisis response counselors have employed assertion training procedures. Rehabilitation counselors have conducted assertion training groups with disabled persons, particularly focusing on how the participants can deal assertively with persons who treat them in an overly protective or solicitous manner. The positive nature of assertion training and its focus on maintaining personal strengths and improving less effective qualities leaves many participants with a greater sense of self-worth.

Police have also participated in assertion training groups to help them to be more effective in their relations with all segments of the public, often within extremely tense situations, e.g., intervening in marriage conflicts, dealing with accident scenes, handling verbal abuse to themselves. The assertive behaviors policemen practice are more appropriate to being in a powerful authority position, recognizing the need for quick and decisive control of situations in an assertive, rather than aggressive, manner.

BUSINESS MANAGEMENT

The recent application of assertion training to business and governmental organizations is a most exciting development. Assertion training procedures can be utilized to help colleagues function more effectively with each other. Supervisors and managers learn to be more effective with their staffs, in conducting meetings, in confronting their staff members with problems or criticisms, in dealing with others as a representative of the company.

Assertion training can be easily integrated into ongoing personnel or management training programs, particularly those which focus on organizational development. The National Training Labs (NTL) people have opened some important doors in the business world with mixed success. Assertion training, however, offers a more direct, behavioral approach to the same goal: increasing personal effectiveness within the organization. Some enterprises (particularly those offering professional services such as medical and dental offices) have had their entire staff participate in assertion training to help the staff members function more effectively with each other and their clientele. Assertion training can also focus on business interactions outside the company itself, such as with salesmen, consultants, or service personnel. Many personnel training programs incorporate a number of the principles of cognitive restructuring and behavior rehearsal.

PROFESSIONAL ORGANIZATIONS

A number of associations have arranged assertion training groups and workshops for their membership either at conventions, regional meetings, or independently. Such groups as the American Association of University Women, the Junior League, an Ananda Marga Yoga society, affirmative action groups, city and county committees and organizations, teachers organizations, and mental health and medical services organizations.

WOMEN'S MOVEMENT

Assertiveness as a personal quality has become a major focus of the women's movement. Assertion groups for women are often conducted in conjunction with some form of consciousness-raising (see Chapter 10). In addition to a number of the contexts already cited, women's assertion groups are offered through the many women's centers located throughout the country. Two important outcomes of women's assertion groups is that women are recognizing and standing up for their personal rights and they are seeking each other out more frequently to fulfill a wider range of their needs. In this sense, assertion training is a valuable experience for persons working toward increased personal freedom.

Some women's groups have focused on very specific concerns. For example, one group dealt with assertiveness in regard to sexuality and worked on situations like initiating contacts with others, accepting and rejecting the initiatives of others, communicating to sexual partners what is enjoyable and what is not, and getting complete information from a gynecologist. Another group focused on assertiveness in their professional positions, not only dealing with being more assertive in their work, but also dealing with colleagues who supported their nonassertive behavior and who were uncomfortable with the women's new assertive behaviors.

In a time when increased personal freedom is an obtainable goal, assertion training becomes even more valuable as the participants recognize their ability to accept such freedom and to act assertively with it.

SUMMARY

The contexts and populations for which assertion training might be helpful are virtually limitless. Particularly exciting are the applications of assertion training in business and government (with supervisors, fellow workers, and persons having public contact) and with service professionals (nurses, teachers, university faculty and staff, lawyers, police, corrections personnel, mental health professionals, physicians).

In addition, families, couples, students, children, and individuals in general are participating in assertion groups conducted through women's centers, mental health centers, private practitioners, growth centers, universities, residential mental health facilities, and pastoral counseling services.

REVIEW QUESTIONS

Identify a segment of the population (business persons, families, educators) and cite specific ways that assertion training might be beneficial.

12
Assertion Training for Job Interviewing and Management/Staff Development
by Thomas V. McGovern

> You can't eat for eight hours a day nor drink for eight hours a
> day nor make love for eight hours a day—all you can do for eight
> hours is work. Which is the reason why man makes himself and
> everybody else so miserable and unhappy.
>
> William Faulkner
> (Quoted in *Working,* by Studs Terkel)

For many people, Faulkner's description of work rests upon their inability or unwillingness to choose other alternatives. They often feel powerless to change. However, change becomes conceivable and even attainable when we can shift our expectations and acquire the skills necessary to realize them. There is a significant difference in the quality of our occupational experiences when we seek satisfaction and do not settle for less. We have a right to look for the personal growth which comes from fully utilizing our talents and abilities. Such a belief necessitates an awareness of our needs, an understanding of what specific work environments can offer, and the ability to communicate our needs to those with whom and for whom we work. It is to this end that assertion training is particularly effective in career development groups. The training paradigm combines cognitive and affective self-awareness with behavioral skills. For this reason, assertion training can be used with diverse populations and problems of career development. The common denominator is that the potential for finding fulfillment in our work lives will be increased by the ability to communicate thoughts, opinions, and feelings in a personally satisfying and effective manner.

245

The following sections will describe several groups and settings in which assertion training techniques are particularly helpful. A systematic training program for job interviewers and interviewees will be presented to illustrate the step-by-step application of these skills.

POTENTIAL APPLICATIONS

College Students

Many students seem locked into a pervasive indecisiveness; to make any choice is viewed as potentially catastrophic. In such a frozen state, educational or occupational information is not heard or integrated, much less actively pursued.

While such a general behavior pattern may be labeled as a clinical problem rather than a vocational one, it can be initially addressed in the context of career choice. Even with generally nonassertive people, the assertion training focus on specific situations provides a starting point for movement out of an established pattern. In the career counseling framework, the selection of a college major, a particular job position, or a work setting can provide a concrete issue around which the client and counselor can develop a hierarchy of specific behavioral tasks. What is more difficult in working with these individuals than with a situational skills group is the greater amount of time spent on cognitive-affective exploration and restructuring. A case example may be helpful here.

Frances is a young woman whose parents were both college educated and in the medical profession. Her two older sisters and one brother pursued academic degrees in the sciences and were in graduate and medical school programs. During her first two years at school, Frances frustrated a series of academic advisors by her apparent inability to choose any major field. Many of the advisors simply programmed her into introductory level courses hoping that something would tap her interests and inspire some motivation. She was finally advised to see a career development counselor before registering for her junior year.

Frances was well aware of the resources available to her on campus. She knew exactly where to seek information about majors and departmental requirements. Yet, she vigorously defended her undecidedness and was unwilling to move from that position. After several sessions devoted completely to Frances' self-exploration, it became apparent to both Frances and the counselor that parental expectations dictated that she pursue a medical or scientific career. Frances hated every course she had ever taken in that area, but accomplished good grades out of fear of offending her parents. Through self-exploration, Frances identified the anxiety which sprang up every time she even considered a different career path. This anxiety was clearly tied to her cognitive expectations about her parents' reactions to a deviant occupational choice. The anxiety made the process of seeking information about other fields impossible.

As Frances gradually became more aware and accepting of her lack of interest in the sciences, she was more willing to look at alternatives. The results of her interest assessment inventory presented a profile of a person much more interested in artistic and helping-social occupations than in scientific ones. Although she had made the decision to explore other alternatives, Frances still construed each act of information-seeking as turning away from her parents' wishes. There remained a great deal of anxiety in taking the steps to change. Since the goal of assertion training is for individuals to respond to their needs and communicate those needs more effectively, it was at this point that assertion skills became applicable for Frances.

In seeking information about major fields, Frances chose art as her starting point. With the counselor, she constructed a hierarchy of tasks, which included: (1) writing a letter to a national association for information on careers in art, (2) asking the secretary in the art department for their handout on curriculum requirements, (3) talking with a graduate student in the art program, (4) calling to make an appointment to discuss courses, (5) talking with the art department advisor about a major, (6) talking with an art graduate who now runs a business, (7) declaring to the art department advisor her intent to major in that area, and (8) registering for courses with her new major. At each step, the counselor used a combination of structured assertion exercises and behavior rehearsal. Her anxiety began to decrease until step five when the discussion with an advisor about a major brought home her movement towards personal independence. Actually registering for the courses was another "crossing the Rubicon" event. Yet with each task, her confidence and ability to communicate her opinions and feelings increased. The assertion training for specific tasks had the effect of making a tentative decision to choose art, not science, more gradual and manageable. It also enhanced her interpersonal skills so that the subsequent work on asserting herself with her parents became easier.

Working with groups of students who are pervasively indecisive can be equally productive. There will be the same initial focus on self-exploration and cognitive restructuring with an emphasis on peer learning in the process. Some common sharing by students of the heavy expectations laid upon them by others starts off as griping. When they have vented their spleen, some active work in behavioral change can occur and is facilitated by the mutual support in the group. After exploring and tentatively understanding some of the common bases for indecisiveness, the group members are encouraged to define a set of reasonable goals to be achieved by them during the life of the group. These goals are then structured into specific behavioral tasks implemented on a weekly basis. The tasks generally involve a range of information-seeking activities which require some form of personal interaction. The interactions range from asking a librarian a question to interviewing a faculty member about departmental requirements or major career opportunities.

The use of assertion skills in a group is grounded both in the nature of the career development tasks and the goals of the training paradigm. Career development as a process of expanding self-awareness and information-seeking via personal communication can be broken down into a series of specific tasks. The anxiety aroused by each of these tasks, or all of them taken together, can be addressed effectively by assertion training. The desired outcome is for individuals to gather increased confidence through success in situation-specific problems, and thereby increase their potential for independent decision-making in the overall career development process.

University Personnel Staff

While the major emphasis in student career development is on planning for satisfying work experience, persons already employed are more concerned with actual job satisfaction. Some of the major issues for these persons are morale, supervisor-employee relations, feedback on work performance, and the conditions of the physical and interpersonal work environment. Most are reasonably content with their selection of an occupational area and their current job position. However, they do voice fears and some anxiety over handling specific interpersonal conflicts which arise on the job. It is to this end that assertion training is especially helpful.

The emphasis on skills training also provides an approachable experience for many who have reservations and stereotypes about what goes on in a "group." It is important for the trainer to be sensitive to these stereotypes and consequent fears. In the first session, it is useful to stress that the group will be using training as a professional development lab in which the members control which issues will be raised. The prohibition on negative feedback to one another and the stress on specific, positive feedback raises some skepticism at first, but has been recalled by members at follow-up sessions as a principal factor in reducing fearful expectations.

The training format follows closely the one described in Chapter 8. The first three sessions are structured and integrate assertion exercises with cognitive material on the rationale of the skills and discrimination between assertive, nonassertive, and aggressive responses. Subsequent sessions (typically three) are devoted to behavior rehearsals in which the members bring to the group specific situations in which they would like to change or expand their ways of responding. Homework between sessions focuses on applying the material covered in the session to their individual work setting (e.g., recognition of nonverbal components of behavior, identification of personal rights, and possible responses to a conflict situation).

Several comments about the process of an assertion training group with this population are appropriate here. Drawing upon the encounter group research by Lieberman, Yalom & Miles (1973), the most successful training experiences have been those in which the trainer has been able to communicate both insight about the skills as well as a caring for each member's attempts to try them in real life. Even more importantly, members learn most significantly from one another in an atmosphere that is safe and fairly unrestricted in content. In practical terms, this often means that the trainer should allow a group of secretaries or supervisors to trade common experiences and to offer one another alternatives for dealing with the worker who burps too loudly or the boss who expects too much. Such a discussion is not just advice or chatter, but the nuts and bolts of daily job satisfaction. Such an exchange gives a member the opportunity to hear a range of alternatives, establish a conviction that change is possible, *then* concentrate on the behavioral means of more effective communication.

There is a final note about a general assertion training program. When it comes to being assertive in situations which may have serious consequences on an individual's employment (e.g., loss of job), the trainees should understand that they are always the ones to choose how to respond. This is consistent with the explicit goals of training which stress individuals communicating in their own personally satisfying and effective manner. There are no absolute "shoulds" promulgated by the training or the trainer. This conviction is also important when trainees consider generalizing newly acquired assertion skills from employees at the office to a spouse or close friend in their personal lives. The skills may be tried out with different people, but the impact and ground rules should be carefully assessed for their emotional clout.

In addition to a general assertion program for university personnel, the assertion training model can be useful for more specific job functions. For example, as part of a supervisory management training program, assertion skills can be included to facilitate the giving of positive and critical feedback on employee job performance. It is surprising that many supervisors do not recognize the need or feel comfortable in giving appropriate praise for a job well done. A review of the job satisfaction research clearly shows the importance of employees knowing both what the supervisor expects and how well they meet those expectations. Focusing on positive feedback usually initiates a discussion on the ability (or inability) of the supervisors to receive feedback either from their subordinates or their direct bosses. By becoming more aware of their own sensitivity to feedback, supervisors are better able to understand the employees' right to know their personal evaluation. Supervisors are then able to focus on the skills necessary to communicate their evaluation in a direct, honest, and appropriate manner.

There is an interesting side effect in using the assertion training model with supervisory staff. While some bring the expectation that assertiveness is equated with the ability to be tough (spelled *aggressive*) with their employees, the opposite can become evident. Much of the need to be tough arises from the fear of being unable to handle conflict or pressure situations. The anxiety of the situation and the ego involvement can encourage an overkill response. Through assertion training, supervisors can become more aware of the causes of their anxiety and practice being assertive in specific contexts. As their sense of control and confidence in handling a situation increases, their ability to be empathic and respond first to the employees' feelings or needs also increases. Their capacity to listen and still communicate their feelings and opinions grows in tandem.

One of the most difficult problems to deal with during assertion training with employed persons is unresolvable conflict. The caveat that being assertive means control over one's own behavior but not of another is little solace in an "unbearable" situation. Whether the trainee is a supervisor or an employee, there will be times when the very best and most consistent of responses falls upon deaf ears. I have seen individuals try to escalate the issue and almost come to blows or to depression over their inability to have any impact. For an employee faced with such a situation, the most assertive response may very well be to seek another position if the environment is unyielding. For a supervisor, the most assertive response may be to terminate an individual for just causes. This is one of the realities which makes assertion training so applicable to so many contexts—there is no packaged set of responses. Individuals must literally struggle sometimes to keep communication with one another open and direct. Yet, just that willingness to struggle may produce a satisfaction and honesty during work hours which was seldom previously experienced.

ASSERTION TRAINING FOR JOB INTERVIEWS*

For many people, a job interview is an important event which can provoke a great deal of anxiety and immobilize a person's ability to communicate effectively. Both the new interviewer and the inexperienced interviewee can perceive similar importance for the interview, and thereby suffer the same anxiety. For the interviewer, each interview is a measure of the ability to assess a qualified candidate and relate to that candidate in such a way that one's employer is well represented. Good judgment is expected of the interviewer; poor judgment may come back to haunt. For the typical interviewee, an interview becomes a proving ground both for personal self-esteem and career goals. The success of a job interview is often perceived as a validation that four years of college preparation or years of prior work experience mean something tangible. With such ego involvement of interviewer and inter-

* The material in this section on training interviewees is based in part on T. McGovern, D. Tinsley, N. Liss-Levinson, R. Laventure & G. Britton. Assertion training for job interviews, *The Counseling Psychologist*, in press.

viewee in this process, it is not surprising to see perspiration output by the bucket preceding and following thirty minutes in the arena!

A systematic program to prepare individuals to handle the role of either interviewer or interviewee can be divided into four basic components:

1. Explanation of the stages and specific objectives of an interview.
2. Discrimination of aggressive, assertive, and nonassertive ways of responding.
3. Definition of personal rights for the interviewer and interviewee.
4. Application of specific training exercises and assertion skills to meet the demands of the interview context.

The first three components of the program are cognitive in nature and can therefore be handled in a didactic manner in a large group. The fourth component, which includes exercises and behavior rehearsal, should be restricted to a small group setting with approximately six to eight members per trainer. The smaller the group, the more opportunities for the members to experience new ways of responding and discover for themselves a personally satisfying, assertive means to handle the interview.

The following is an example of how a trainer might introduce this program for interviewers or interviewees:

An interview is like any other interaction between two relative strangers. The quality of the experience depends a great deal on the skill of the two participants. However, there is a certain intangible chemistry in mixing together two personal styles. Because this chemistry is so unpredictable, it would be a disservice to either interviewer or interviewee to be programmed with a packaged set of questions/responses. There is a plethora of "how to—do's & don'ts" literature in the popular market which perpetuate stereotypes rather than encourage individual differences.

The goal of this training program is for the interviewer or interviewee to discriminate what is assertive, to develop a wide repertoire of verbal and nonverbal skills applicable to the interview (and more), and to be able to choose an appropriate response based upon the criteria of personal preference and satisfaction.

The trainer will facilitate the accomplishment of these goals by placing minimal emphasis on modeling a correct way of handling a particular interview situation. Rather, a variety of ways can be elicited from the group members, with every individual responsible for choosing one consistent with personal style. The norm of positive feedback between group members reinforces these goals. Each member comes to the interview with some level of sensitivity and skill. The training serves to identify these skills, enhance them, and facilitate their use as a means of inhibiting the anxiety of the interview. The extent to which any interviewer/interviewee can internalize their own criteria for a successful interaction will be a good indicator of their ability to handle the unpredictable job interview.

1. Stages and Objectives of an Interview

Some basic objectives of an interviewee would include: to communicate information about oneself, to seek information about the particular job position and employer, and to be able to make a tentative decision about the match between personal needs and what the job offers. The interviewer's objectives are similar: to gather relevant information about the candiate's qualifications, to assess how well these qualifications match the job requirements, and to promote the organization and thereby attract the best people for the position. While these objectives sound fairly concrete, the process of accomplishing them remains less specific. The assessment by the interviewer tends to be impressionistic and based a great deal upon the quality of the interviewee's communication.

In trying to provide some benchmarks for the ongoing process of communication and assessment, it is helpful to define four stages of an interview. The stages are not meant to be hard and fast boundaries, but a basic framework within which the objectives of both interviewer and interviewee can be accomplished.

Stage 1 "Breaking the Ice" / Because this is an interaction between two strangers, small talk chatter quite literally serves to "break the ice." The interviewer ought to take primary responsibility for initiating this conversation; the interviewee can be responsive. While there is an initial urge to get down to business right away, "breaking the ice" ought to be seen as an investment in relaxing both participants to facilitate the best possible communication flow later on.

253

Stage 2   Sharing of General Information / Once the interview has gotten off the ground and some degree of rapport has been established, the second stage focuses on a mutual sharing of information. Hopefully, the interviewer will have had an opportunity to review the candidate's resume before starting the interview. This preparation will allow the interviewer to flesh out the interviewee's qualifications and background. The interviewer can begin to share information about the overall organization and the particular job position for which this interview is being held. Using either the interviewee's specific experience or relevant information, the interviewer begins to gather more and more concrete information about the candidate.

For the interviewee, this stage can be seen as the first opportunity to communicate personally relevant information. Keeping in mind that the interviewer is motivated to match candidate with position, the interviewee must be aware of the job requirements and communicate specific skills or experience which meet them. Concise self-descriptive statements provide the interviewer with the best data for making a judgment on the interviewee's resourcefulness and self-confidence.

Stage 3   Amplification and Sharpening the Focus / Stage 2 provides both the interviewer and interviewee some general sense about each other's "goodness of fit." During Stage 3, effective interviewers will limit their initiative to sharpening the focus on critical information. This information may be a more detailed description of qualifications or an exploration of the candidate's personal goals, work values, and aspirations. An assessment of these characteristics can really identify individual differences, especially when a stack of resumes all show similar backgrounds.

It is at this stage of an interview that there becomes a clear difference between the interviewee who hopes that an interviewer will like him, and the interviewee who has the reasonable conviction that this is a mutual decision-making process. In response to the interviewer's decreasing structure, the interviewee can assume more initiative and amplify self-communication. In addition to providing broader and deeper information, the interviewee can take the lead and ask a series of direct questions about the position and its potential to meet his concrete needs. The effective interviewee will have a great deal of control over the interaction at this point. Not only will he receive the necessary data to make a decision, but he will be communicating to the interviewer a genuine sense of enthusiasm and independence.

254

Stage 4 Tying It Together / The final stage of the interview allows both participants to clarify any needed information and make some closing comments which tie the interview together. The interviewer and interviewee may find it helpful to summarize their impressions and reactions to the interview process. The interviewee can seek information concerning what will happen next in the recruitment process (e.g., notification by what date, second interview scheduling, etc.). While the interviewer may not be in the position to give extensive feedback to interviewees about their chances, some feedback will be both educational and satisfying, if handled effectively. Finally, the interviewee may want to express continued interest in the job position if, indeed, that is genuine.

These four stages can be followed in the traditional thirty-minute interview. Some of the anxiety aroused by the interview can be eased by giving it some structure so that interviewer and interviewee have clear expectations about the form and content of the process.

2. Discrimination Between Assertive, Nonassertive and Aggressive Ways of Responding

After the participants have learned the stages of an interview, the training can shift its focus to actual assertive skills. Many individuals who behave in an unassertive manner (either nonassertive or aggressive) often do so because they feel there is no other way to respond. One of the general purposes of training is to make people cognitively aware that they have a range of responses which can fit an occasion.

The trainer should begin this section of the training program by giving a brief description of the differences between the three ways of responding. The important aspect to stress for this part of the training is that assertive behavior maximizes the communication process between two individuals. In contrast to nonassertiveness in which the person shuts down, or aggressiveness in which one person shuts the other down, assertiveness strives to keep the channels open. Either the interviewer or interviewee may choose to respond in an unassertive way during the interview. However, after this discrimination training, they can better understand the consequences of that behavior and recognize potential alternatives consistent with their own personal needs and response style.

Following the description of the ways of responding, the trainer might use the filmed vignettes (Jakubowski-Spector, Pearlman &

255

Coburn, 1973) described earlier in this book. If trainers have access to video tape equipment, they may want to develop their own set of vignettes which are directly applicable to the job interview context. After each vignette is shown, the trainer asks the members to express several responses and assess whether each would be considered non-assertive, assertive, or aggressive. The purpose of this exercise is to have the group begin to form a criterion for assertive communication. Most often, they have difficulty in the discrimination of assertive and aggressive ways of responding. It is from this work on discrimination that the members first recognize some of their personal rights and how assertive communication is sensitive to those rights and to the other individual. A discussion of personal rights now adds more depth and clarity to the members' criteria (see Chapters 2, 3, and 4 for more detailed sections on discrimination and personal rights training).

3. Definition of Personal Rights

Assertion training has popularized the concept that there are basic human rights which an individual can choose not to have violated. For a more specific context, such as a job interview, it is helpful to zero in on some particular rights applicable for the interviewer and interviewee. It should be noticed that many of the rights are parallel for both participants in the interview since both share similar objectives and can expect to be treated as persons during the interaction.

a. Rights of the Interviewee:

Right to assume that one will be listened to

Right to communicate important information about oneself

Right to seek as much necessary information about the job in order to make a good decision

Right to answer questions in one's own manner and style

Right to say no to an unreasonable request without feeling guilty

Right to have specific needs and to express them

Right to expect truthfulness and accurate information from the interviewer

Right to be treated fairly, without discrimination due to sex, race, age, or previous experience

Right to express a healthy self-confidence and feel good about one's accomplishments

Right to make mistakes

b. *Rights of the Interviewer:*

Right to assume that one will be listened to

Right to seek information from a candidate about her qualifications

Right to ask questions about values, attitudes, goals

Right to communicate information about the job position and organization

Right to determine the length of the interview

Right to expect truthfulness and accurate information from the interviewee

Right to say no to an unreasonable request without feeling guilty

Right to be enthusiastic and expressive

Right to evaluate and make judgments about a candidate's qualifications

Right to make mistakes

These are some fairly specific personal rights which each participant in the interview may pursue. A discussion of personal rights should be done in a large group as a brainstorming session with the trainer soliciting rights from each member (see Exercise 9, Chapter 4). It is important for the interviewer and the interviewee to identify a nucleus of rights which they consider as critical to their own growth and satisfaction. As was discussed earlier in this book, these personal rights form the belief system upon which the behavioral skills or assertive communication are based.

Whether it is a group of interviewers or interviewees, it is helpful for the members to identify the rights of both participants. This serves two integrated purposes. The first is to demonstrate the parallel nature of the personal rights. For example, some are exactly the same. Others are interrelated. The right of the interviewer to ask "personal" questions about a candidate's values, attitudes, or goals must be balanced with the interviewee's right to be treated fairly, without discrimination due to sex, race, age, or previous experience. The male interviewer asking a female interviewee about her views on contraception or child rearing practices demonstrates a conflict. What can be learned so well from this example is the second purpose of identifying both sets of rights. Assertiveness involves communication of needs, but not at the expense of another. Members can begin to see more sharply the differences between assertiveness and aggressiveness as they struggle to define the boundaries of their own rights and those with whom they interact. It is a cognitive process of continually defining the criteria for assertive communication. The trainer will find it necessary to return to these rights often when the members begin work in the structured exercises and behavior rehearsal.

4. Training Exercises and Behavior Rehearsal

The structured exercises and behavior rehearsal should be handled in a small group with six to eight members per trainer. For each exercise, the trainer describes the rationale and purpose of the skill for the interview. The group members are asked to individually practice the skill and receive positive feedback on their communication from other members and the trainer. The participants are encouraged to share their feelings and experiences about the particular skills and interview situations. After the structured exercises, extended behavior rehearsal can be pursued based upon the needs of the group.

While an actual training program would be held separately for interviewers and interviewees, some of the structured exercises apply to both groups. Some apply only to one or the other. The objectives and methodology for each exercise will be presented here with its application for either or both participants in the interview. The sequencing of the exercises follows the stages of the interview already discussed. Once again, the reader is referred to Chapter 4 for a more detailed description of some of these exercises, which have been modified to fit this particular group.

"Breaking the ice" topics (interviewee and interviewer) / The purpose of this exercise is for both participants to feel relaxed and confident in "breaking the ice" conversations. The means by which this is accomplished is practice in an awareness of the nonverbal components of assertive communication (eye contact, facial expressions, tone of voice, body movement, hand gestures, energy level). The aware-

258

ness of these nonverbal components also provides the substance for all specific, positive feedback given by one member to another in the sessions.

Interviewee / It is important for interviewees to identify the specific nonverbal skills they have when engaging in a conversation. This identification serves the dual purpose of fostering self-confidence as well as becoming aware of some cues which indicate nervousness. The latter should not be stressed at this early stage of the training, but can be emphasized during behavior rehearsal which follows the structured exercises. Instead, the focus of this exercise should be on positive feedback such as an interviewee's effective eye contact or a smile and hand gestures which come across as genuinely expressive. Becoming more aware of effective nonverbal communication will serve as an important asset not only for "breaking the ice" conversation but throughout the interview.

Interviewer / It is just as important for the interviewer to identify a personal style of nonverbal communication which comes across effectively. However, in addition to receiving feedback which increases self-confidence, interviewers become more aware of how an interviewee will respond to the atmosphere which they set. In "breaking the ice," the interviewer seeks to relax the interviewee in order to maximize subsequent communication. It should be noted that this emphasis on the interviewer being able to set the interviewee at ease reflects a value inherent in this entire training program. In contrast to an approach which would have the interviewer maximize stress and observe the interviewee's ability to respond under pressure, the assertion training format minimizes either participant's need to be "one-up." Instead, interviewers will elicit the best data upon which to make a decision when their assertive communication has facilitated the interviewee's opportunities to be assertive and take initiative. If interviewees do not have the level of confidence or drive which an interviewer is looking for, this will be discovered just as easily in a nonthreatening atmosphere set by the interviewer.

Method / The trainer distributes to every member of the small group a "breaking the ice" topic (e.g., weather, food, campus activities) on which they will speak for one to two minutes (see Exercise 2, Chapter 4). The trainer then elicits from the group a variety of nonverbal components of communication and directs them to focus their positive feedback on these specific components. After an individual has

259

talked about the topic, the partner (or group) gives feedback on what was effective. The trainer may also ask the individual to simply be *aware* of any nervousness and how it was communicated nonverbally. The exercise is completed when every member has had an opportunity to talk on a topic and receive feedback. The trainer should conclude this exercise by clarifying for the group members the place of this skill in the interview. Most often, the interviewer initiates the topic of conversation in "breaking the ice." The interviewee takes this cue and is responsive. At the close of the interview, both participants may engage in small talk, but each should be aware of the other's nonverbal cues that the interaction should be concluded shortly.

Carrying on conversations (interviewee and interviewer) / While the "breaking the ice" exercise gets an individual started on a conversation, this exercise emphasizes the skills necessary to keep it going. Carrying on a successful conversation involves an interaction between two people who can effectively ask open-ended questions, listen and respond to information provided by the other, and paraphrase when seeking clearer or additional information. For the job interview, these skills are used as the process moves from "breaking the ice" to mutual information sharing. In a sense, this exercise enables an individual to know when and how to pick up the ball, run with it, and pass it off when stuck!

Interviewee / The goal for the interviewee in this exercise is to learn how to listen to an interviewer's questions or information about the job position and respond effectively with some personal data. Interviewees are often frustrated because the pressure of the interview blocks their ability to listen or understand a question. Sometimes they may accurately hear the question but not know where to begin in answering it "right." This exercise develops a capacity to listen more easily and pick up the converation in whatever way seems most comfortable.

Interviewer / It will be recalled that the interviewer may want to assume the initiative in the first two stages of the interview. This exercise is especially important for interviewers in learning how to facilitate the process of information sharing in a way which will allow them to gradually say less and less.

Asking open-ended questions increases the opportunity for the interviewee to talk more and share personal qualifications. Active listening focuses on exactly what the interviewee says to form the direction of the interaction. It involves balancing one's own agenda about securing necessary information with responding to what the interviewee has considered as her most important qualification or experience. By paraphrasing from time to time what the interviewee has said, interviewers not only communicate that they have listened and understood, but also encourage the interviewee to then choose in what way to broaden or deepen the conversation. The desired outcome of this exercise is for the interviewer to be able to get much more relevant information while having to say much less.

Method / After a brief description of the skills which will be covered for both groups (interviewees: active listening and free responding; interviewers: asking open-ended questions, active listening, free responding, paraphrasing), the trainer may choose several ways of approaching this exercise (see Exercise 5, Chapter 4).

For the interviewee group, one way to approach this exercise is to ask the members to form triads. One member of the triad serves as observer of the interaction between the other two. One of the interacting members takes the role of the interviewer, the other the interviewee. The content of the role play could be on the interviewee's college major, course work, or general educational background as it applies to choosing an occupation. The goal of the interviewee is to educate the interviewer about the nature of the academic background and his personal investment in it. The interviewer role is structured to keep the interviewee talking as much as possible. The observer acts as the principle source of feedback for both what the interviewee said (clarity, concreteness, etc.) and how it came across (the nonverbal components already learned). The triad rotates roles until all have had an opportunity to be the interviewee and receive some positive feedback. The role play content can be varied based upon the background and needs of the interviewee group. It is important, however, to choose topics which will be directly applicable to the information typically communicated in the interview. Following the work in triads, the trainer may want to have the interviewees share their reactions on an effective sequence to communicate this factual information about themselves.

A similar process can be followed for the interviewer group: a brief description of the three skills, brainstorming examples of open vs. close-ended questions, modeling the paraphrasing technique, then work in triads. The goal of the interviewer is to integrate the three skills in order to facilitate an interviewee's sharing of relevant information. In the triad, one role is that of interviewer, the others are interviewee and observer. It is best to focus on information directly applicable to the interview as the content of the role play. After every member has had an opportunity to be the interviewer in an extended interaction, the trainer may want to have the members share their own approaches to information-gathering. This may also be an appropriate time to brainstorm ways of handling problems like the frozen interviewee, the interviewee who despite every interviewer attempt, answers every open-ended question with a yes or no response.

Giving a compliment (interviewer) / Specific, enthusiastic feedback on an interviewee's accomplishments is an effective means of education and confidence-building. The purpose of this exercise is to recognize that genuine compliments are important to give. They serve as another means for the interviewer to maximize the positive nature of an interview and thereby increase the potential for rapport and better communication.

Method / There are two parts to this exercise. The first has the members experience giving a compliment to one another. This can have the side effect of adding to group cohesiveness by sharing some genuine "warm fuzzies." The second part considers what areas are appropriate as the basis for giving a compliment to an interviewee (see Exercise 3, Chapter 4). The first part is done by asking each group member to turn to the person on the right and give a specific compliment on some aspect of that person's sensitivity or skill demonstrated during the training. When the circle is complete, each receiver of a compliment then shares with the giver what was effective. The second part is handled as a discussion with every interviewer being asked to suggest what they consider an appropriate area for a compliment to the interviewee. Typical areas include: outstanding letters of recommendation, good grades, quality and diversity of prior work experience, ability to communicate during the interview, enthusiasm, motivation. After discussing a variety of potential areas, the trainers should ask every interviewer to verbalize a concise and satisfying way of giving a compliment in one or several areas.

Receiving a compliment (interviewee) / Many of us have been taught to be pervasively humble, to respond to a compliment with a

262

blush and to reply, "Oh, it's nothing." The purpose of this exercise is to do some cognitive restructuring with the interviewees. An interviewer expects an interviewee to have a realistic assessment of personal skills and abilities. It is therefore permissible to recognize these talents and feel OK when someone else pays us a compliment.

Method / The trainer can ask all of the interviewees the one area in their overall qualifications which is special. The trainer gives each member a compliment on that area. For example, "Your resume shows several excellent positions of responsibility which you've held," or "These letters of recommendation from your teachers and supervisors are consistent in their recognition of your independence and creativity." The interviewee should respond to the compliment in a manner which acknowledges the praise and demonstrates some sense of feeling comfortable with it. After responding to the compliment, the member receives feedback from the group on the effective verbal and nonverbal parts of the response. The desired outcome of the exercise is for the interviewee to be able to respond assertively to a compliment and expand upon it, when appropriate.

Making a positive self-statement (interviewee) / Like the previous exercise which works on receiving a compliment, this skill may also require some cognitive restructuring. Interviewees often express the fear of sounding too "pushy" or coming across like an aggressive or obnoxious braggart. This fear can be minimized through increased self-awareness on the part of the interviewee and practice in making a clear, concise, positive self-statement.

Method / The trainer asks the interviewees to pause for a moment and consider a job position or setting for which they would most likely interview. Having anchored into a specific position or setting, the interviewees are then asked to identify some concrete talents or abilities which would apply. Every interviewee is given the opportunity to respond to an open-ended question like, "Well, Mr./Ms. _____, I wonder if you could tell me some of the special qualifications you have for this position." After one interviewee has responded to the question with a positive self-statement, the other group members give feedback on the assertive behaviors demonstrated. The exercise continues until every interviewee has had an opportunity to respond and receive feedback. Depending upon the needs of the group and time constraints, the trainer may want to pose another similar question for practice, e.g.,

"What are some of your long-range career goals and how have you prepared yourself to achieve them?"

This exercise is helpful in giving the interviewee an opportunity to define strengths and learn how to communicate them in an assertive manner. The skill is used during both Stage 2 and Stage 3 when personal information is being shared and amplified by the interviewee.

Making a request/Seeking specific information (interviewee and interviewer) / This exercise really makes the interview participants aware of what they define as personal rights and how this affects specific behavior. The purpose of the exercise is to define the interview as a mutual decision-making process. Whatever information is necessary to make a fair and substantive decision can be legitimately requested during the interview by either the interviewer or the interviewee.

Interviewee / There is a skill involved in asking clear, concrete questions when seeking information about a job position or organization. For interviewees, it requires an awareness of their specific needs in an occupation and some prior preparation about the job. It should be understood by the interviewee that a series of direct questions about the position not only gathers required information about a position, but communicates to the interviewer an attitude of independence, enthusiasm, and self-confidence.

Interviewer / Recalling the personal rights of the interviewer, one stands out for this exercise in particular—the right to ask questions about values, attitudes, and goals. More than resume information, these personal qualities are the real substance of a qualified candidate. Also, interviewers may have special difficulty in asking questions for which the answers may be embarrassing or threatening to the candidate. Examples of these topics include poor grades, large gaps in an interviewee's work history, changing jobs often, or terminations. There are two things to stress for these situations: (1) the manner in which the question is asked can convey a lot in allowing the interviewee to feel less defensive, and more importantly, (2) the interviewer can potentially gain valuable information on how this candidate has handled adversity and can now handle a sensitive area. One example is that of an interviewer who must assess a handicapped person's capacity for physical activity. Avoiding such a question encourages stereotypes; for example, handicapped persons will be embarrassed by such a question, or it is safe to assume their lack of ability to do any significant physical activity. Asking it may reveal a person who has a realistic awareness of both strengths and liabilities.

Method / Whether for interviewers or interviewees, it is beneficial to start this exercise by focusing on the personal rights which are essential to the individual. After identifying these rights, the members can break up in pairs to practice asking direct questions. The person in the pair who plays the role of respondent should be encouraged to supply minimal information as a first response to the interviewer or interviewee question. This will facilitate the practicing individual's discovery of alternative ways of probing or making the decision that the question is not going to be answered.

The second part of the exercise can shift from the form of seeking information as a question, to making a request or stating a minimum requirement. This also involves the identification of personal rights. For example, the first part of the exercise may encourage a question such as, "What opportunities do you have for employees to continue their education while working for you?" The second part of the exercise may emphasize another manner, "One of the important aspects of a job I want is that it provides time or compensation for furthering my education. How might that be possible?" Initially, interviewees will feel more comfortable with the open question. However, some in the group may have developed a level of awareness and a belief system which makes the second style appropriate for them.

For interviewers, a similar format can be followed. In addition to seeking more specific information about the interviewee's qualifications, the interviewer must be able to clearly state the requirements of the job position. Therefore, the first part of the exercise can be devoted to interviewer pairs practicing the asking of questions which seek specific, concrete information. The second part of the exercise should stress that the interviewers must define the job requirements for the particular position. They must then be able to communicate those requirements in a way in which the interviewee can appropriately respond. The two ways of doing this are again similar to the interviewee section. For example, "Have you made any plans to continue your graduate education while working with us?" An even more definite question will clarify the job's requirements, "We place a high value on our employees completing their master's degree during the first several years of work with us. How do you plan to accomplish this?" The interviewers should be able to develop their personally effective style of stating requirements and eliciting interviewee reaction through this exercise.

Saying no (interviewee and interviewer) / One of the consequences of identifying personal rights is having to say no to a request which infringes upon them. However, a very important consideration should be emphasized in introducing this exercise. The individual interviewer or interviewee has the right to sometimes choose not to assert those rights in a particular situation. Given the nature of the job market, whether jobs are scarce or candidates are scarce, individuals must choose which of their needs are more important. The goal of this exercise and assertion training in general is not to prescribe behavior, but to provide alternatives so that we do not have to settle for something because we cannot communicate better.

Interviewee / This exercise clarifies even further the interviewee's primary needs in a job position. In some extreme cases, it may simply be getting one job no matter what. One of the real fears which interviewees have is that any assertiveness which involves saying no will be automatic ground for disqualification. After exploring with the interviewees some of the possible and realistic consequences of saying no during the interview, the trainer should suggest that the results don't necessarily have to be catastrophic. The way in which the interviewee communicates the refusal of an interviewer's request and perhaps combines firmness on an issue with willingness to discuss alternatives may come across positively. It may not. In sum, the interviewees must decide whether principle or employment is their bottom line after trying to negotiate both.

Interviewer / One situation which interviewers must confront is clarifying unrealistic expectations which an interviewee may have about a job position or organization. It would be very nonassertive to say nothing about these expectations with the idea that reality will catch up with the interviewee on the job. The interviewee has the right to know what to expect and the interviewer has the right to communicate a more realistic picture.

Method / Saying no is one of the more difficult exercises to simulate and to implement with inexperienced interviewees (see Exercise 15, Chapter 4). Since the context is so foreign to them, they are usually at a loss to define unreasonable requests. The trainer can help this process by role playing with every member some requests which drastically infringe upon the interviewee's time, safety, or career goals.

266

For example, in working with a group of students who majored in home economics education, I asked them to consider outlandish duties as part of their job responsibilities. The requests ranged from preparing the dinner for every faculty function to mending the band's uniforms on personal time throughout the football season.

For either group, the initial skill is to firmly say the word, "no." In role plays with the trainer or in pairs, the interviewees or interviewers gradually expand upon the single word reply and can add reasons for their refusal or suggest some alternative ways of meeting the request.

Interviewers must necessarily expand upon the reply of no, in order to clarify for the interviewee company policy or alternatives which are available. The straight, factual answers are fairly easy to handle. Interviewers have more difficulty responding to interviewee statements which deal with values, attitudes, or an organizational philosophy. The critical skill in handling these situations is recognizing that interviewers have the right to express their organization's position and that this can be communicated assertively without criticizing the interviewee's position. So often, both interviewer and interviewee labor under the assumption that a good interview is defined by no disagreement. While it is true that there has to be a goodness of fit on perhaps eighty percent of the issues, total agreement is unrealistic. One of the rights common to both participants is the expectation of truthfulness and accurate information on the part of the other.

Behavior rehearsal (interviewee and interviewer) / The structured exercises provide interviewees and interviewers with a set of individual assertion skills applicable to the four stages of the interview. The major work left to be done at this point in the training program is to have the people integrate these skills into a personally effective style. The trainer should determine the content of the remaining sessions based upon the group's needs.

The session immediately following the last structured exercise can be used to allow individual members the opportunity to do a behavior rehearsal on a specific skill which is still difficult. (The reader is encouraged to review Chapter 6 for a detailed description of behavior rehearsal procedures.) If video tape equipment is available, it can be used very effectively for this part of training. The trainer can demonstrate the steps of the rehearsal with the entire small group, then break down into triads, with each triad alternating work with the trainer and work with the video tape as sources of feedback. At the close of this session, interviewers or interviewees should be asked to assess how well the skills are integrated and what further work needs to be done.

An assessment of work which still needs to be done is easier when the interviewer or interviewee has had the opportunity to do an actual job interview. This gives members the opportunity to test out the skills under the pressure and anxiety for which they were designed. Very often, the members will report that their nervousness still got in the way of their communication. This is the perfect opportunity for the trainer to provide valuable help in cognitive restructuring (see Chapter 5). The trainer can address the group as follows:

Half the battle of handling anxiety can be won by recognizing that we are nervous, and accepting that it is to be expected given the pressure. The other half is won by the behavioral skills we've practiced during training. For example, what usually runs through our minds when the anxiety in an interview becomes greatest? "That other person will think I'm a dummy." "If I don't get this job, I won't get any." Have you had any others you'd like to share with the group? (Pause for some reactions.)

It's my belief that when we tend to really catastrophize, our anxiety level gets out of control. The first way to get a handle on that can be done prior to the interview by clearly setting out your expectations. This probably won't be the last job for which you interview. Most people make mistakes. We're probably no different. We'd like to minimize the mistakes we make by some practice. What are some of the specific nonverbal behaviors which can cue you that you're nervous? Do you talk very fast? Voice become squeaky? Do you withdraw and take a long time to respond? Do you squirm a lot in your chair or avoid eye contact? You know you can channel this nervous energy into an asset. Now that you're aware of your own nonverbal behaviors, recognize them when they occur during the interview. This doesn't mean hiding them or shutting down. Instead, use these nonverbal behaviors as a cue for some cognitive work. After hearing yourself answer a question so fast that it was hard to understand, check out your SUDS level. If it is very high, why? "I'm nervous because this is important to me." "I'm eager to make a good impression and can't wait to do that." By the cues you've recognized the anxiety.

268

The internal messages let you accept the nervousness as expected in the situation. With this recognition and acceptance, the communication skills which you've developed during training won't be blocked by the anxiety and will now flow more freely.

This work on nonverbal behaviors as a cue to cope is one example of the content which is appropriate following the structured exercises sessions. In the absence of an opportunity to do an actual interview, the trainer can use these sessions to simulate the experience with members getting additional practice and feedback from the trainer, the video tape, and other interviewers or interviewees. The members might also practice specific ways of closing the interview, tying it together, and recognizing the nonverbal cues which indicate that the interaction is dragging on too long.

Review of Training Format
Assertion training for job interviews combines the guidelines and trainer techniques described in the previous chapters to help people deal with the anxiety of one particular situation. Individuals enter this training program with little understanding of the demands of the interview. Many of their expectations are global and frequently catastrophic! The main difference, therefore, in the program described in this chapter is the more frequent focus on information about interviewees, interviewers, and the interview itself. This focus is evident in the format of the whole training package as well as the additional discussion time following many of the structured exercises.

A typical training program for interviewees or interviewers can be structured in the manner presented in Figure 4 (p. 271). The times indicated for each component may be adapted for individual groups. However, the times represent a realistic, maximum boundary which allows the trainer to cover the material and the group members to both practice and discuss.

SUMMARY
This chapter began with Faulkner's gloomy observation. If nothing else, the possibility that that description is accurate should be enough motivation to try to change. The use of assertion training programs can enhance the growth of people in career development groups. The groups have ranged from a focus on the undecided individual, to the job seeking person, to the employer/employee concerned with job satisfac-

tion and professional development. Each of these people brings to assertion training a different level of skills and experience. What is common is the excitement and personal satisfaction generated as every person discovers a sense of their competency and new ways to handle situations. The outcomes of their assertiveness are not always the most desirable. People cannot change some work environments. Interviewees do not always get the job they want the most. Yet, I am constantly encouraged to see people, with only limited reinforcement, begin to have the sense that one person can make a difference.

REVIEW QUESTIONS

1. How can assertion training be applied to the career choice process for some people?

2. How can assertion training be helpful to employees and supervisors in the working relationship?

3. Briefly describe the four stages of a job interview?

4. What are the personal rights of interviewers and interviewees?

5. What exercises might be employed within a group focusing on job interviewing?

6. How could the cognitive restructuring principles and procedures of Chapter 5 be utilized in such a group?

Figure 4
Format for Interviewee/Interviewer
Assertion Training Program

Session	Topic	Time
1	Stages of the Interview	1 hour
	Discrimination Training	1 hour
2	Discussion of Personal Rights and Integration with Discrimination Training	2 hours
3	*Interviewees*	
	"Breaking the Ice" Topics	20 minutes
	Carrying on Conversations	40 minutes
	Receiving a Compliment	30 minutes
	Making a Positive Self-Statement	30 minutes
	Making a Request/Seeking Specific Information	30 minutes
	Saying No	30 minutes
3	*Interviewers*	
	"Breaking the Ice" Topics	20 minutes
	Carrying on Conversations	60 minutes
	Giving a Compliment	30 minutes
	Making a Request/Seeking Specific Information	40 minutes
	Saying No	30 minutes
4	Behavior Rehearsal	2 hours
	(One or more actual interview experiences)	
5-6	Behavior Rehearsal and/or Interview Simulation	2-4 hours

13
Assessment Procedures

Assessment procedures are used throughout the course of assertion training to determine whether (1) an individual's problems are appropriate for group assertion training, (2) progress is being made during the course of the training, (3) behavior has changed and is maintained after formal assertion training has ended, and (4) assertive behavior has generalized to new situations.*

ASSESSMENT ISSUE 1: SCREENING PROCEDURES
Conducting screening interviews is one of the main ways in which trainers can assess whether a prospective group member is likely to benefit from assertion training. In addition, such screening interviews also enable the trainer to compose a more compatible group of individuals, to clarify purposes of the group, to start establishing therapeutic norms such as confidentiality, self-disclosure, giving support to others, and helping others, and to identify idiosyncratic assertion needs of the prospective members.

Specifying Specific Problem Situations
A first step in the screening process involves identifying specific situations in which a prospective group member has difficulty acting assertively. This helps the trainer ascertain whether the planned assertion training group will meet the person's needs. In the process, individuals become more active in delineating their problems and setting personal goals for change.

* Parts of this chapter are taken from Jakubowski & Lacks (in press).

The individuals may be simply asked to describe specific situations in which they act nonassertively or aggressively, or they may complete one of the available paper-and-pencil assertion measures (see p. 283). The latter method often helps people become more aware of their assertion problems. Another method involves using the Wolpe-Lazarus Assertiveness Questionnaire (Wolpe & Lazarus, 1966) to identify and analyze an individual's problems in acting assertively. This questionnaire has been effectively used to identify assertive and nonassertive individuals (McFall & Marston, 1970; Eisler, Miller & Hersen, 1973). The questionnaire consists of thirty questions which the trainer asks the prospective group member. Examples of these questions are:

Do you avoid complaining about the poor service in a restaurant or elsewhere?

If a friend unjustifiably criticizes you, do you express your resentment there and then?

Are you able to contradict a domineering person?

The person's answers on a paper-and-pencil assertion measure, the Wolpe-Lazarus Assertiveness Questionnaire, or to the trainer's request to simply describe specific problem situations are analyzed by the trainer and the assertion training candidate to determine nonassertive or aggressive patterns of behavior.

In analyzing these patterns, trainers need to keep in mind the conditions which can affect the ability to be assertive. MacDonald (in press) has noted that an individual's ability to be assertive in different situations depends on (1) the degree to which the other person is an intimate or a stranger, (2) the number of people present who will observe the behavior, (3) the status and sex of the other person, and (4) the extent to which one has time to prepare for assertive behavior. Additional conditions have been specified by Jakubowski & Lacks (in press): (1) whether one initiates the assertive encounter or instead is responding to the other person's initiated aggression or manipulation, (2) whether the situation calls for a type of assertive behavior one can enact, e.g., expressing affection, refusing requests, making requests, defending personal opinions, and finally, (3) whether the other person in the interaction controls significant reinforcers, such as the power to withhold affection, job raises, recommendations, etc. Those prospective group members who cannot identify specific problem situations are likely to be poor candidates for group assertion training.

Identifying Conditions that Prevent Assertive Behavior

When these patterns of nonassertive and aggressive behavior are identified, a next important step is to identify the causes of the nonassertion and aggression. Although there are many causes of nonassertion and aggression (as discussed in Chapter 2), we see the following as four basic causes:

1. People may simply lack information or practice in acting assertively. In some cases, people may lack awareness of their own preferences, desires, and feelings.
2. People may not view their own or others' nonassertive, aggressive, and assertive behavior accurately. In such cases, they may feel unreasonably guilty after appropriate expressions of irritation because they inaccurately view it as aggression, may inhibit spontaneous assertive behavior because they see this as aggressive, may react aggressively because they consider assertion as too weak and therefore nonassertive.
3. The belief system may be such that it does not support assertive behavior. For example, people may not believe that they or other people are entitled to express certain feelings, opinions, etc.
4. People may lack strategies for coping with their own excessive anxiety, anger, and guilt—feelings which interfere with their ability to act assertively.

In identifying the major causes of a person's nonassertion and aggression, the trainer can use such probes as: How are you most likely to act in this situation? If that failed, what would you do? What would you like to be able to say? What stops you from acting the way you'd like? How can you tell whether you've acted nonassertively or aggressively in this situation? What methods do you use to lower your anxiety in this situation?

While it is unlikely that during the screening interview a trainer will be able to do a full analysis of a prospective group member's problems in acting assertively, getting some sense of the chief causes of nonassertive and aggressive patterns can help trainers to better plan the assertion training experiences for an individual. It also helps the trainer determine whether an individual's needs are likely to be satisfied in a specific assertion training group. For example, when a person's basic problem is lack of information on how to act assertively, an assertion training group which emphasizes skill acquisition is likely to be more appropriate than one which emphasizes consciousness-raising. Or if the prospective group members mainly lack self-awareness of their needs and preferences, the trainer could develop a training program which includes more awareness-building activities.

Other Factors to Consider in Selecting Members

Situational vs. general problems in assertion / Alberti & Emmons (1974) differentiate between generally and situationally aggressive and nonassertive individuals. They caution against including generally aggressive or nonassertive individuals in assertion training groups until these persons have received therapy or possibly assertion training on a one-to-one basis. Before discussing their recommendation, we would like to clarify our understanding of assertion problems as "situational" or "general."

The available research evidence* does not support the view of assertion as a unitary and pervasive personality trait but rather that assertion is a situation-specific set of behaviors. Thus in a sense all assertion, nonassertion, and aggression can be considered as situationally determined. Some individuals are occasionally nonassertive or aggressive in a few specific situations while others have frequent problems across a vast spectrum of different types of situations. We see this latter group as generally nonassertive or aggressive. Our use of these terms does not imply a personality trait position.

Returning to Alberti & Emmons' caution about people who have general problems with assertion, it is our observation that some people are merely nonassertive or aggressive across many situations while other individuals have this problem *plus* other characteristics; for example, motor retardation, being unable to even imagine themselves acting assertively, being virtually out of contact with their feelings and preferences, or being extremely explosive. Sometimes a person's inability to act assertively is part of a much larger syndrome, like the "pampered child syndrome" (Rattner, 1971) in which individuals resent having to

---

* For example, factor analysis of the Rathus Assertiveness Scale (Rathus, personal communication, 1973), Lawrence Assertive Inventory (Lawrence, 1970), the Assertion Inventory (Gambrill & Richey, 1975), and the College Self-Expression Scale (Galassi & Galassi, 1974) all revealed no general factors of assertion. Eisler et al. (1975) likewise supported the view that individuals who are assertive in one situation may not be assertive in a different interpersonal context.

make their wants known to others, resent having to depend on others to figure out what their unexpressed needs are, and feel powerless to change their own passive-manipulative behavior patterns.

The upshot of all of this is that people who have general problems in assertion, which are complicated by some additional problems, would be more appropriately seen in therapy. These persons could receive assertion training after their more basic problems and ambivalences have been resolved. Generally nonassertive or aggressive individuals who are not so incapacitated by other complicated problems may be appropriately placed in group assertion training. However, as we will discuss later in this chapter, these individuals may be better served by being in a homogeneous group composed of other persons who are also generally nonassertive or aggressive.

Motivation to change / It is important to determine whether prospective members are really interested in changing their behavior and becoming more assertive. When membes are very ambivalent about changing, they often end up spending a lot of group time simply discussing their ambivalence. In addition, the unmotivated or ambivalent group member may sabotage the assertion training group. For example, when a person is not interested in becoming employed and is in an assertion training group to acquire assertion skills to get a job, that person may end up sabotaging his own training. The entire group may also be hurt by one member's sabotaging efforts.

Commitment to work / Another important consideration concerns assessing prospective members' willingness to actually work on changing their behavior through homework assignments, behavior rehearsals, etc. It is usually desirable to screen out those individuals who are merely curious about assertion training and are not committed to changing their behavior.

Willingness to self-disclose / It is important to ascertain that individuals are willing to talk about those situations in which they have trouble acting assertively. When people report that it is difficult for them to be self-disclosive in groups but that they are willing to do so, the trainer can ask them to consider what would help make it easier for them to self-disclose. Individuals who resent self-disclosing and strongly believe that others should be able to figure out what they need would generally not be appropriate for assertion training groups until they have resolved this issue.

Ability to talk in groups / People who are extremely uncomfortable during the individual screening interview—who can barely be heard, who avoid eye contact, who are vague and brief in their answers—stand a good chance of being even more uncomfortable in the group setting. Such painfully shy individuals usually would be more appropriately seen in individual assertion training.

Realistic expectations / It is important that the prospective members' expectations about the training group are appropriate. Individuals who hold magical expectations of personality transformation or who expect an encounter experience are likely to be disappointed and possibly disruptive in the training group.

Triadic factors / Yalom & Lieberman's (1971) research in encounter groups indicates that people may become "group casualties" when they have the following three characteristics: (1) very low anxiety about being in the group, (2) great vulnerability and low self-esteem, *and* (3) great motivation to change. It is reasonable to believe that such individuals may prematurely disclose deeply personal problems before a sufficient trust level has been established in the group. Thus they would be unprepared for any negative group reaction. We believe that these triadic factors are likely to be less important in assertion training groups than in personal counseling and encounter groups. In assertion training groups, the emphasis is on skill acquisition rather than on psychological probing and personal therapy. Also, the members in assertion training groups are encouraged to provide positive feedback, support, and information instead of negative confrontation and strong negative feelings.

Prior bad group experience / When prospective members have had a prior bad experience in a group, the trainer needs to ascertain whether their bad experience was due to the leader or group—or whether the individuals caused their own bad experience. For example, people who expect the leader to be 100 percent attentive to all their needs, who cannot "stand" any confrontation, or who interpret any suggestions for improvement as unwarranted attacks set themselves up to have a negative group experience. In selecting individuals for assertion training groups, it is important to avoid those who are likely to repeat their self-defeating pattern of behavior and end up having another "bad group experience."

Other issues / Individuals who see the trainer as a power figure to be rebelled against, whose obvious anger is denied and covered by a thin veneer of sweetness, who are highly manipulative, who have a borderline hold on reality, who are paranoid or psychopathic, who deny their obvious anger, who are overadaptive and take the position, "Just tell me exactly what I should do in the group and I'll do it," are generally poor candidates for group assertion training.

Balancing the Group

Sex factors / Brummage & Willis (1974) found that single sex groups and mixed sex assertion training groups significantly improved their assertive behavior as measured by a paper-and-pencil measure of assertion (Rathus Assertiveness Schedule). The single sex groups improved more than those single sex groups which later added members of the opposite sex, which in turn improved more than the mixed sex groups. Group leaders rated the single sex groups as having greater cohesiveness and self-disclosure than the mixed sex groups. Our own experience with assertion training groups also supports these observations. Although the data are limited, it appears that having males and females in the same assertion training group will not reduce the overall effectiveness of the group experience; however, cohesiveness and self-disclosure are usually greater in single sex groups. Needless to say, when the assertion training group consists of members of both sexes, ideally there would be roughly equal numbers of males and females.

Age factors / Age factors are usually not considered to be very important in encounter and personal counseling groups. However, in assertion training groups whose members are greatly different in age, group cohesiveness often suffers. In such groups, the members are likely to be dealing with very different assertion issues (e.g., trying to establish independence from parents vs. becoming more assertive at work), and the members frequently have trouble being supportive of each other's concerns. In general, it is better to have the group members in roughly similar age groups, where they are dealing with similar assertion issues. A side benefit is that the greater homogeneity of members' problems makes planning the group experiences far easier.

Situational and general problems / Mixing individuals who are extremely nonassertive with those who are extremely aggressive usually creates division within the group and may result in members dropping out. Likewise, mixing people who are generally nonassertive with those who have a few assertion issues also poses a problem. In such groups, generally nonassertive individuals often start emotionally withdrawing when the trainer does behavior rehearsals with the situationally nonassertive members. For example, in one group when a situationally nonassertive member practiced refusing a request, a generally nonassertive member crossed her arms, frowned, and turned her face away. This member felt that the person had no right to refuse the request in the first place. The trainer had to continually stop the process to deal with the issue of personal rights. In a sense, the generally nonassertive individual was still at the stage of learning the distinction between assertion, aggression, and nonassertion and accepting personal rights, while the other group members were ready to develop assertion skills through behavior rehearsal. In other cases, the group mixture of generally nonassertive and situationally nonassertive people may result in the generally nonassertive individuals devaluing themselves, feeling even more inadequate as they compare their slow progress with that of the more situationally nonassertive individuals, or becoming even more entrenched in their belief that assertive behavior is destructive.

Thus persons with general problems in assertion may be better served in a homogeneous group with others who share their problems. Trainers who mix general and situational persons need to be aware that this group composition is likely to result in some group management problems and may well be a disservice to the person with general problems in assertion.

Screening Prospective Group Members Who Have Clinical Problems

For at least three reasons trainers need to know how to screen individuals who have clinical problems: (1) other therapists may refer their clients to a trainer for an assertion group, (2) trainers who are also therapists need to know the conditions under which assertion training may help their own clients, and (3) individuals may wish to join an assertion group for help with their clinical problems.

The assertion training case study literature has established that assertion training—often in combination with other therapeutic procedures—is a useful behavior change procedure for a wide variety of clinical problems:

> Abdominal spasms (Lazarus, 1965)
> Addictions (Salter, 1949, pp. 200-201)
> Agrophobia (Lazarus, 1966b; Rimm, 1973)

Asthma (Gardner, 1968; Wolpe & Lazarus, 1966, case no. 3)
Depression (Bean, 1970; Cameron, 1951; Katz, 1971; Lazarus &
Serber, 1968; Piaget & Lazarus, 1969; Stevenson & Wolpe, 1960,
case no. 3; Wolpe, 1958, case no. 2)
Dermatological problems (Seitz, 1953)
Hallucinations (Nydegger, 1972)
Headaches (Dengrove, 1968)
Marital problems (Fensterheim, 1972a; Eisler et al., 1974)
Phobias (Rimm, 1973; Lazarus, 1971; Cautela, 1966)
Sex problems (Edwards, 1972)
Urinary retention (Barnard, Flesher & Steinbook, 1966)

Unfortunately the case study literature does not explicitly
address itself to an important assessment question: Under what
conditions would these clinical problems be likely to benefit from assertion training? Let's take a mother who abuses her child. Under what
conditions might assertion training be of help with this psychological
problem? First, when a mother ricochets between nonassertive and
aggressive behavior with her child. Second, when she nonassertively
denies her own needs and feels like she is sacrificing herself for her
child. Then, when she's drained, aggressively overreacting to the feelings of helplessness and inadequacy which are triggered when the child
cries or is disobedient and seems to be demanding yet more of her. In
summary, assertion training would be appropriate when the child abuse
is at least partially caused by a mother's failure to accept and assert her
own needs, to constructively express her anger and disappointment
with her child and others, and to be assertive with her own parents and
husband who may be highly critical of her and who therefore contribute to her feelings of inadequacy (Jakubowski, in press, a).

Since the assertion training case study literature does not
explicitly describe these conditions, it is up to trainers to make this
decision based upon their knowledge of the prospective member's assertion problems. Trainers can ask themselves: If the person were to act
more assertively in certain specified situations, what changes would I
expect to happen in the person's life, and are these changes likely to
affect the person's presenting complaints? (Jakubowski & Lacks, in
press). For example, if a trainer discovered that an alcohol-dependent
client used alcohol in order to (1) escape from conflict situations with
other people who are easily able to overpower the client; (2) indirectly
express hurt and anger towards significant others; and (3) relax so that

the client could express thoughts and feelings which ordinarily would have been suppressed, it would be reasonable that the client would benefit from assertion training (Jakubowski, in press, a). It could be anticipated that as a result of assertion training, the client would be able to effectively handle interpersonal conflicts and directly express hurt and anger. Thus, a major need for drinking alcohol would be reduced.

Using this approach in trying to ascertain whether a person's clinical problem would be likely to benefit from assertion training, is it likely that a widow *who seeks assertion training to ease her sadness* would benefit from such training? Not when her predominant concern is that she suffered a loss that no one else—except other widows—could appreciate; when she holds magical expectations about assertion training; when she cannot specify specific situations where she wants to become more assertive. Would a homosexual male *who wants assertion training to help him keep his lover* likely to be substantially helped? Again no—if the man has a history of his love relationships gradually deteriorating due to his increasing possessiveness, jealousy, and incessant demands for fidelity; when he demands that he be loved by everybody; when he refuses to do anything which would jeopardize others' approving of him. While such a man probably needs some additional assertion skills, it is unlikely that simple assertion would help him achieve his goal of keeping a lover forever.

ASSESSMENT ISSUE 2:
PROCEDURES FOR DETERMINING PROGRESS

A second assessment issue involves determining whether individuals are making progress in the course of assertion training.

In assertion training groups there are three main ways in which this information is obtained. Noting the types of situations which the group members ask to rehearse in the group can provide a rough indication of their progress. For example, trainers can note whether these situations are ones which involve increasing risk for the participants, e.g., being assertive with clerks to being assertive with an employer or mate. Another method involves having the members verbally report their assertion experiences during the group meetings. A more systematic method involves having the members keep a daily log of all their assertion experiences, or keeping logs on just those behaviors which they had earlier specified as major ways in which they wished to change (Hedquist & Weinhold, 1970). Roszell (1971) has developed a check list of various assertive behaviors on which the group members daily check those assertions they emitted and their accompanying level of anxiety. Interestingly, he found that keeping this type of log reduced the members' anxiety about acting assertively. When behavioral logs are kept, trainers can analyze the types and frequency of attempted assertion to determine an individual's progress.

ASSESSMENT ISSUE 3:
PROCEDURES FOR ASSESSING CHANGE
Paper-And-Pencil Measures
Besides assessing specific assertion problems, paper-and-pencil assertion measures may be used to assess whether the members have made gains in assertion as a result of training. A number of paper-and-pencil measures have been recently developed for college students: Constriction Scale (Bates & Zimmerman, 1971), Conflict Resolution Inventory (McFall & Lillesand, 1971), Assertive Inventory (Lawrence, 1970), Assertiveness Schedule (Rathus, 1973a, 1973b), and College Self-Expression Scale (Galassi et al., 1974; Galassi & Galassi, 1974). The Adult Self-Expression Scale (Gay, Hollandsworth, & Galassi, 1975) and the Assertion Inventory (Gambrill & Richey, 1975) have been developed for noncollege adults. Several other measures are in the process of being developed for adults (MacDonald, 1975; Jakubowski & Wallace, 1975) and adolescents (McCarthy & Bellucci, 1975). Lastly, Warren (1975) is developing a measure of assertive expressions of tenderness and affection. Although space limitations prohibit an extensive analysis of these various measures, some comments are in order so that trainers can decide which of these measures to use.

The Bates-Zimmerman scale has not often been used in assertion training research. It does have extensive statistical and conceptual analysis. However, it still needs additional cross-validation and normative data.

Although the Lawrence scale has been used in several assertion training studies, it has several disadvantages. Most importantly, its scores appear to be significantly influenced by social desirability. Lacks & Connelly (1975) found a significant correlation ($r = .28$, $p < .01$) between the Lawrence scale and the Marlowe-Crowne Social Desirability Scale. They also found that this scale takes longer to complete than is desirable—average time is 24 minutes with a range of 13 to 48 minutes for college students.

The Rathus scale likewise has been used in several research studies, but it also has a significant relationship (r = .27, p < .01) with social desirability (Lacks & Connelly, 1975). Furthermore, Rathus (1973a) reports a moderate correlation (.34) with assertiveness as measured by correlating subjects' assertion test scores with friends' ratings of their behavior on a factor-analyzed scale. Finally, a visual inspection of the Rathus scale reveals that several of the items appear to measure aggressive rather than assertive behavior, e.g., "There are times when I look for a good, vigorous argument."

The McFall-Lillesand scale measures a single type of assertive behavior, that of refusing requests. It is methodologically sound and scores on the paper-and-pencil measure of refusal behavior are highly related to actual behavior in a behavior situations test (Loo, 1971).

The College and Adult Self-Expression Scales appear to be methodologically sound. The former scale has been shown to be unrelated to aggression, as measured by a subscale of the Adjective Check List (Galassi et al., 1974); however, the Adult Scale is significantly correlated (Gay, Hollandsworth & Galassi, 1975). The College Self-Expression Scale is not significantly related to social desirability (r = .18) (Lacks & Connelly, 1975).

Lastly, the recently published Gambrill-Richey scale has an interesting format which makes it useful for assessment of assertion problems as well as for the measurement of change. With this scale, a trainer can collect three types of information about a person's assertive behavior: (1) how uncomfortable a person feels in specific assertion situations, (2) how likely the person is to react assertively in specific situations, and (3) the specific situations in which the person would like to act more assertively.

In summary, the Adult and College Self-Expression Scales appear to be the most useful for measuring a wide variety of different types of assertive behaviors. The Conflict Resolution Inventory is an excellent measure of one type of assertive behavior, that of refusing requests. Lastly, the format of the Gambrill-Richey scale makes it potentially valuable as an assessment instrument as well as a method to measure change. It should be noted that none of these measures has a separate scale to measure aggressive behavior and that all were normed on a white population.

Behavioral Measures

Behavioral measures enable the trainer to more precisely assess actual changes in the group members' behavior—before and after assertion training. A behavioral measure involves the trainer creating six to ten real-life situations which could be simulated through role play and which would elicit the kind of behavior the assertion training program is designed to increase (specific kinds of assertive behavior) or decrease (aggressive behavior). The role play situations would typically be short (one to two minutes) and would tap common assertion problems of the group members. Trainers could use the situations developed by McFall (McFall & Marston, 1970; McFall & Lillesand, 1971) and Eisler (Eisler, Miller & Hersen, 1973) or could devise their own role play situations which would be appropriate for their particular assertion training group.

Trainers who develop their own behavioral situations need to know in advance the common assertion problems shared by the group members. In creating these role play situations, the first step involves identifying at least fifteen common problems of the target population. From this larger group of common situations, six to ten problems are chosen, using the following criteria: (1) Is this a situation with which most of the target population have difficulty? (2) Is there reason to believe that this is an important situation for the group members to learn to deal with? (3) Is the situation one which would be comparatively easy to set up in role play?

Following this general model of developing behavioral role play situations, Janice Van Buren and Leon Ashford of Washington University and Patricia Jakubowski developed the following behavioral situations for black college students who were learning to become more assertive with authority figures:

1. One of your instructors has just offered you a job working on a research project. The job, however, will be in addition to your duties as a library aide. You decide to decline the offer.
2. It is late at night and you have just left the library after spending several hours studying. As you slowly walk across the campus, a campus policeman approaches you and asks to see your identification card. You have lost your card and have not yet requested a new one.
3. You are in the dean's office. You have been notified that you will not be allowed to register next semester because of your poor academic performance during the last two terms. You want to remain in school and think you have some valid reasons for being allowed to continue next semester.

285

4. You are receiving financial aid from the school for tuition and living expenses (e.g., room and board). Your parents have usually paid for your books and other supplies. However, because of a recent emergency, your family will not be able to help you. So you have come to the financial aid office to ask for the money you need.

5. During a lecture on measurement and intelligence tests, your instructor makes the following statement: "The literature indicates that blacks are somewhat less intelligent than whites and this is evident by their scores on intelligence tests." You think his statement is too general and inaccurate. You have read recent publications that give a different interpretation of these test scores. You have decided to approach him in his office after class to express your disagreement.

6. You and your advisor are meeting to select the courses you will take next semester. After examining your transcript, your advisor suggests that you take chemistry, calculus, English, sociology, and philosophy. You are apprehensive about taking chemistry and calculus together. Your grades have been good, but you don't feel that your background preparation has been adequate in these areas. You decide to express this concern to your advisor.

7. You are finding it difficult to understand some material presented in one of your courses. You have taken good notes and studied hard. You've also tried to get help from friends and classmates. Now you have come to get help from the instructor.

In the behavioral role playing measure, a tape recording usually sets the context of the situation, or the member may read a descriptive statement of the context of the situation, as shown in the above seven statements. A role playing confederate then enacts the situation with the member. One of the easiest ways to create the confederate's role (e.g., of a financial aid officer) is to have two or three members from the target population enact the role play situations with the trainer. By analyzing tape recordings of these interactions, the trainer can select key statements which will become part of the confederate's role (for further details see Whiteley & Jakubowski, 1969). (Incidentally, when assertive members of the target population enact these role plays, transcripts of their audio tapes can often be edited and eventually made into video or audio modeling tapes of assertive behavior.)

Instead of a live confederate role player, some trainers use a tape recording which describes the context of the situation and presents the confederate's prompting statements. For example, "You're in a crowded grocery store, in a hurry, and have one item to check out. You're next to be waited on when a woman with a cart full of groceries tries to cut in line, 'You don't mind if I cut in here do you? I'm in a hurry.' " (Eisler, Hersen & Miller, 1973).

The member's behavior in the behavioral situations are usually video taped and various verbal and nonverbal behaviors are rated. Eisler, Miller & Hersen (1973) have developed fairly straightforward ratings of the nonverbal components of assertive behavior.

1. Duration of Looking: Length of time that the group member looks at the confederate (from the delivery of the confederate's prompting statement to the end of the member's response).
2. Duration of Reply: Length of time the member speaks to the confederate. Pauses longer than three seconds terminate timing until the member begins speaking again.
3. Loudness of Speech: Loudness is rated on a five-point scale from 1 (very low) to 5 (very loud).
4. Affect: Affect is rated on a five-point scale from 1 (very flat, unemotional tone of voice) to 5 (full and lively tone that is appropriate to the situation).

Research has generally supported the importance of these behaviors as components of assertion (Hersen, Eisler & Miller, 1973; Galassi, Galassi & Litz, 1974).

In contrast, the ratings of verbal assertion are more crude and considerably less objective. Researchers have used a simple dichotomous rating of whether the assertive behavior occurred or not (Eisler, Hersen & Miller, 1973), paired the member's responses on the pre- and post-test situations and simply rated which of the two paired responses was more assertive (McFall & Marston, 1970), rated the member's assertion in the behavioral situation on a seven-point scale with 7 indicating maximum assertiveness (Rimm et al., 1974), or in the case of refusal behavior have used a five-point scale from 1 (unqualified acceptance) to 5 (unqualified refusal) (McFall & Twentyman, 1973). Obviously, increases in the quality of the assertive behavior would be hard to demonstrate with some of these rating procedures. A more refined rating, The Extended Interaction Test, has been developed by

McFall & Lillesand (1971) to measure the member's ability to continue refusing requests while under pressure to accede. The member's responses to each successive request is rated on a five-point scale, and the request to which the member finally responds with an unequivocal refusal becomes the member's final measure of assertion.

When both paper-and-pencil assertion measures and behavioral assertion measures have been used together to assess changes in members' assertive behavior, there have been contradictory findings with respect to how the self-report measures correlate with behavioral measures of assertion (Hersen, Eisler & Miller, 1973). Some researchers have found a substantial relationship (e.g., McFall & Lillesand, 1971) while others have found a low relationship (Friedman, 1971a). Sometimes individuals change their overt assertive behavior, but do not significantly change on a self-report measure of assertion (Hersen et al., 1973) while just the reverse may occur in other cases (McFall & Marston, 1970).

Supplementary Measures

Besides using paper-and-pencil assertion measures and behavioral measures, trainers may wish to use additional measures to assess group members' changes.

In general, global personality measures have not been found to be sensitive to the rather specific changes that occur as a result of assertion training, as the following studies indicate: Guildford-Zimmerman Temperament Survey (Perkins, 1972), Internal-External Locus of Control (Snyder, 1973; Rimm et al., 1974), Jacob's Survey of Mood and Affect (Snyder, 1973), Leary Interpersonal Check List (Lomont et al., 1969), Marlow-Crowne Social Desirability Scale (Roszell, 1971; Snyder, 1973), Repression-Sensitization Scale (Snyder, 1973), and Rosenzweig Picture Frustration Test (Snyder, 1973). The following show some promise as supplementary pre-post measures of assertion training: Personal Orientations Inventory (Roszell, 1971) and Willoughby Personality Schedule (Kazdin, 1974). In addition, measures of self-esteem, self-concept, moral development, or self-disclosure would be conceptually related to assertion and may be helpful to include as additional measures of assertion. Indeed, Bellucci (1975) has found that self-disclosure accounts for almost half of the variance of assertion.

Anxiety measures have often been used as supplementary evaluation measures since it is reasonable to believe that anxiety about acting

288

assertively would be reduced after assertion training. However, a review of the literature in this area indicates that thus far anxiety measures have not proved sensitive to anxiety reductions that may be occurring (Lacks & Jakubowski, 1975). In addition, a problem in using anxiety measures is that merely exposing the group members to the behavior pre-test may reduce their anxiety reactions at post-testing (Galassi, Galassi & Litz, 1974).

Two final measures may be very useful to assess change as a result of assertion training. Schwartz & Gottman (1974) at Indiana University have developed a 34-item questionnaire, the Assertive Self-Statement Test, which measures how frequently people make different kinds of negative and positive self-statements in the course of acting assertively. Their research suggests that after assertion training there ideally would be significant changes in the frequency of negative and positive self-statements that group members make in the course of assertion training.

The Discrimination Test in Chapter 2 may be used to measure the extent to which the group members have increased their ability to accurately discriminate between aggressive, assertive, and non-assertive behavior after assertion training.

Whatever measures the trainer uses to assess changes in the members' assertion can also be used at the follow-up period. Needless to say, in attempting to find out whether the group members' gains in assertive behavior have been maintained after formal assertion training has ended, it is more appropriate to administer the same measures that were used at post-testing, rather than to simply call the participants on the phone and check on their progress.

Trainers should be aware that the assertion training case study literature reports that clients' gains in assertive behavior have been almost invariably maintained at follow-up periods, some of which were six years after completing therapy. Likewise Mayo, Bloom & Pearlman (1975) found in their questionnaire follow-up study of clinical assertion training groups, six to eighteen months after training, that 95 percent of the members reported they were able to maintain or increase their level of assertion skills. Generally the experimental studies report short follow-up periods of a month or, with Galassi, Kostka & Galassi (1975) reporting an exceptionally long follow-up of one year. In general, the experimental studies report that the subjects' gains in assertive behavior have also been maintained at follow-up.

ASSESSMENT ISSUE 4:
PROCEDURES FOR DETERMINING
THE GENERALIZATION OF ASSERTION SKILLS

The case study literature usually reports that clients were able to transfer their assertion skills to some new situations. In their follow-up of assertion training groups, Mayo, Bloom & Pearlman (1975) found that over 90 percent of their group members reported that they adapted the assertion skills to completely novel situations or to new situations which were similar to those practiced in the training sessions. The experimental literature, however, reports much more limited generalization or transfer of training effects. Generally speaking, the experimental studies have found some generalization effects within one kind of assertive behavior. McFall & Lillesand (1971), for example, found that when subjects were trained to refuse requests, they showed generalization of training to refusal situations on which they had received no training. On the other hand, little generalization has been found across different kinds of assertive behavior. For example, Lawrence (1970) found that training subjects to express disagreement with others' opinions did not generalize to another kind of behavior, that of expressing their honest agreement with others' opinions.

The failure to find more significant transfer of training effects in the experimental studies may be due to several factors: (1) these studies are very tightly controlled and usually bear little resemblance to clinical assertion training groups in that they lack the group cohesiveness, group support, and the unique combination of reinforcement, behavior rehearsals, modeling, cognitive coping strategies, homework assignments, and vicarious learning that occur in clinical assertion training groups; (2) the subjects in the studies are often persons who are not strongly motivated to change their behavior; (3) the measures of generalization may be too crude to measure transfer of training effects that may actually be occurring; and (4) subjects' assertion experiences in the experimental studies are usually of much shorter duration than usually occur in clinical assertion training.

To date, researchers have developed two basic methods for assessing transfer of assertion skills. The most common method involves giving the members a behavioral role play test which consists of several situations (e.g., five) on which the individuals received training during the course of the group, plus a limited number of situations (e.g., two) on which no training was received. By analyzing the gains made from the behavioral pre-test to the behavioral post-test, the trainer can assess whether the group members' assertion skills transferred to untrained situations.

A more stringent measure of generalization has been developed by McFall (McFall & Marston, 1970; McFall & Lillesand, 1971). In his creative measure, a confederate telephones subjects who have completed assertion training and pressures them to buy magazine subscriptions, help in a worthy cause, or lend their class notes (McFall & Twentyman, 1973). The subjects' responses are audio taped and then rated. Some generalization effects have been obtained with this measure (e.g., McFall & Marston, 1970), although they generally have been weak. Further measures which are unobtrusive and approximate real-life encounters are sorely needed.

SUMMARY

One of the first assessment steps in assertion training involves ascertaining whether an individual's problems are appropriate for group assertion training. Making this determination usually involves various kinds of screening procedures, with the screening interview being an important procedure. Such interviews may also involve using various paper-and-pencil assertion measures. A critical issue for trainers of such groups is determining whether a particular individual's clinical or psychological problems are likely to benefit from assertion training.

The second assessment issue concerns determining whether an individual is making progress during the course of assertion training. Various methods for dealing with this assessment issue were presented.

The third assessment issue concerns ascertaining whether an individual's behavior has changed as a result of assertion training, and whether these changes are maintained after formal assertion training has ended. Various paper-and-pencil measures of assertion which could be used to make this determination were discussed, as well as methods for using behavioral role playing measures.

The fourth assessment issue deals with the issue of generalization of the newly acquired assertive skills.

REVIEW QUESTIONS AND EXERCISES

1. What are some conditions which affect a person's ability to be assertive in specific situations?

2. Should generally nonassertive or aggressive individuals be included in assertion training groups? Explain your answer.

3. What are some factors to consider in deciding whether to accept an individual in an assertion training group?

4. What are some factors to consider in balancing a group?

5. Describe several procedures which can be used to assess whether an individual is making progress in the course of assertion training.

6. What does the term "behavioral role play measure" mean?

7. Describe one method for assessing whether transfer of training has occurred in training groups.

8. Administer and score two of the paper-and-pencil assertion measures. Analyze the test information to determine patterns of assertion problems.

9. Conduct a screening interview with a friend. Assess the degree to which you established a comfortable atmosphere, asked clear questions, and got the information needed to make a screening decision.

14
Ethical Considerations

A number of ethical issues regarding the training of assertion trainers, the process of training, the potential consequences of training for participants and others, and the researching of training groups warrant discussion here.

We have recommended a three-stage training sequence and have cited other important expertise prospective assertion trainers should possess (see Chapter 8). As with the encounter group movement, many people who are not academically or professionally trained are likely to be conducting assertion groups. Although academic credentials are not a guarantee of competence, we wish to express cautions to those persons who have had limited supervised experience in doing counseling, psychotherapy, or assertion training. First, the process of assertion training (particularly when the goal is personal growth, as opposed to more intensive psychotherapy) is not difficult to understand, but it is quite a complex procedure and requires practice with supervision to do it well. Essentially, our concern is that the participants may not profit from their experience and the trainers may not have a successful experience nor learn from it.

Second, the leaders in any psychologically focused group should be prepared to respond effectively to the variety of dysfunctional dynamics which might occur ranging from disruptions, attention-seeking, and gamey resistances to intense emotional reactions and withdrawals. Although the structured nature of much of assertion training minimizes the expression of interpersonal dysfunction within the group, participants still often engage in "gamey" or ineffectual behaviors in the group. The trainers not only need to know how to recognize such dysfunctions, but also must know how to respond to them. We have offered a number of suggestions for handling such behaviors. However, trainers should have previous experience in supervised group work before conducting a group alone. Trainers with little counseling or therapy experience also should have a more experienced person available for supervision and consultation.

Trainers should also assess their personal goals for doing assertion training as with any helping relationship. Probably everyone who leads groups seeks personal fulfillment through such work. Some leaders, however, may be seeking excessive recognition as a potent, "healthy," "together" person. For example, the "charismatic" leader described by Yalom & Lieberman (1971) may be more interested in having the group members leave with the thought, "Gee, she's really an amazing leader; she's so together" than with the thought, "I made some important changes for myself in the group today." We do not need to belabor the possible personal needs of trainers which might negatively affect the group process. Trainers should, however, look for their own tendencies to "show off" their assertiveness to the relatively nonassertive group members or to impress the group with their perceptiveness.

Before beginning the group, trainers have ethical responsibilities regarding two issues presented earlier: advertising and screening participants (see Chapter 8). Trainers have an ethical responsibility not only to adhere to a professional, informational mode of notifying people about the group, but also to exercise great care to avoid making unwarranted claims, for example, that assertion training will produce major personality changes, resolve marital problems, or enhance love life. Trainers are not selling toothpaste, but rather are offering professional services. We would also like to note the ethical responsibility trainers have for screening prospective group members. Screening has more than the functional purpose of increasing the likelihood of a good group; it allows trainers to responsibly exclude persons who are not seeking such an experience or who are in need of more intensive psychotherapy.

Either during the screening session (as suggested in Chapters 8 and 13) or at the outset of the first session, the trainers should clearly explain what is going to happen in the group (the focus on cognitive restructuring, personal rights, and rehearsal; the group procedures). The trainers also should explain what is not going to happen, for example, it will not be an encounter or sensitivity group focusing on interactions between members; nor will it be a heavily confrontational group; nor will it be a therapy group where deep intrapsychic dynamics, developmental patterns, and heavy investments in maintaining dysfunctional behavior would be the focus.

In most instances, participants initiate interest in joining an assertion group. However, we have seen persons, particularly within institutional settings, strongly pressured by a supervisor or friend into joining a group. At the screening session, this fact usually becomes apparent. It is important that the trainers communicate to both the candidate and the supervisor or friend that participation in the group must be voluntary. If pressured into the group, the person is likely to be resistive and have a negative effect on other participants. It is possible that the person is setting up a victim game which would be reinforced by being in the group under such conditions. Trainers may either refuse to allow such persons into the group, or establish an agreement directly with them on their assertion training goals. To support having someone in the group without their own commitment violates the very definition of assertiveness.

During the first session, the trainers should make a brief statement regarding confidentiality among group members. The message should essentially be that anything that is discussed in the group should stay in the group. It is all right to tell others about the specific exercises or how the group works on problem situations. No references should be made to specific individuals, even anonymously, nor to the specifics of a situation on which someone worked in the group. Some situations are not so personal that anyone would mind if others knew it was practiced in the group. Nevertheless, the blanket rule of confidentiality rules out the need for individuals to have to make such discriminations and seems to help participants be more comfortable working on highly personal situations.

Our primary ethical guidelines for trainer behavior during the group are to be direct and honest in whatever you do and to respect the personal rights of all group members. More specifically, trainers should explain not only what they are doing (e.g., when conducting an exercise), but also why they are doing it that way (using positive feedback at first so that the group's first interactions will be supportive; doing the exercises so that participants will learn various components of the rehearsal procedures to come; phrasing feedback during rehearsals in the form of suggestions so that the person working takes greater responsibility for deciding to make each change). In addition, trainers should avoid being provocative or negatively manipulative toward participants in an effort to elicit a particular response (unless of course it is part of a role play). Participants usually respond to such provocative techniques by withdrawing. For example, one participant wanted to work on not changing his mind as soon as someone else offered an alternative. He had two situations on which to work and selected one of them, whereupon the trainer attempted to convince him to work on the other (which he did). At that point, the trainer noted how easy it was to convince him, and the participant became embarrassed and probably angry, although he did not express it directly. There was no need for the trainer to create examples of nonassertiveness within the group, particularly when the participant had already chosen a situation to work on. The trainer was at least negatively manipulative and might have been supporting a "gamey" transaction to meet both his and the participant's dysfunctional needs for control and susceptibility, respectively. In another situation, a trainer asked a woman in the group if she wanted to continue working on a particular situation which she had just practiced several times. She said "OK, I guess," whereupon the trainer asked the same question with a somewhat critical tone. The woman became more anxious, paused, and said "If you think so." The trainer repeated his exact question several more times as the participant communicated increasing confusion and discomfort. The trainer finally asked her to say "Yes or No" and she said "No." The trainer later explained that he was trying to get her to recognize that her responses were not expressions of her own decisions, but rather adaptations to the trainer's wishes. In fact, however, he never explained to her what he was doing. The trainer also recognized later that he felt she was "acting" dumb by not understanding his repeating the question with greater emphasis on what *she* wanted to do.

Our interpretation of the interaction is that the trainer was not clear with the participant as to what he wanted and became angry when the participant became anxious and confused. In observing the interaction, we also believed the participant was shutting down as a protective behavior. A more effective way to deal with highly adaptive behavior in the group is to share your perception that the person may not be thinking of what she wants to do and then ask her if that is an accurate perception. Thus, a direct and open interaction could lead to an important refocusing of the participant's thinking in a noncritical, nonpressured context. Incidentally, the participant in this incident did not

296

return to the group. Trainers do not have to "walk on eggs" in the way they respond to participants but mutual respect and direct, honest communication are crucial. Trainers *are* models.

Another issue regarding the process of assertion training has to do with the term manipulation. Some people react negatively to the use of "techniques" for more effective behavior as opposed to being "spontaneous." Moreover, some persons believe that they are being manipulative (and therefore bad) by assessing a situation and planning their behavior. Since some participants might resist intentionally trying to influence others for fear of being manipulative (and therefore bad), trainers should be able to discuss this issue and hopefully clarify the participants' thinking regarding the goodness or badness of manipulation. The term itself has come to take on a pejorative quality in our society. We believe, however, that attempts to shape another person's behavior in a positive direction or to influence interactions to turn out the way one would like are forms of manipulation *and* are not "bad." Actually, we are constantly attempting to manipulate ourselves and our world in all kinds of ways which we would not label manipulative. The critical issue, however, seems to be: Am I respecting my own personal rights *and the rights of others*. Thus, the real issue is not whether we consciously attempt to influence our world, but rather whether we are responsibly and ethically assertive as we attempt to exercise influence. On the other side of the coin, we have worked with participants who initially viewed assertion training as a way to get better at getting things from people with little regard for the personal rights of those people. We both spent considerably more time discussing the belief system issues regarding empathy and regard for the personal rights of others with these participants. Merely introducing such a different belief system is not enough to change a person's moral reasoning or belief system. Moreover, persons with a very rigid and insensitive perspective toward others often are quite fearful or angry and might best be helped in individual or group therapy. Assertion training might later be appropriate to help such a person begin to act on the newly developed belief system.

Assertion training can become manipulative in the negative sense when, for example, a person pays someone a compliment so that the person will pay him a compliment in return, or a person disagrees with his colleague so that the boss will be impressed. Recall that we defined assertiveness as a *direct, honest,* and *appropriate* expression of opinions,

297

beliefs, needs, or feelings. These two examples were neither direct nor honest in the expression of needs. Unfortunately, it is not always easy to recognize what is actually prompting our own overt behavior or the behavior of others. We believe that through the cognitive assessment procedures suggested in this book, we can more easily recognize our own internal dialogs and what is prompting our behavior. At this point we also feel the need to reiterate a point made by Albert Ellis (personal communication) that we do not *have* to be assertive all the time nor do we have to be on guard in case we "fall back" into unassertive behaviors. Persons who make this mistaken belief have simply substituted a new "should" ("I *should* be assertive *always*"; "I *should* be *perfectly* assertive") which they can use to castigate themselves when they are not assertive. Thus, although we may choose to strive for being as assertive and interpersonally effective as we can be, we should not use assertiveness as a new absolute criterion for our OK-ness or not OK-ness.

Another area for ethical concern is the question of the legitimate definition of assertion training. We have specified a procedure combining cognitive and behavioral principles and techniques (Chapter 5) as well as process and outcome goals (Chapter 1). We believe it is important to define what assertion training is, not in order to exclude effective treatment modes nor to generate semantic conflict over terms. Rather, our concern is with the present popularity and proliferation of groups being labeled assertion training when they do not remotely represent the use of cognitive and behavioral principles and techniques. For example, we have learned of a person who calls her group assertion training and is actually doing something like advanced "feminine wiles" training. Confusion seems to exist between the process goals and the outcome goals of groups. Many treatment modes or group experiences may eventuate in more effective interpersonal communication; however, the procedures and group process vary considerably. We believe it is important for professionals to have a clearer understanding of what is legitimately labeled assertion training. Although combinations of cognitive and behavioral components may vary from trainer to trainer or group to group, we believe that clinical—as opposed to experimental—assertion training is a combination of these components. Trainers have an ethical responsibility to use psychological terminology appropriately; they should not conduct training groups under whatever label happens to be currently popular. Such "opportunism" is irresponsible to participants and to the profession. Admittedly, there is no recognized entity which passes judgment on what one may call his work, particularly if the person does not call it psychology or psychotherapy and is not a member of the American Psychological Association. The Committee on Scientific and Professional Ethics and Conduct of APA will make informal, educative efforts to inform members of inaccurate labeling of their work and, of course, take more formal action if the work is of questionable psychological value. The existence of a more formal committee would have its assets *and* its great liabilities. We believe that the members of the psychological and educational professions do have an ethical responsibility to clarify the labeling of their professional services. Caveat emptor is not enough.

Often in assertion groups, participants will reveal a number of psychological problems which are more appropriate for in-depth psychotherapy. As noted earlier, many psychological concerns include assertiveness components which are correctly dealt with in training groups. An ethical issue, however, emerges when trainers begin to do in-depth psychotherapy in what is offered as assertion training for personal growth. A most frustrating factor in explaining these ethical concerns is the problem of discriminating between assertion training (as a personal growth, learning, and therapy experience) and a more in-depth therapeutic procedure. Two directions might help to clarify the distinctions: the material attended to, and the manner in which the material is handled. Assertion training appropriately includes cognitive restructuring and behavior rehearsal procedures and several behavioral techniques such as relaxation and contracting.

An experienced therapist will also be able to recognize and interpret participants' psychological dynamics, historical origins of dysfunctional behaviors, or repression of feelings. If the trainers are offering an assertion training group for personal growth, these therapeutic practices are clearly going beyond such training. In effect, assertion therapy, rather than training, is being offered. If trainers decide they wish to pursue such psychological material utilizing additional therapeutic procedures, it is critical that participants be informed at the outset of the specific procedures to be used and that the group is also a therapy group. Assertion training may be used in conjunction with an assessment of the participants' behavioral-developmental patterns (e.g., in transactional analysis terms: assessment of games or scripts). Such procedures fit the third type of assertion training group which combines training with other procedures. Needless to say, in such groups, it is also important that the participants be advised of these procedures prior to joining the group.

We have shared our clinical observations with participants both within the group and individually when referrals seemed appropriate. For example, as a participant was working on speaking up in groups, it became clear that she was also not allowing herself to think. The trainer helped her identify some of the irrational thinking ("Never say anything stupid"), clarified her rights to express her opinions, and had her practice several situations. After the group, the trainer noted to the participant that she also seemed to keep herself from thinking and asked if she was aware of that. She agreed. The trainer asked if she could recall any support for not thinking as she was growing up. She did. The trainer suggested that if she wished to work on this, she might do so with a counselor. She felt there was something important to her shutting off and decided to work on it with a counselor. The trainer skillfully clarified what was appropriate for the assertion group and what was not. The trainer also was willing to make the confrontation and to recommend a source of resolution.

If the trainers wish to assess the impact of the group on its participants or to conduct other research, several ethical issues arise. First, participation in the research should be voluntary; it should not be contingent on doing the research if the group is offered as a service (as opposed to a research project). The participants should be informed of what they are required to do (without contaminating the data) for the project. They should be guaranteed anonymity beyond the researchers. If a no-treatment control group is offered, the trainers should be prepared to offer those persons training as soon as possible. The trainers should also share the individual results for that participant and the anonymous global results of the study with any participant who wants them.

Assertion training intentionally seeks behavior change for participants. Many of the participants' important relationships may have been based on their being unassertive in many situations. Helping persons change involves a number of ethical issues regarding the consequences of increased assertiveness to the participant as well as to significant others in that person's life.

It has already been noted that one should assess the consequences of being assertive; for example, in the work setting, possible consequences may be getting fired, demoted, or passed over for promotion or pay raises. Depending on the alternatives available, one might choose not to behave in a manner which, although assertive, would also lead to serious negative consequences. Trainers should make this issue clear and distinguish between such reasonable assessment and rationalizations which justify avoiding a situation that may result in negative consequences. With reasonable assessment, the person is choosing to behave based on reason; with rationalization, the primary motive is anxiety.

People are not assertive in a vacuum. Therefore, participants should always assess the likely consequences of their behavior. Trainers can make the point that one may choose not to stand up for one's rights when the consequences of such behavior outweigh the benefits of doing so. An important distinction can be made between individuals who reasonably choose not to be assertive (although they could be if they chose to) and individuals who avoid being assertive out of anxiety. For example, one of the authors checked into a New York hotel to attend a national convention. The desk clerk gave the room key to a bellman who picked up his bag. Art explained that he would rather carry his bag up himself. The clerk quickly escalated the situation by stating: "Well, I won't stand for this! If he doesn't take your bag up, I'll cancel your reservation right now!" Art was taken aback by such an overreaction, but realized some important facts: (1) just a moment earlier a person with no reservation had requested a room and was told the hotel was full as were the others in the immediate area, (2) that person was still at the desk when the incident occurred and would have been delighted to take the empty room. Consequently, Art agreed to permit the bellman to take his bag up.

Although Art agreed to something he did not want to do, he judged that his other options were less desirable. Thus, the decision was made out of reason and not out of anxiety. Such reasoning is not to be confused with "rationalizing" which sometimes accompanies avoidance behavior, i.e., "post hoc" reasons why avoidance made sense yet the actual motivating force for the behavior was anxiety.

In this incident, Art might have confronted the desk clerk at a later time. He might have expressed irritation at the manner in which he was treated. He might also have reported the clerk's behavior to his supervisor, if the clerk persisted in overreacting. At the moment, however, he judged his behavior to be appropriate.

In some instances, participants have realized that several of their closest relationships have become disrupted as they increased their assertiveness. Often these relationships symbiotically required the participant to stay nonassertive; when the person changed, the relationship was out of balance. Trainers should be prepared to respond to participants who find they are losing some of their closest relationships. The participants (assuming they wish to continue such changes) can practice in the group discussing changes with the important people in their lives. Trainers should help participants assess what is happening in their relationships: Are others not liking the more assertive participant because of their own needs to perpetuate the earlier relationship, or is the participant behaving in ways that really are disruptive and does the participant wish to work on such behaviors? What does the participant think about this newly acquired assertive behavior?

The impact on others as one becomes more assertive is probably most serious in marriages, families, and other intimate relationships. Trainers should not only help participants assess the impact of their assertiveness on such relationships, but they should also help participants to deal with the reactions of intimates. We believe trainers have an ethical responsibility not to take a person out of an intimate living situation (especially children), teach that person to be assertive, and return the person to that "system" when others in that system are unprepared to handle these new behaviors. Clearly, we are not suggesting that such a person not seek or receive assertion training. Rather, the trainers should raise such concerns in the group and help participants to help others to understand their changes. Often the dialog carried on between intimates regarding the changes one of them is currently making help to strengthen the relationship. In some cases, the relationship does not continue when a mutually satisfactory basis is not found.

Moreover, we believe trainers should be prepared to offer consultation, counseling, or make referrals for intimates seriously influenced by a participant's increased assertiveness. The trainer's role in such a consultation is to help the person explore how the participant's assertiveness is affecting him and to provide information to him on what assertiveness is about. Essentially, the message is that the participant is becoming more aware of her personal rights and working toward being more direct in expressing her thoughts, feelings, and needs. More subtly, we believe that such a consultation is reassuring; the person can better understand that assertion training is not a conspiracy against him, but rather a process that results in renegotiations within the relationship. The trainer might also discuss how to go about renegotiating in a way that allows both persons to feel OK about themselves.

At the same time, trainers should be alerted to several potentially negative outcomes of such a meeting: (1) the trainer might become too much of a spokesperson for the participant and thereby "rescue" him from expressing his own thoughts, (2) the other person might use the meeting to blow up or to make provocative accusations. Nevertheless, we believe that these consultations can be a very valuable experience for all involved and, therefore, support their occurrence and caution trainers to be sensitive to the fears and intentions of the others involved.

Our concern with changing someone who is functioning within a small system is even greater when the person has relatively little control in the system and the potential for negative reaction to assertiveness is great. Children and adolescents who are participating in assertion groups often cannot behave assertively without severe recriminations from their parents or other persons exercising control. The trainer's ethical responsibility here is to discuss these realities with the participant and to work on situations in such a way that the person can maximize the likelihood of being assertive at a level which minimizes the potential for punishment. Ideally, consultation with the entire family would be preferred but is not always available. We believe it would be highly unethical to train a young person to be assertive without realistic regard for the likely consequences.

SUMMARY

Trainers should be sensitive to the potential effect on others of the participants' increased assertiveness. This is not a caution to hold participants back in any way. Rather, we believe that trainers should: (1) be prepared to respond to participants' concerns about the effects of their increased assertiveness, (2) help participants to clarify for others how and why they are changing when they wish to explain, (3) be available for consultation or make referrals for close persons who recognize the changes in the participant, wish to understand more fully, and possibly make some changes in the way they have been relating to the participant, and (4) help participants to recognize and accept that some relationships are based on their being nonassertive and that these relationships are unlikely to change.

REVIEW QUESTIONS

1. Identify and discuss the issues regarding the accurate explanation of what assertion training is and is not.

2. Identify and discuss the ethical issues regarding trainer preparation and capability.

3. Identify and discuss the issues regarding the potential impact of being assertive. How can trainers handle these issues when conducting groups?

4. Discuss how trainers might deal with the problem of participants presuming they should *always* be assertive.

References

Aiduk, R. A comparison of replication techniques in the modification of nonassertive behavior. Doctoral dissertation, University of Cincinnati. *Dissertation Abstracts International,* 1973, *33,* (9-B), 4498.

Alberti, R. E. & Emmons, M. L. *Your perfect right: A guide to assertive behavior* (2nd ed.). San Luis Obispo, CA: Impact Press, 1974.

Ascher, L. M. & Phillips, D. Guided behavior rehearsal. *Journal of Behavior Therapy and Experimental Psychiatry,* 1975, *6,* 215-218.

Atkinson, D. Effect of selected behavior modification techniques on student-initiated action. *Journal of Counseling Psychology,* 1971, *18,* 395-400.

Bach, G. & Deutsch, R. *Pairing.* New York: Avon Books, 1970.

Bach, G. & Wyden, R. *The intimate enemy.* New York: William Morrow & Co., 1968.

Balson, P. The use of behavior therapy techniques in crisis-intervention: A case report. *Journal of Behavior Therapy and Experimental Psychiatry,* 1971, *2,* 297-300.

Bancke, L. L. Background antecedents of aggressiveness and assertiveness found in academically achieving women. Doctoral dissertation, University of Cincinnati. *Dissertation Abstracts International,* 1972, *33* (6-B), 2800.

Bandura, A. Vicarious processes: A case of no trial learning. In L. Berkowitz (Ed.), *Advances in experimental social psychology* (Vol. 2). New York: Academic Press, 1965.

Bandura, A. *Principles of behavior modification.* New York: Holt, Rinehart and Winston, 1969.

Bandura, A. Analysis of modeling processes. In A. Bandura (Ed.), *Psychological modeling.* Chicago: Aldine Atherton, 1971.

Bandura, A., Grusec, J. E. & Menlove, F. L. Vicarious extinction of avoidance behavior. *Journal of Personality and Social Psychology,* 1967, *5,* 16-23.

Bandura, A. & Jeffery, R. W. Role of symbolic codes and rehearsal processes in observational learning. *Journal of Personality and Social Psychology.* 1973, *26,* 122-130.

Barnard, G., Flesher, C. & Steinbook, R. The treatment of urinary retention by aversive stimulus cessation and assertive training. *Behaviour Research and Therapy,* 1966, *4,* 232-236.

Bates, H. D. & Zimmerman, S. Toward the development of a screening scale for assertive training. *Psychological Reports,* 1971, *28,* 99-107.

Bean, K. L. Desensitization, behavior rehearsal, the reality: A preliminary report on a new procedure. *Behavior Therapy,* 1970, *1,* 542-545.

Beck, A. Cognitive therapy: Nature and relation to behavior therapy. *Behavior Therapy,* 1970, *1,* 194-200.

Beech, H. R. *Changing man's behavior.* Middlesex, England: Penquin, 1969.

Bellucci, J. E. The prediction of counselor assertion from a combination of self-disclosure variables. Unpublished manuscript, University of Cincinnati, 1975.

Blanchard, E. B. Relative contributions of modeling, informational influences, and physical contact in extinction of phobic behavior. *Journal of Abnormal Psychology,* 1970, *76,* 55-61.

Bloom, L. Z., Coburn, K. & Pearlman, J. *The new assertive woman.* New York: Delacorte Press, 1975.

Bloomfield, H. H. Assertive training in an outpatient group of chronic schizophrenics: A preliminary report. *Behavior Therapy,* 1973, *4,* 277-281.

Booker, A. The effect of dominance status on aggression in kindergarten aged children. Doctoral dissertation, University of Texas, Austin. *Dissertation Abstracts International,* 1973, *33,* (7-B), 3334.

Booraem, C. D. & Flowers, J. V. Reduction of anxiety and personal space as a function of assertion training with severely disturbed neuropsychiatric inpatients. *Psychological Reports*, 1972, *30*, 923-929.

Brumage, M. E. & Willis, M. H. *How three variables influence the outcome of group assertive training.* Paper presented at the American Personnel and Guidance Association, New Orleans, April 1974.

Cameron, D. E. The conversion of passivity into normal self-assertion. *American Journal of Psychiatry*, 1951, *108*, 98-102.

Carter, D. *Developmental stages of feminism.* Unpublished paper, University of Iowa, 1974.

Cautela, J. R. A behavior therapy approach to pervasive anxiety. *Behaviour Research and Therapy*, 1966, *4*, 99-109.

Corsini, R. *Roleplaying in psychotherapy: A manual.* Chicago: Aldine, 1966.

Creer, T. L. & Miklich, D. R. The application of a self-modeling procedure to modify inappropriate behavior: A preliminary report. *Behaviour Research and Therapy*, 1970, *8*, 91-92.

Curran, J. P. An evaluation of a skills training program and a systematic desensitization program in reducing dating anxiety. Unpublished manuscript, 1973.

Dengrove, E. Behavior therapy of headaches. *Journal of the American Society of Psychosomatic Dentistry and Medicine*, 1968, *15*, 41-48.

Dorman, L. Assertive behavior and cognitive performance in pre-school children. Doctoral dissertation, Boston University Graduate School. (University Microfilms, 1969, No. 69-18, 782)

Doty, D. W. Role playing and incentives in the modification of the social interaction of chronic psychiatric patients. *Journal of Consulting and Clinical Psychology*, 1975, *43*, 676-682.

D'Zurilla, T. & Goldfried, M. Problem solving and behavior modification. *Journal of Abnormal Psychology*, 1971, *78*, 107-126.

Edwards, N. B. Case conference: Assertion training in a case of homosexual pedophilia. *Journal of Behavior Therapy and Experimental Psychiatry*, 1972, *3*, 55-63.

Eisler, R. M., Hersen, M. & Agras, W. S. Effects of videotape and instructional feedback on non-verbal marital interactions: An analogue study. *Behavior Therapy*, 1973, *4*, (1), 1-6. (a)

Eisler, R. M., Hersen, M. & Agras, W. S. Videotape: A method for the controlled observation of non-verbal interpersonal behavior. *Behavior Therapy*, 1973, *4*, 420-425. (b)

Eisler, R. M., Hersen, M. & Miller, P. M. Effects of modeling on components of assertive behavior. *Journal of Behavior Therapy and Experimental Psychiatry*, 1973, *4*, 1-6.

Eisler, R. M., Hersen, M., Miller, P. M. & Blanchard, E. F. Situational determinants of assertive behaviors. *Journal of Consulting and Clinical Psychology*, 1975, *43*, 330-340.

Eisler, R. M., Miller, P. M. & Hersen, M. Components of assertive behavior. *Journal of Clinical Psychology*, 1973, *29*, 295-299.

Eisler, R. M., Miller, P. M., Hersen, M. & Alford, H. Effects of assertive training on marital interaction. *Archives of General Psychiatry*, 1974, *30*, 643-649.

Ellis, A. *Reason and emotion in psychotherapy*. New York: Lyle Stuart, 1962.

Ellis, A. *Growth through reason*. Palo Alto, CA: Science and Behavior Books, 1971.

Ellis, A. *Humanistic psychotherapy: The rational-emotive approach.* New York: Julian Press, 1973. (New York: McGraw-Hill Paperbacks, 1974)

Ellis, A. *Disputing irrational beliefs (DIBS).* New York: Institute for Rational Living, 1974.

Ellis, A. *How to live with a neurotic.* New York: Crown Publishers, 1975.

Ellis, A. & Harper, R. A. *A new guide to rational living.* Englewood Cliffs, NJ: Prentice-Hall, 1975.

Farrell, W. *The liberated man.* New York: Random House, 1975.

Fensterheim, H. Assertive methods and marital problems. In R. D. Rubin, H. Fensterheim, J. D. Hendersen & L. P. Ullmann (Eds.), *Advances in behavior therapy.* New York: Academic Press, 1972. (a)

Fensterheim, H. Behavior therapy: Assertive training in groups. In C. J. Sager & H. S. Kaplan (Eds.), *Progress in group and family therapy.* New York: Brunner/Mazel, 1972. (b)

Fensterheim, H. & Baer, J. *Don't say yes when you want to say no.* New York: David McKay Co., 1975.

Field, G. D. & Test, M. A. Group assertive training for .severely disturbed patients. *Journal of Behavior Therapy and Experimental Psychiatry*, 1975, *6*, 129-134.

Flowers, J. & Guerra, J. The use of client-coaching in assertion training with large groups. *Community Mental Health Journal*, 1974, *10* (4), 414-417.

Foy, D. W., Eisler, R. M. & Pinkston, S. Modeled assertion in a case of explosive rages. *Journal of Behavior Therapy and Experimental Psychiatry*, 1975, *6*, 135-137.

Frank J. *Persuasion and healing*. Baltimore: Johns Hopkins University Press, 1961.

Frayn, D. H. A relationship between rated ability and personality traits in psychotherapists. *American Journal of Psychiatry*, 1968, *124*, 1232-1237.

Freiberg, P. Modeling and assertive training: The effect of sex and status of model on female college students. Doctoral dissertation, University of Maryland, 1974.

Friedman, P. H. The effects of modeling and role-playing on assertive behavior. In R. D. Rubin, H. Fensterheim, A. A. Lazarus & C. M. Franks (Eds.), *Advances in behavior therapy*. New York: Academic Press, 1971. (a)

Friedman, P. H. The effects of modeling, role-playing and participation on behavior change. In B. Maher (Ed.), *Progress in experimental personality research* (Vol. VI). New York: McGraw-Hill, 1971. (b)

Fuhriman, A. & Pappas, J. Behavioral intervention strategies for employment counseling. *Journal of Employment Counseling*, 1971, *8*, 116-124.

Galassi, J. P., Delo, J. S., Galassi, M. D. & Bastien, S. The College Self-Expression Scale: A measure of assertiveness. *Behavior Therapy*, 1974, *5*, 165-171.

Galassi, J. P. & Galassi, M. D. Validity of a measure of assertiveness. *Journal of Counseling Psychology*, 1974, *21*, 248-250.

Galassi, J. P. & Galassi, M. D. Relationship between assertiveness and aggressiveness. *Psychological Reports*, 1975, *36*, 352-354.

Galassi, J. P., Galassi, M. D. & Litz, M. C. Assertive training in groups using video feedback. *Journal of Counseling Psychology*, 1974, *21*, 390-394.

Galassi, J. P., Hollandsworth, J. C., Radecki, J. C., Gay, M. L., Howe, M. R. & Evans, C. L. Behavioral performance in the validation of an assertiveness scale. *Behavior Therapy*, 1975, in press.

Galassi, J. P., Kostka, M. P. & Galassi, M. D. Assertive training: A one year follow-up. *Journal of Counseling Psychology*, 1975, *22*, 451-452.

Galassi, M. D. & Galassi, J. P. The effects of role playing variations on the assessment of assertive behavior. *Behavior Therapy*, in press.

Gambrill, E. D. & Richey, C. A. An assertion inventory for use in assessment and research. *Behavior Therapy*, 1975, *6*, 350-362.

Gardner, J. E. A blending of behavior therapy techniques in an approach to an asthmatic child. *Psychotherapy: Theory, Research, and Practice*, 1968, *5*, 46-49.

Gay, M. L., Hollandsworth, J. G. & Galassi, J. P. An Assertiveness Inventory for Adults. *Journal of Counseling Psychology*, 1975, *22*, 340-344.

Geisinger, D. Controlling sexual and interpersonal anxieties. In J. D. Krumboltz & C. E. Thoresen (Eds.), *Behavioral counseling*. New York: Holt, Rinehart and Winston, 1969.

Gentry, W. D. & Kirwin, P. M. Constriction, aggression, and assertive training. *Psychological Reports*, 1972, *30*, 297-298.

Gerst, M. Symbolic coding processes in observational learning. *Journal of Personality and Social Psychology*, 1971, *19*, 7-17.

Gibbs, D. N. Reciprocal inhibition therapy of a case of symptomatic erythema. *Behaviour Research and Therapy*, 1965, *2*, 261-266.

Gittelman, M. Behavior rehearsal as a technique in child treatment. *Journal of Child Psychology and Psychiatry*, 1965, *6*, 251-255.

Glass, C. Response acquisition and cognitive self-statement modification approaches to dating behavior training. Doctoral dissertation, Indiana University, 1974.

Goldfried, M., Decenteces, E. & Weinberg, L. Systematic rational restructuring as a self-control technique. *Behavior Therapy*, 1974, *5*, 247-254.

Goldfried, M. & Goldfried, A. Cognitive change methods. In F. Kanfer & A. Goldstein (Eds.), *Helping people change*. New York: Pergamon Press, 1975.

Goldfried, M. & Sobocinski, D. Effect of irrational beliefs on emotional arousal. *Journal of Consulting and Clinical Psychology*, 1975, *43*, 504-510.

Goldstein, A. J., Serber, M. & Piaget, G. Induced anger as a reciprocal inhibitor of fear. *Journal of Behavior Therapy and Experimental Psychiatry*, 1970, *1*, 67-70.

Goldstein, A. P. Case conference: Conflict in a case of frigidity. *Journal of Behavior Therapy and Experimental Psychiatry*, 1971, *2* (1), 51-59.

Goldstein, A. P., Martens, J., Hubben, J., Van Belle, H. A., Schaaf, W., Wiersma, H. & Goedhart, A. The use of modeling to increase independent behavior. *Behaviour Research and Therapy*, 1973, *11*, 31-42.

Goldstein, A. P., Sprafkin, R. P. & Gershaw, N. J. *Skill training for community living*. New York: Pergamon Press, in press.

Goodman, D. & Maultsby, M. *Emotional well-being through rational behavior training*. Springfield, IL: Charles Thomas, 1974.

Goodwin, S. E. & Mahoney, M. J. Modification of aggression through modeling: An experimental probe. *Journal of Behavior Therapy and Experimental Psychiatry*, 1975, *6*, 200-203.

Gordon, T. *Parent effectiveness training*. New York: Peter H. Wyden, 1970.

Gormally, J. A behavioral analysis of structured skills training. *Journal of Counseling Psychology*, 1975, *22*, 458-460.

Gormally, J., Hill, C. E., Otis, M. & Rainey, L. A microtraining approach to assertion training. *Journal of Counseling Psychology*, 1975, *22*, 299-303.

Green, A. H. & Marlatt, G. A. Effects of instructions and modeling upon affective and descriptive verbalization. *Journal of Abnormal Psychology*, 1972, *80*, 189-196.

Green, R. A. & Murray, E. J. Expression of feeling and cognitive reinterpretation in the reduction of hostile aggression. *Journal of Consulting and Clinical Psychology*, 1975, *43*, 375-383.

Gutride, M. E., Goldstein, A. P. & Hunter, M. F. The use of modeling and role playing to increase social interaction among asocial psychiatric patients. *Journal of Consulting and Clinical Psychology*, 1973, *40*, 408-415.

Hedquist, F. J. & Weinhold, B. K. Behavioral group counseling with socially anxious and unassertive college students. *Journal of Counseling Psychology*, 1970, *17*, 237-242.

Hersen, M., Eisler, R. M. & Miller, P. M. Development of assertive responses: Clinical measurement and research considerations. *Behaviour Research and Therapy*, 1973, *11*, 505-521.

Hersen, M., Eisler, R. M., Miller, P. M., Johnson, M. B. & Pinkston, S. G. Effects of practice, instructions, and modelling on components of assertive behavior. *Behaviour Research and Therapy*, 1973, *11* (4), 443-451.

Hewes, D. D. On effective assertive behavior: A brief note. *Behavior Therapy*, 1975, *6*, 269-271.

311

Holt, R. R. On the interpersonal and intrapersonal consequences of expressing or not expressing anger. *Journal of Consulting and Clinical Psychology*, 1970, *35*, 8-12.

Homme, L. *How to use contingency contracting in the classroom.* Champaign, IL: Research Press, 1970.

Jacobson, E. *Progressive relaxation.* Chicago: University of Chicago Press, 1938.

Jakubowski, P. A discrimination measure of assertion concepts. Unpublished manuscript, University of Missouri-St. Louis, 1975.

Jakubowski, P. Assertive behavior and clinical problems of women. In D. Carter & E. Rawlings (Eds.), *Psychotherapy for women: Treatment towards equality.* Springfield, IL: Charles Thomas, in press. (a)

Jakubowski, P. Self-assertion training procedures for women. In D. Carter & E. Rawlings (Eds.), *Psychotherapy for women: Treatment towards equality.* Springfield, IL: Charles Thomas, in press. (b)

Jakubowski, P. & Lacks, P. Assessment procedures in assertion training. *The Counseling Psychologist,* in press.

Jakubowski, P. & Wallace, G. Adult Assertion Scale. Unpublished manuscript, University of Missouri-St. Louis, 1975.

Jakubowski-Spector, P. *An introduction to assertive training procedures for women.* Washington, D.C.: American Personnel and Guidance Association, 1973. (a)

Jakubowski-Spector, P. Facilitating the growth of women through assertive training. *The Counseling Psychologist,* 1973, *4*, 75-86. (b)

Jakubowski-Spector, P., Pearlman, J. & Coburn, K. *Assertive training for women: Stimulus films.* Washington, D.C.: American Personnel and Guidance Association, 1973.

James, M. & Jongeward, D. *Born to win.* Reading, MA: Addison-Wesley, 1971.

Johnson, S. M. & White, G. Self-observation as an agent of behavior change. *Behavior Therapy,* 1971, *2,* 488-497.

Kagan, N. *Interpersonal Process Recall: A method of influencing human interaction.* East Lansing, MI: Michigan State University, 1975.

Kagan, N. & Krathwohl, D. *Studies in human interaction.* Research Report 20, East Lansing, Michigan State University, Educational Publications Services, 1967.

Kanfer, F. & Seider, M. Self control factors enhancing tolerance of noxious stimulation. *Journal of Personality and Social Psychology*, 1973, *25*, 381-389.

Katz, R. Case conference: Rapid development of activity in a case of chronic passivity. *Journal of Behavior Therapy and Experimental Psychiatry*, 1971, *2*, 187-193.

Kaufman, L. M. & Wagner, B. R. Barb: A systematic treatment technology for temper control disorders. *Behavior Therapy*, 1972, *3*, 84-90.

Kazdin, A. E. Covert modeling and the reduction of avoidance behavior. *Journal of Abnormal Psychology*, 1973, *81*, 87-95.

Kazdin, A. E. Effects of covert modeling and model reinforcement on assertive behavior. *Journal of Abnormal Psychology*, 1974, *83*, 240-252.

Kazdin, A. E. Covert modeling, imagery assessment, and assertive behavior. *Journal of Consulting and Clinical Psychology*, 1975, *43*, 716-724.

Keat, D. B. Broad-spectrum behavior therapy with children: A case presentation. *Behavior Therapy*, 1972, *3*, 454-459.

Lacks, P. & Connelly, J. Analysis of four self-report measures of assertion. Unpublished manuscript, Washington University, 1975. Cited in P. Jakubowski & P. Lacks, Assessment procedures in assertion training. *The Counseling Psychologist*, in press.

Lacks, P. B. & Jakubowski, P. A critical examination of the assertion training literature. Unpublished manuscript, Washington Universtity, 1975.

Lange, A. & Jakubowski, P. *Cognitive-behavioral group assertion procedures.* Paper presented at the American Psychological Association, Chicago, 1975.

Lange, A., Rimm, D. C. & Loxley, J. C. Cognitive and behavioral procedures for group assertion training. *The Counseling Psychologist*, in press.

Lawrence, P. S. The assessment and modification of assertive behavior. Doctoral dissertation, Arizona State University. (University Microfilms, 1970, No. 70-11, 888)

Laws, D. R. & Serber, M. Measurement and evaluation of assertive training with sexual offenders. In R. E. Hosford & S. Moss (Eds.), *The crumbling walls.* Urbana, IL: University of Illinois Press, in press.

Lazarus, A. A. The treatment of a sexually inadequate man. In L. P. Ullmann & L. Krasner (Eds.), *Case studies in behavior modification.* New York: Holt, Rinehart and Winston, 1965.

Lazarus, A. A. Behavior rehearsal vs. non-directive therapy vs. advice in effecting behavior change. *Behaviour Research and Therapy,* 1966, *4,* 209-212. (a)

Lazarus, A. A. Broad spectrum behavior therapy and the treatment of agrophobia. *Behaviour Research and Therapy,* 1966, *4,* 95-97. (b)

Lazarus, A. A. Behavior therapy in groups. In G. M. Gazda (Ed.), *Basic approaches to psychotherapy and group counseling.* Springfield, IL: Charles Thomas, 1968. (a)

Lazarus, A. A. Variations in desensitization therapy. *Psychotherapy: Theory, Research, and Practice,* 1968, *5,* 50-52. (b)

Lazarus, A. A. *Behavior therapy and beyond.* New York: McGraw-Hill, 1971.

Lazarus, A. A. *Clinical behavior therapy.* New York: Brunner/Mazel, 1972.

Lazarus, A. A. On assertive behavior: A brief note. *Behavior Therapy,* 1973, *4,* 697-699.

Lazarus, A. A. *Assertion training.* Paper presented at the American Personnel and Guidance Association, New York, April 1975.

Lazarus, A. A. & Abramovitz, A. The use of "emotive imagery" in the treatment of children's phobias. In L. P. Ullmann & L. Krasner (Eds.), *Case studies in behavior modification.* New York: Holt, Rinehart and Winston, 1965.

Lazarus, A. A. & Fay, A. *I can if I want to.* New York: William Morrow & Co., 1975.

Lazarus, A. A. & Serber, M. Is systematic desensitization being misapplied? *Psychological Reports,* 1968, *23,* 215-218.

Leibowitz, G. Comparison of self-report and behavioral techniques of assessing aggression. *Journal of Consulting and Clinical Psychology,* 1968, *32,* 21-25.

Lieberman, M., Yalom, I. & Miles, M. *Encounter groups: First facts.* New York: Basic Books, 1973.

Liberman, R. P. A behavioral approach to group dynamics: I, Reinforcement and prompting of cohesiveness in group therapy. *Behavior Therapy,* 1970, *1,* 141-175.

Liberman, R. P. Behavioral methods in group and family therapy. *Seminars in Psychiatry.* Oxnard, CA: Camarillo State Hospital, Laboratory of Behavior Modification, May 1972, *4* (2), 145-156. (a)

Liberman, R. P. Behavior therapy with neurotics: Assertive training. *A guide to behavioral analysis and therapy.* New York: Pergamon Press, 1972. (b)

Linehan, M. & Goldfried, M. Assertion training for women: A comparison of behavior rehearsal and cognitive restructuring therapy. Paper presented at the Association for the Advancement of Behavior Therapy, San Francisco, 1975.

Lomont, J. F., Gilner, F. H., Spector, N. J. & Skinner, K. K. Group assertive training and group insight therapies. *Psychological Reports,* 1969, *25,* 463-470.

Longin, H. & Rooney, W. M. Assertion training as a programatic intervention for hospitalized mental patients. *Proceedings of the 81st Annual Convention of the American Psychological Association,* 1973, *8,* 459-460.

Longin, H. E. & Rooney, W. M. Teaching denial assertion to chronic hospitalized patients. *Journal of Behavior Therapy and Experimental Psychiatry,* 1975, *6,* 219-222.

Loo, R. M. Y. The effects of projected consequences and overt behavior rehearsal on assertive behavior. Doctoral dissertation, University of Illinois. Urbana, IL. (University Microfilms, 1971, No. 72-6988)

Lovaas, O. I., Freitas, K. N., Nelson, K. & Whalen, C. The establishment of imitation and its use for the development of complex behavior in schizophrenic children. *Behaviour Research and Therapy,* 1967, *5,* 171-181.

Ludwig, L. D. & Lazarus, A. A. A cognitive and behavioral approach to the treatment of social inhibition. *Psychotherapy: Theory, Research, and Practice,* 1972, *9,* 204-206.

MacDonald, M. L. Teaching assertion: A paradigm for therapeutic intervention. *Psychotherapy: Theory, Research, and Practice,* in press.

MacDonald, M. L., Lindquist, C. U., Kramer, J. A., McGrath, R. A. & Rhyne, L. D. Social skills training: Behavior rehearsal in groups and dating skills. *Journal of Counseling Psychology,* 1975, *22,* 224-230.

MacPherson, E. L. R. Selective operant conditioning and deconditioning of assertive modes of behavior. *Journal of Behavior Therapy and Experimental Psychiatry,* 1972, *3,* 99-102.

Mahoney, M. *Cognitive and behavior modification.* Cambridge, MA: Ballinger Publishing Co., 1974.

Maish, J. The use of an individualized assertive training program in the treatment of depressed in-patients. Doctoral dissertation, Florida State University. *Dissertation Abstracts International*, 1972, *33* (6-B), 2816.

Malott, R. *Contingency management.* Kalamazoo, MI: Behaviordelia, Inc., 1972.

Martorano, R. D. Effects of assertive and nonassertive training on alcohol consumption, mood, and socialization in the chronic alcoholic. *Proceedings of the 81st Annual Convention of the American Psychological Association*, 1973, *8*, 393-394.

Masters, J. C. & Branch, M. N. Comparison of the relative effectiveness of instruction, modeling, and reinforcement procedures for inducing behavior change. *Journal of Experimental Psychology*, 1969, *80*, 364-368.

Maultsby, M. C., Jr. *More personal happiness through rational self counseling.* Lexington, KY: Author, 1971. (a)

Maultsby, M. C., Jr. Systematic, written homework in psychotherapy. *Psychotherapy: Theory, Research, and Practice*, 1971, *8*, 195-198. (b)

Maultsby, M. C., Jr. *How and why you can naturally control your emotions.* Lexington, KY: Author, 1974.

Maultsby, M. C., Jr. *Help yourself to happiness.* New York: Institute for Rational Living, 1975.

Maultsby, M. C., Jr. & Ellis, A. *Technique for using rational-emotive imagery* (REI). New York: Institute for Rational Living, 1974.

Maultsby, M. C., Jr., Stiefel, L. & Brosky, L. A. Theory of rational behavioral group process. *Rational Living*, 1972, *7*, 28-34.

Mayo, M., Bloom, M. & Pearlman, J. Effectiveness of assertive training for women. Unpublished manuscript. Cited in L. Z. Bloom, K. Coburn, & J. Pearlman. *The new assertive woman.* New York: Delacorte Press, 1975.

McCarthy, D. J. & Bellucci, J. A. Adolescent Self-Expression Scale. Unpublished manuscript, Loras College, 1975.

McFall, R. M. & Lillesand, D. B. Behavior rehearsal with modeling and coaching in assertive training. *Journal of Abnormal Psychology*, 1971, *77*, 313-323.

316

McFall, R. M. & Marston, A. R. An experimental investigation of behavior rehearsal in assertive training. *Journal of Abnormal Psychology,* 1970, *76,* 295-303.

McFall, R. M. & Twentyman, C. T. Four experiments on the relative contributions of rehearsal, modeling, and coaching to assertion training. *Journal of Abnormal Psychology,* 1973, *81,* 199-218.

McGovern, K. B., Arkowitz, H. & Gilmore, S. K. Evaluation of social skill training programs for college dating inhibitions. *Journal of Counseling Psychology,* 1975, *22,* 505-512.

McNamara, J. R. The broad based application of social learning theory to treat aggression in a preschool child. *Journal of Clinical Psychology,* 1970, *26,* 245-247.

Mehrabian, A. *Nonverbal communication.* Chicago: Aldine/Atherton, 1972.

Meichenbaum, D. H. Examination of model characteristics in reducing avoidance behavior. *Journal of Personality and Social Psychology,* 1971, *17,* 298-307.

Meichenbaum, D. H. Cognitive modification of test anxious college students. *Journal of Consulting and Clinical Psychology,* 1972, *39,* 370-380.

Meichenbaum, D. H. Cognitive factors in behavior modification: Modifying what clients say to themselves. In C. Franks and T. Wilson (Eds.), *Annual review of behavior therapy: Theory and practice.* New York: Brunner/Mazel, 1973. (a)

Meichenbaum, D. H. Therapist manual for cognitive behavior modification. Unpublished manuscript, University of Waterloo, 1973. (b)

Meichenbaum, D. H. *Cognitive behavior modification.* Morristown, NJ: General Learning Press, 1974.

Meichenbaum, D. H. The cognitive-behavioral management of anxiety, anger, and pain. In P. Davidson (Ed.), *Behavioral management of anxiety, depression and pain.* New York: Brunner/Mazel, 1976.

Meichenbaum, D. H. Self instructional methods (How to do it). In A. Goldstein & F. Kanfer (Eds.), *Helping people change: Methods and materials.* New York: Pergamon Press, 1975. (a)

Meichenbaum, D. H. Toward a cognitive theory of self control. In G. Schwartz & D. Shapiro (Eds.), *Consciousness and self-regulation: Advances in research.* New York: Plenum, 1975. (b)

Meichenbaum, D. H. & Cameron, R. Stress innoculation: A skills training approach to anxiety management. Unpublished manuscript, University of Waterloo, 1973.

Meichenbaum, D. H. & Cameron, R. The clinical potential of modifying what clients say to themselves. In C. Thoresen & M. Mahoney (Eds.), *Self-control: Power to the person.* New York: Brooks/Cole, 1974.

Meichenbaum, D. H., Gilmore, B. & Fedoravicious, A. Group insight vs. group desensitization in treating speech anxiety. *Journal of Consulting and Clinical Psychology,* 1971, *36,* 410-421.

Melnick, J. A comparison of replication techniques in the modification of minimal dating behavior. *Journal of Abnormal Psychology,* 1973, *81,* 51-59.

Mitchell, S. A psychological approach to the treatment of migraine. *British Journal of Psychiatry,* 1971, *119,* 533-534.

Mummery, D. V. Family backgrounds of assertive and non-assertive children. *Child Development,* 1954, *25,* 63-80.

Neuman, D. Using assertive training. In J. D. Krumboltz & C. E. Thoresen (Eds.), *Behavioral counseling.* New York: Holt, Rinehart and Winston, 1969.

Novaco, R. W. A treatment program for the management of anger through cognitive and relaxation controls. Unpublished doctoral dissertation, Indiana University, 1974.

Novaco, R. W. *Anger control: The development and evaluation of an experimental treatment.* Lexington, MA: D. C. Heath & Co., Lexington Books, 1975.

Nydegger, R. V. The elimination of hallucinatory and delusional behavior by verbal conditioning and assertive training: A case study. *Journal of Behavior Therapy and Experimental Psychiatry,* 1972, *3,* 225-227.

Orenstein, H., Orenstein, E. & Carr, J. E. Assertiveness and anxiety: A correlational study. *Journal of Behavior Therapy and Experimental Psychiatry,* 1975, *6,* 203-207.

Osborn, S. M. & Harris, G. G. *Assertive training for women.* Springfield, IL: Charles Thomas, 1975.

Palmer, R. D. Desensitization of the fear of expressing one's own inhibited aggression: Bioenergetic assertive techniques for behavior therapists. *Advances in behavior therapy.* New York: Academic Press, 1972.

Patterson, R. L. Time-out and assertive training for a dependent child. *Behavior Therapy,* 1972, *3,* 466-468.

318

Pearlman, J., Coburn, K. & Jakubowski-Spector, P. *A leader's guide to assertive training for women.* Washington, D. C.: American Personnel and Guidance Association, 1973.

Perkins, D. G. The effectiveness of three procedures for increasing assertiveness in low assertive college students. Doctoral dissertation, North Texas State University. (University Microfilms, 1972, No. 72-24, 200)

Perls, F. S. *Gestalt therapy verbatim.* Moab, UT: Real People Press, 1969.

Phelps, S. & Austin, N. *The assertive woman.* San Luis Obispo, CA: Impact Press, 1975.

Piaget, G. W. & Lazarus, A. A. The use of rehearsal-desensitization. *Psychotherapy: Theory, Research, and Practice,* 1969, *6,* 264-266.

Potter, S. *One upmanship.* New York: Holt, Rinehart and Winston, 1970.

Prazak, J. A. Learning job-seeking interview skills. In J. D. Krumboltz & C. E. Thoresen (Eds.), *Behavioral counseling.* New York: Holt, Rinehart and Winston, 1969.

Rachman, S. Systematic desensitization. *Psychological Bulletin,* 1967, *67,* 93-103.

Rappaport, J., Gross, T. & Lepper, C. Modeling, sensitivity training, and instruction: Implications for the training of college student volunteers and for outcome research. *Journal of Consulting and Clinical Psychology,* 1973, *40,* 99-107.

Rathus, S. A. An experimental investigation of assertive training in a group setting. *Journal of Behavior Therapy and Experimental Psychiatry,* 1972, *3,* 81-86.

Rathus, S. A. A 30-item schedule for assessing assertive behavior. *Behavior Therapy,* 1973, *4,* 398-406. (a)

Rathus, S. A. Instigation of assertive behavior through video-tape mediated assertive models and directed practice. *Behaviour Research and Therapy,* 1973, *11,* 57-65. (b)

Rattner, L. The pampered lifestyle. In A. G. Nikelly (Ed.), *Techniques for behavior change.* Springfield, IL: Charles Thomas, 1971.

Rausbaum-Selig, M. Assertion training with young people. *The School Counselor,* in press.

Rimm, D. C. Assertive training used in the treatment of chronic crying spells. *Behaviour Research and Therapy,* 1967, *5,* 373-374.

319

Rimm, D. C. Thought stopping and covert assertion. *Journal of Consulting and Clinical Psychology,* 1973, *41,* 466-467.

Rimm, D. C., Hill, G. A., Brown, N. N. & Stuart, J. E. Group assertive training in the treatment of expression of inappropriate anger. *Psychological Reports,* 1974, *34,* 791-798.

Rimm, D. C., Keyson, M. & Hunziker, J. Group assertive training in the treatment of anti-social aggression. Unpublished manuscript, Arizona State University, 1971.

Rimm, D. C. & Masters, J. C. *Behavior therapy: Techniques and empirical findings.* New York: Academic Press, 1974.

Rimm, D. C., Saunders, W. & Westel, W. Thought stopping and covert assertion in the treatment of snake phobics. *Journal of Consulting and Clinical Psychology,* 1975, *43,* 92-93.

Ross, D. M., Ross, S. A. & Evans, T. A. The modification of extreme social withdrawal by modeling with guided participation. *Journal of Behavior Therapy and Experimental Psychiatry,* 1971, *2,* 273-279.

Roszell, B. L. Pretraining, awareness, and behavioral group therapy approaches to assertive behavior training. Doctoral dissertation, University of Minnesota. Minneapolis, MN. (University Microfilms, 1971, No. 72-378)

Russell, P. & Bradsma, J. A theoretical and empirical integration of the rational-emotive and classical conditioning theories. *Journal of Consulting and Clinical Psychology,* 1974, *42,* 389-397.

Salter, A. *Conditioned reflex therapy.* New York: Farrar, Straus & Giroux, 1949.

Sarason, E. G. & Sarason, B. R. *Constructive classroom behavior: A teacher's guide to modeling and role-playing techniques.* New York: Behavioral Publications, 1974.

Sarason, I. Verbal learning, modeling, and juvenile delinquency. *American Psychologist,* 1968, *23,* 254-266.

Sarason, I. & Ganzer, V. J. Modeling and group discussion in the rehabilitation of juvenile delinquents. *Journal of Counseling Psychology,* 1973, *20,* 442-449.

Sarbin, T. Imagining as muted role-taking: A historical-linguistic analysis. In P. Sheehan (Ed.), *The function and nature of imagery.* New York: Academic Press, 1966.

Schacter, S. The interaction of cognitive and physiological determinants of emotional state. In C. Spielberger (Ed.), *Anxiety and behavior.* New York: Academic Press, 1966.

Schwartz, R. & Gottman, J. A task analysis approach to clinical problems: A study of assertive behavior. Unpublished manuscript, Indiana University, 1974.

Seitz, P. F. D. Dynamically-oriented brief psychotherapy: Psychocutaneous excoriation syndromes. *Psychosomatic Medicine,* 1953, *15,* 200-242.

Serber, M. Teaching and nonverbal components of assertive training. *Journal of Behavior Therapy and Experimental Psychiatry,* 1972, *3,* 179-183.

Serber, M. & Nelson, P. The ineffectiveness of systematic desensitization and assertive training in hospitalized schizophrenics. *Journal of Behavior Therapy and Experimental Psychiatry,* 1971, *2,* 107-109.

Sherman, A. R., Mulac, A. & McCann, M. Synergistic effect of self-relaxation and rehearsal feedback in the treatment of subjective and behavioral dimensions of speech anxiety. *Journal of Consulting and Clinical Psychology,* 1974, *42,* 819-828.

Shmurak, S. Design and evaluation of three dating behavior training programs utilizing response acquisition and cognitive self-statement modification techniques. Unpublished doctoral dissertation, Indiana University, 1974.

Smith, M. J. *When I say no I feel guilty.* New York: Dial Press, 1975.

Snyder, O. W. Assertive training: A comparison of behavior rehearsal, modeling, and silent reading, and the relationship. Doctoral dissertation, West Virginia University. (University Microfilms, 1973, No. 73-12, 978)

Sperber, D. F. S. A comparison of two intervention techniques for decreasing aggressive behavior. Doctoral dissertation, The American University. Washington, D.C. (University Microfilms, 1972, No. 73-5193)

Steel, C. & Hochman, J. *Assertion skill training: A group procedure for women.* Washington, D.C.: American Personnel and Guidance Association, in press. (a)

Steel, C. & Hochman, J. *Improving personal relationships: Assertive training for high school women, stimulus films.* Washington, D.C.: American Personnel and Guidance Association, in press. (b)

Steel, C. & Hochman, J. *A leader's guide to assertion training with high school women.* Washington, D.C.: American Personnel and Guidance Association, in press. (c)

Stevens, J. O. *Awareness.* Lafayette, CA: Real People Press, 1971.

Stevenson, I. Direct instigation of behavioral changes in psychotherapy. *AMA Archives of General Psychiatry*, 1959, *1*, 99-107.

Stevenson, I. & Wolpe, J. Recovery from sexual deviations through overcoming of nonsexual neurotic responses. *American Journal of Psychiatry*, 1960, *116*, 737-742.

Sturm, I. The behavioristic aspect of psychodrama. *Group Psychotherapy*, 1965, *18*, 50-64.

Sturm, I. Implications of role-playing methodology for clinical procedure. *Behavior Therapy*, 1971, *2*, 88-96.

Tophoff, M. Massed practice, relaxation and assertion training in the treatment of Gilles de la Tourette's syndrome. *Journal of Behavior Therapy and Experimental Psychiatry*, 1973, *4*, 71-73.

Twentyman, C. & McFall, R. Behavioral training of social skills in shy males. *Journal of Consulting and Clinical Psychology*, 1975, *43*, 384-395.

Ullmann, L. P. Making use of modeling in the therapeutic interview. In R. D. Rubin & C. M. Franks (Eds.), *Advances in behavior therapy*. New York: Academic Press, 1968.

Varenhorst, B. Helping a client to speak up in class. In J. D. Krumboltz & C. E. Thoresen (Eds.), *Behavioral counseling*. New York: Holt, Rinehart and Winston, 1969.

Wagner, M. K. Comparative effectiveness of behavioral rehearsal and verbal reinforcement for effecting anger expressiveness. *Psychological Reports*, 1968, *22* (3, Pt. 2), 1079-1080. (a)

Wagner, M. K. Reinforcement of the expression of anger through role-playing. *Behaviour Research and Therapy*, 1968, *6*, 91-95. (b)

Wallace, C. J., Teigen, J. R., Liberman, R. P. & Baker, V. Destructive behavior treated by contingency contracts and assertive training: A case study. *Journal of Behavior Therapy and Experimental Psychiatry*, 1973, *4*, 273-274.

Warren, N. A behavioral test for the measurement of tenderness expression. Master's thesis, St. Louis University, 1975.

Weinman, B., Gelbart, P., Wallace, M. & Post, M. Inducing assertive behavior in chronic schizophrenics. *Journal of Consulting and Clinical Psychology*, 1972, *39*, 246-252.

Weintraub, M., Segal, R. & Beck, A. An investigation of cognition and affect in the depressive experiences of normal men. *Journal of Consulting and Clinical Psychology*, 1974, *42*, 911.

Wells, W. P. Relaxation-rehearsal: A variant of systematic desensitization. *Psychotherapy: Theory, Research, and Practice*, 1970, *7*, 224-25.

Whalen, C. Effects of a model and instructions on group verbal behaviors. *Journal of Consulting and Clinical Psychology*, 1969, *33*, 509-521.

Whiteley, J. M. & Jakubowski, P. A. The coached client as a research and training resource in counseling. *Counselor Education and Supervision*, 1969, *9*, 19-30.

Whiteley, R., Becker, P., Craig, M., Cohen, J., Hotchner, B., Jakubowski-Spector, P. & Sobota, L. Women in groups. *The Counseling Psychologist*, 1973, *4*, 27-43.

Wolfe, J. Short-term effects of modeling/behavior rehearsal, modeling/behavior rehearsal-plus-rational therapy, placebo, and no treatment on assertive behavior. Doctoral dissertation, New York University, 1975.

Wolpe, J. *Psychotherapy by reciprocal inhibition.* Stanford: Stanford University Press, 1958.

Wolpe, J. *The practice of behavior therapy.* New York: Pergamon Press, 1969.

Wolpe, J. The instigation of assertive behavior: Transcripts from two cases. *Journal of Behavior Therapy and Experimental Psychiatry*, 1970, *1*, 145-151.

Wolpe, J. *The practice of behavior therapy* (2nd ed.). New York: Pergamon Press, 1973. (a)

Wolpe, J. Supervision transcript: V—Mainly about assertive training. *Journal of Behavior Therapy and Experimental Psychiatry*, 1973, *2*, 141-148. (b)

Wolpe, J. & Lazarus, A. A. *Behavior therapy techniques.* New York: Pergamon Press, 1966.

Wolpin, M. On assertion. *The Counseling Psychologist*, 1975, *5*.

Yalom, I. & Lieberman, M. A study of encounter group casualties. *Archives of General Psychiatry*, 1971, *25*, 16-30.

Yarnell, T. Symbolic assertive training through guided affective imagery in hypnosis. *American Journal of Clinical Hypnosis*, 1972, *14*, 194-196.

Yates, D. Relaxation in psychotherapy. *Journal of General Psychology*, 1946, *34*, 213-238.

Young, E. R., Rimm, D. C. & Kennedy, T. D. An experimental investigation of modeling and verbal reinforcement in the modification of assertive behavior. *Behaviour Research and Therapy*, 1973, *11*, 317-319.